Scottish Popular Politics

Scottish Popular Politics

From Radicalism to Labour

W. Hamish Fraser

POLYGON
AT EDINBURGH

To Ian MacDougall

without whose work many of the records of working people's
activities would have disappeared.

© W. Hamish Fraser, 2000

Polygon at Edinburgh
An imprint of Edinburgh University Press Ltd
22 George Square, Edinburgh

Typeset in Garamond
By Bibliocraft Ltd, and
Printed and bound in Great Britain by
The Cromwell Press, Trowbridge, Wilts

A CIP record for this book is available from the British Library

ISBN 1 902930 11 8 (paperback)

Contents

Acknowledgements

Much of this book is the product of happy hours spent in libraries and archives over many years. My thanks are due to the many librarians and archivists who provide such excellent service often in increasingly difficult circumstances. Particular thanks are due to the staff of the National Library of Scotland, the National Archives of Scotland (in the days when it was less grandly the SRO), the University libraries of Aberdeen, Edinburgh, Glasgow and Strathclyde, the Mitchell Library and Archives in Glasgow and the British Library in London.

A great deal of the research and writing was accomplished during a fruitful semester as a Fellow of the Institute of Advanced Study in the Humanities of the University of Edinburgh. Peter Jones and his colleagues together with the visiting Fellows at the Institute help generate an environment which is wonderfully conducive to research and my warm thanks are due to them for their hospitality and support.

Colleagues in the Department of History at the University of Strathclyde gave time, lent books, took extra students and shouldered more administration to allow space for study leave. I am grateful to them all for their help and their company. Most of all I have to thank my wife, Helen, for tolerating the cancellation of Christmas and Easter as I battled to meet deadlines and EUP for being patient.

Introduction

Professor Christopher Smout in 1986 ended his *A Century of the Scottish People* on a gloomy note:

> Few today are as concerned as their forefathers were with the meanings of liberty or democracy, or would understand the meaning of the motto that the joiners of Glasgow carried on their banner in their demonstrations from 1832 to 1908.[1] The Friends of the People, the Chartists, the Liberal Working Man, Keir Hardie and the Clydesiders shared a common belief that, at the close of the twentieth century, we are in danger of losing: by the exercise of political will, the people hold their own future in their own hands, and in the last analysis, no one can be blamed for our predicament but ourselves.[2]

The despondency was unnecessary. Within eighteen months, the Constitutional Steering Committee of the Campaign for a Scottish Assembly's *A Claim of Right for Scotland* was reacting to what it saw as 'a drive to diminish democracy' and declaring,

> There is a profound hypocrisy in saying that the Scots should stand on their own feet while simultaneously denying them management of their own political affairs, and that denial is a clear deprivation of choice for Scots. Scots can stand on their own feet only by refusing to accept the constitution which denies them the power to do so.[3]

Eleven years later, as this introduction is being written, the Scots are electing a Scottish Parliament, the child, albeit much battered, bruised and wayward, of that declaration.

The Scotland Act of 1998 which brought the Parliament into being was passed by a Labour government dominated by Scots most of whom had come belatedly and sometimes grudgingly to accept the need for major constitutional change. Not all were agreed on how much real power was to be devolved from what was now the Labour bastion of Westminster. While no doubt political expediency played a crucial part in persuading the Labour leadership to commit itself to a Scottish Parliament, they could claim to be inheritors of a tradition of which the founding of the Labour Party a century ago was a part. It is that tradition which Christopher Smout felt had disappeared in 1986, 'the belief ... that, by the exercise of political will, the people hold their own future in their own hands'. The creation of the Labour Party, in substantial part a Scottish creation, was one such reflection of a people's will, but it was built on earlier campaigns for the creation of political structures which listened to the 'people below'.

The aim of this book is to look at some of those movements and campaigns in Scotland which, from the eighteenth century, by their commitment to the spread of democracy, contributed language, tradition and personnel to the formation of the Labour Party at the beginning of the twentieth century. The Labour Party in Scotland was the inheritor of a distinctively Scottish radical thread. Added to it were elements of socialism, but the moral reforming tone which was so much part of it, would have been recognisable to its Liberal radical predecessors. It created a distinctive liberal social democratic tradition in Scotland.

It could be a justifiable criticism to suggest that the title *Popular Politics* is in fact a misnomer, since most of the time the politics being examined were far from popular in the sense of always commanding majority support. But the extra-parliamentary movements looked at here are, none the less, about the politics of the popular. They were trying to mobilise popular support to bring constitutional change which would lead towards greater democracy. Limited at first to demands for checks on arbitrary executive power, they broadened into assertions of the right to universal suffrage. Middle-class campaigns expanded into movements which embraced working-class radicalism. With some advances towards the goal of universal suffrage achieved by the last decades of the nineteenth century, the attention switched to getting political representation which was more representative of working people. The result was the formation of parties for independent labour which eventually merged into the Labour Party. Their advance was not easy, since loyalty to Liberal radicalism remained tenacious, and by continuing to use the language of radicalism – anti-privilege, anti-aristocracy, anti-war, anti-drink – the proponents of independent labour politics were slow to find a discourse which interpreted the world differently.

However, because of the crisis of Liberalism created by the first world war, for a brief moment, the Labour Party could claim to have incorporated almost all the earlier issues of radical protest into its programme – temperance, land reform, abolition of the House of Lords, home rule, municipal socialism, pacifism and added to it a commitment to tackling social problems through some redistribution of wealth. In the economic blizzard of the inter-war years, however, much of the radical element was lost as the social problems of the declining industrial areas came to the fore. The Labour Party became identified only as the party of the industrial working class. It also became as much a supporter of centralisation of power as its Conservative rival. The radical elements were suppressed. As the brief concluding chapter of this study suggests, this allowed others to challenge for the mantle of radicalism. As a result, by the last forty years of the the twentieth century, the demands for democratic change became inextricably linked with the demands for devolution of power away from Westminster.

While throughout the book there are plenty of references to the middle class and working class, the conclusion must be that political change has not come about through the activities of social classes, but rather through the commitment of relatively small groups of individuals and families who have struggled against apathy and hostility to stir a belief in the possibility of change through the democratic will. A striking feature are the elements of continuity from one reform movement to another. Survivors of the reform movements of the 1790s were in the great reform demonstrations of 1832. Many who came into political activity in the first reform campaign continued through Chartism and other campaigns and helped create the Liberal radicalism of the mid-nineteenth century. Unitarianism, Quakerism, family connection run through these developments from the Peddies and the Christies to the Wighams and the McLarens and many others. As the Liberal radical tradition both reacted with and responded to socialism to feed into independent labour, again key individuals can be found spanning the reform movements from the 1860s through to the early twentieth century. Land reform, anti-landlordism, anti-imperialism, support for home rule became the central tenets of radicalism as well as of early Labour. Popular pressure was always at its most effective when it united groups from all social classes.

As the twentieth century advanced, the Labour Party, for much of the time, was usually able to take a majority of seats, but this was often achieved with the support of a shrinking proportion of the electorate. There were always those who were not convinced that the process of democratisation had been completed as long as power remained centralised at Westminster. Once again small groups of radicals were able to mobilise support for devolution of power to a Scottish Parliament, against the views of most politicians, and, through the power of argument and debate, convince those in authority to concede to 'the settled will of the Scottish people'. Thanks to a reformed electoral system the result is a new Scottish Parliament with no single political party commanding an overall majority, but with all using some of that Scottish radical discourse inherited from the past.

Notes

1. 'They are unworthy of freedom, who hope for it from hands other than their own.'
2. T. C. Smout, *A Century of the Scottish People 1830–1950* (1986), p. 275.
3. *A Claim for the Right of Scotland* (Edinburgh, July 1988), p. 11.

CHAPTER ONE

Politics Discovered 1770s–1802

Popular protest was not uncommon in eighteenth-century Scotland. The Edinburgh mob, which came from many different sections of the community, had long had a notoriety that made the authorities wary of challenging it. It did not hesitate to make its views known on individuals, on taxation, on tolls, on religious issues and on the behaviour of the public authorities. A Glasgow crowd in 1725 burned down Shawfield House and ran riot over the next two weeks when the local MP, Duncan Campbell, supported the imposition of an excise duty on malt. Most notorious of all was the Porteous riot of 1736, immortalised in Scott's *Heart of Midlothian*, when Captain Porteous, captain of the Edinburgh city guard, was lynched in the Grassmarket by the Edinburgh crowd of tradesmen and apprentices after ordering his men to fire on a crowd trying to rescue a smuggler. Food shortages and the accompanying rise in prices could lead to meal mobs and the forced sale of hoarded grain, such as those which spread through Galloway and Tayside in 1771 and 1772. Their actions reflected a widely shared view that there was a a limit to authority and a duty to ensure that food was available and that it was at a price which people could afford. Those in power could be reminded of their duties and responsibilities by united community action.

Social protest was common; political protest was rarer, but certainly not absent. Recent work has challenged earlier accounts which, under the influence of early nineteenth-century Whiggish history, saw eighteenth-century Scottish politics as confined to a small and generally venal élite, with the only alternative being reactionary Jacobitism. The growth of urban settlement inevitably led to challenges, to irritations and to tensions between the town and the neighbouring landowners over boundaries and common land. Within established royal burghs the political battles were usually fought out within trade incorporations and merchants' guildries and between the incorporations and the town councils. Town councils were self-perpetuating, often corrupt, bodies frequently dominated by single families or business groups, but disputed elections were not uncommon. Trade incorporations often offered one of the few ways in which alternative views could be made known and town-council dominance could be challenged. Rab Houston has shown how in-fighting within Edinburgh's trade incorporations in the 1730s and 1740s was not just about conflicting economic interests but had political significance and involved challenging the dominating groups. Alex Murdoch's work illustrates how merchants, professionals, tradesmen and labourers could join in demanding change in the closed system of burgh politics in Dumfries, Ayr, Glasgow as well as Edinburgh, appealing to the Convention of Royal Burghs and to the courts for the voices of the burgesses to be heard in burgh affairs.[1]

Merchants and tradesmen in many places wanted the opening up of representation in their towns and calls for changing the sett or constitution of the burgh to achieve this was the most common form of political protest. There was resentment, for example, at the way in which town councils usually exercised some control over the selection of deacons of trades by insisting on approving a short leet. In 1761 an Edinburgh pamphlet, *The Free Thoughts of a Burgher*, pressed for the burgesses in the Merchant Company to be allowed to elect the seventeen merchants who sat on the town council. When in the following year a London banker was imposed as MP, 'without the knowledge or consent of the inhabitants', it led to protests at the presumption 'by persons who assume a right of determining for us, which constitution and independency of Scotland, and its capital, does not allow them'.[2] In 1763 there were again attempts to select deacons who would stand up to the dominant group on the town council.

Mid-eighteenth-century Scotland was a stable and relatively prosperous society. Between the 1740s and the 1780s the Scottish economy was transformed. The quality of buildings, both public and private, by the 1780s is an indication of how a formerly poor, underdeveloped country was being transformed. The fine streets of Glasgow, the start of the new town in Edinburgh were good examples, but so also was the new elegance of places like Dumfries in the south and the new villages like Grantown and Fochabers in the north. A building boom brought prosperity to many others and, by the 1780s, the gap between traditionally low Scottish wages and those of the north of England was narrowing. It was also a paternalistic society. With many of the great aristocrats now in London, it was a country run by the gentry anxious to maintain stability and order. Older patterns of paternalism survived in Scotland with various mechanisms to ensure that food shortages could be dealt with. The famine years of the 1690s were powerfully etched in the collective memory. Trade incorporations and local authorities would bulk buy food at times of shortage. This did not prevent incidents of protest at the export of grain or against hoarders, and Chris Whatley has identified meal riots in every decade from the 1720s until the 1790s, but they seem to have been rarer in Scotland than in England, where the market was allowed to prevail. Even in the always delicate field of industrial relations, there was considerable harmony, with associations of workers tolerated and magistrates prepared to interfere to regulate wages and hours – not always to the advantage of employers.[3]

Economic change, however, brought social change. Older patterns of social relationships with their accompanying traditional customs and practices were breaking down. Alongside the prospering gentry a new commercial and professional bourgeoisie was beginning to emerge. The Reverend Alexander 'Jupiter' Carlyle noted that Captain Porteous 'by his skill in many exercises, particularly the golf, and by gentlemanly behaviour, was admitted into the company of his superiors, which elated his mind and added insolence to his native roughness'.[4] Stana Nenadic has documented the signs of changing life styles among those gaining from the new business wealth. The gap between employers and workers was widening and, with new luxuries, there were signs that master tradesmen were 'set up to live like gentlemen'.[5] Towns were growing fast and many of the inhabitants were new comers. The bigger cities were filling with 'straingers' and were all the more frightening for that. The pressure from the middle ranks to escape was strong and was reflected in the growing residential segregations of classes. Edinburgh's New Town is the best example, clearly marking the end of any social cohesion, but Glasgow, Aberdeen and Dundee all had their equivalent new towns. With sharper social relationships, street protest was no longer to be seen as a sign of a breakdown of community relationships, but as a real threat to property. The painter Alan Ramsay, writing in 1781 to Lord Monboddo, bemoaned the increasing insecurity life and property which he saw around him.[6] Public disorder of any kind was more often seen as having the potential for seditious insurrection and, therefore, there was a greater readiness to resort to force in response.

But eighteenth-century Scotland was also a country where orthodoxy was being challenged by a ferment of new ideas emerging from its universities. There was much talk of the need for change, for new rules required for a new commercial society. The problem of the distribution of power in such a modern society was central to many of the concerns of enlightenment thinkers, as was finding the right balance between liberty and subjection to ensure progress and improvement. Key thinkers accepted that adaptation was necessary and developed the idea of law having constantly to adjust to meet the needs of an evolving society. Adam Ferguson, for one, did not see the purpose of laws as being 'to instruct the citizen how to act the part of a virtuous man', but were expedients 'to adjust the pretensions of parties, and to secure the peace of society'.[7] John Millar, Adam Smith's successor in Glasgow, was calling for the abolition of corporate privileges, an end to monopolies and to the restrictions on land sale which came from primogeniture and entail. Young men were coming into contact with liberal ideas, not just home-grown ones but from England and Ireland, in their lectures and in their debating societies and clubs.[8] The Edinburgh literati were not unalloyed in their enthusiasm for a commercial society and, on the whole, their concern was to ensure that traditional values and interests survived, but they recognised that for this to happen changes had to take place.

In national politics there was much to protest about. The thirty county members of parliament in Scotland were elected by fewer than 3,000 voters, increasing numbers of them, thanks to labyrinthine electoral laws, mere nominees of landed grandees. The fifteen burgh representatives were selected by the self-elected, generally corruptible town councils. Through the judicious use of patronage, such a system was relatively easily 'managed' by government. Because of this, Scottish politicians were perceived, with some justification, as the most venal and the most ready to sell their votes in return for government patronage. Both as ministers and as clients they had an unenviable reputation. Also, English radicals found Scotland's Jacobite sympathies suspect and when John Wilkes and his associates in London raised the cause of liberty at the end of the 1760s they saw Scots ministers and their Scottish supporters as among the greatest threat to that liberty. Scots by their nature and their history were assumed to be supporters of reaction and tyranny. In local politics the concern was about the lack of any accountability on the part of those who ran the town councils, who were free to spend the local common good funds and to borrow with little or no check by the burgesses. In most places, burgh finances became increasingly secretive and yet eventual liability could fall on the citizens.

The American War

The Declaration of Independence by the thirteen American Colonies could not but stir immense interest in Scotland where ties of kinship, business, religion and ideas with the colonies were so extensive. Most American patriots, just like Wilkes, regarded the Scots with their Stuart and Jacobite sentiments as natural reactionaries and, indeed, Scots predominated among the loyalists in the thirteen colonies. However, there were plenty who were critical of the war. Francis Hutcheson's *System of Moral Philosophy*, published in 1755 after his death, had been the first to recognise the right of colonists to rebel.[9] Benjamin Franklin had been entertained in Edinburgh in 1771 and David Hume, despite his Toryism, in the weeks before he died would proclaim, 'I am an American in my Principles'. The ideas of political rights emerging from Philadelphia were extensively reported. A letter in the *Aberdeen Journal* of August 1775 noted that 'taxation and representation are inseparably linked.'[10] Adam Ferguson, another friend of Franklin, served as secretary of a Peace Commission in 1778.

Clergymen from the moderate wing of the Church, as ever, preached obedience to secular authority. But among the popular, evangelical wing there was much more sympathy with the rebels. The minister of Old Greyfriars in Edinburgh, John Erskine, wrote pamphlets deprecating the idea of war with the colonies. The Reverend Charles Nisbet in Montrose caused the town council to walk out of his church with his pro-American views, while Dr Thom in Govan and James Lyndsay in Kirkliston also argued the American cause.[11] Thom, on the national days of thanksgiving at the end of the war asked,

> Now, I should like to know what it is we are to give thanks for, is it for the loss of thirteen provinces? Is it for the slaughter of so many thousands of our fellow countrymen? Is is for so many millions of increased national debt?[12]

Inevitably the events in America caused discussion and debate on the principles involved. Adam Smith and John Millar both advocated representation of the colonists in Westminster parliament and the issues were debated in the Edinburgh Speculative Society on numerous occasions before the war broke out. There were a number of reform societies, following the lead of Burke and Pitt in England, calling for shorter parliaments and a wider franchise.[13] When another demand by the trades' incorporations for reform of the Edinburgh burgh sett was again blocked by the Court of Session, a 'congress' of delegates was called, deliberately using the language of America and with the delegates giving one another the names of American rebels, Adams, Hancock, Washington.[14] Once war had broken out, however, there was a general rallying to the government cause, particularly after the French became involved. The fact that Scots regiments were so prominent added to the patriotic sentiments. The radicalism of John Wilkes and his friends in London, not surprisingly in view of its pervasive Scotophobia, stirred little support in Scotland. None the less, the long-drawn-out nature of the war, the claims of corrupt distribution of military contracts, the American victory at Saratoga and the ultimate defeat did raise questions about the quality of government which the existing system was offering and encouraged the first stirrings of demands for political reform.

Religion and politics

What always aroused powerful sentiments were religious matters. The Patronage Act of 1712 left a residue of bitterness which could readily be agitated by ham-fisted management and which drove many into secession. Anti-Burgher seceders led the way in reducing the deference towards the gentry.[15] Richard Sher has shown how the Drysdale affair in Edinburgh between 1762 and 1764 over the placement of a moderate minister by the town council stirred demands for reform in language, which with talk of 'liberty' and 'independence', had much in common with that of Wilkes and English radicals, showing a novel determination to challenge the local élite.[16] Evangelical clerical leaders were also prepared to utilise a 'Popular Party' to resist 'Moderate' domination of the Church, as in 1778–9 when they unleashed a furious anti-popery campaign against the Lord Advocate, Henry Dundas's efforts to push through a Catholic Relief Bill. The Bill would have rescued Scottish Catholics from some of the more extreme disabilities under which they had had to labour since the ousting of James VII and perhaps have encouraged a few more from the Highlands to volunteer for the army.[17] The Reverend John Erskine again led the assault, warning that Catholicism was the enemy of liberty and that concessions to it were part and parcel of wider threats to liberty from a corrupt executive. After riots spread from Edinburgh to Glasgow and Perth, Dundas and the Moderates in the Church were forced to back away. While popular frenzies over religion were often primitive responses to outsiders, as Dundas recognised, a more educated resistance stemmed from a failure on the part of government to have political antennae fully attuned to Scottish political sentiment. Also, patronage was a class issue, a power which a few great landowners had but which the majority of the gentry and 'the middle ranks of men' did not. Ecclesiastical and civil liberty were readily linked and it is no coincidence that demands for political reform coincided with a campaign against patronage by the urban middle classes.[18]

The signs of political stirrings which saw an oligarchic government dominated by an aristocracy as inefficient, corrupt and corrupting were increasingly apparent during the American War years. Smith saw a distinction between the nobility and the gentry and in his *Theory of Moral Sentiments* of 1759 had already questioned by what right a young nobleman could claim 'superiority over his fellow citizens' and, in the *Wealth of Nations*, published as the war was breaking out, he challenged the 'exactions of government' on the individual.

> It is the highest impertinence and presumption, therefore, in kings and ministers, to pretend to watch over the economy of private people, and to restrain their expense. They are themselves always, and without exception, the greatest spendthrifts in the society.[19]

There was no love lost for 'that insidious and crafty animal, vulgarly a statesman or politician, whose councils are directed by the momentary fluctuations of affairs'.[20]

While there were ties between landowners and the new business classes and while the former, as Christopher Smout has shown, were a driving force behind Scottish industrialisation, they wanted to manage change in their own terms. There were many signs of differences in perception between town and country. Dundas's Corn Law of 1778 was seen by the business classes as a blatant manoeuvre to increase the income of the landowning classes. There was a growing sense of a 'landed interest' whose interests were not the same as those of a developing 'middle-class community', with the former seen as idle and unproductive and lacking in civic virtue. There was a perception, which grew with time, that the developing system of taxation was pushing the burden away from the landed class on to the urban middle ranks. A merchant from Irvine in Ayrshire writing to Pitt in 1784 protested at the weight of the new window tax on 'the Industrous [sic] Traders and Merchants ... and on the very Industrius[sic] and Active set of people in any State ... the Industrius and Frugal Merchant and Mechanick'.[21]

Burgh reform

By 1782 two groups were pressing for political reform. Many of the smaller landowners in the counties were calling for an end to the device which allowed proprietors of great estates to grant life rents to their friends and to create so-called 'faggot' voters, 'by which means the votes of the real independent Freeholders were in effect annihilated'. An attempt by the Court of Session in 1768 to block faggot voters had been reversed by the House of Lords with the result that the number of fictitious voters was actually increasing. Scottish county reformers were aware of the demands for parliamentary reform in England coming from bodies like Christopher Wyvill's Yorkshire Association, but declined to make common cause with them, pressing only for a moderate change to ensure that 'a respectable and independent body of proprietors had the vote'.[22]

Burgh reform stirred at the end of the year, when a wealthy merchant, Thomas McGrugar, writing as 'Zeno' in the *Caledonian Mercury*, called for an end to the choosing of MPs by the closed town councils:

> What right, then, have we to boast of a Parliament! to boast of freedom! to boast of being our own legislators! Can that legislature be called *ours*, in which we have no representation? Can that representation be called *ours*, in which we have no voice?

He was careful to exclude 'the dregs of the populace . . . disqualified by a natural ignorance and hebetude, which render them unfit to be their *own* directors and, therefore, they must be directed by *others*'.

> But men in the middle ranks of life, who generally constitute the majority of every free community, cannot be excluded from a voice in the appointment of their representatives, because this would deny them the right to self-government, for which they are qualified by their knowledge and extent of property, which must give them a weight in every free state, and a title to a share in the legislation.

Quoting Montesquieu, he argued that all 'except those who are in so mean a situation as to be deemed to have no will of their own' should have the right to vote. 'These claims,' he argued, 'arise from natural right, and this natural right has been possessed by every free and independent people'.[23]

Despite the rhetoric, the demands of those who led the campaign for burgh reform in the early 1780s were very moderate. The Edinburgh advocate, Archibald Fletcher, who linked reform to the attack on church patronage, was concerned to find a system of election which

> should be highly popular, and should, at the same time, bestow upon land-owners, that share of influence in the election of ministers, to which they are entitled by their rank, their education, and interest in the country; which should produce, among the people, that sense of liberty, so essential to the existence of a free government, and should be exempted, as far a possible,

from those popular disturbances, that are apprehended to the the effects of popular elections.

Not surprisingly, the convention of burgh reformers held in 1785 was concerned to ensure 'against the great and real evil of universal suffrage',[24] although the very fact that it was being mentioned probably indicates that some were talking about. In the end, calls for parliamentary reform were abandoned and the decision was made to press only for more open government in burghs. But Dundas and his acolytes in Parliament would have none of it. To Dundas general elections were 'a species of dissipation' which occurred every seven years. He had led the rejection of a motion in 1784 for parliamentary reform and Richard Sheridan's efforts to get through a bill for reform of the Scottish burghs were contemptuously rejected in 1787, 1789, 1790 and again in 1791. With Dundas so much in control of patronage at many different levels it was hard to find those who would endanger their prospects by providing either leadership or support for oppositional political activities. Also, the parliamentary critics of the government, Charles Fox and his often dissolute Whig aristocratic associates, may well have caused problems for many Scots. Among those concerned with ways of developing the virtuous and moral man, the personal excesses of the Foxite circle were not encouraging. Personal excesses, Sir John Sinclair for one believed, could readily lead to public excesses.[25]

French Revolution

Political debate was already well underway before the Revolution in France exploded its waves of influence, although debate was muted in the prosperity of the late 1780s. The events of 1789 and 1790 in France were viewed with a great deal of sympathy. The Dundee Whig Club dispatched an address to the National Assembly congratulating the French people on having regained their liberty and welcoming the prospects of peace and harmony between the two nations. Dugald Stewart visiting Paris harangued the crowds *pour la liberte*.' France was not seen as a model for change, but rather as a country belatedly moving into the modern age. The anti-clericalism of the French reformers chimed with Scottish views linking Catholicism with tyranny. Glasgow sympathisers toasted, 'May bigotry, superstition, and all manner of religious tyranny, soon come to an end'. The Polish Revolution in July 1791, where the aristocracy had given up their privileges, also found echoes in Scotland.[26]

Not until Burke came along at the end of 1790 were there any warnings that there might be dangers to property in the ideas emerging from France, but they were not taken too seriously. Three months later, Thomas Paine, known to some as a publicist for the American revolutionaries, issued his stirring reply to Burke, *The Rights of Man*, in a language quite different from that of earlier reformers. He dismissed the much-vaunted British Constitution as a fraud, run by banditti who had seized power largely by force, and which was incapable of reform from within. Only a system which gave 'equal representation to the people' could change the situation.

By 1791, there were further reasons for even moderate reformers to be discontented with government. Yet another attempt at burgh reform had been thrown back as had petitions to abolish the slave trade. Parliament had failed to exempt Scots in England from the provisions to the Test Act, which required acceptance of the thirty-nine articles of Anglicanism before being admitted to various public offices, a reform which evangelicals had persuaded the General Assembly to support. The Corn Law had been made even more complex, expensive and unequal in its operation between different parts of Scotland, something which convinced many distillers and brewers of the need for reform. In addition the prolonged period of economic prosperity which Scotland had sustained gave way to the beginnings of economic depression. Intellectual interest in the events in France became linked to real economic grievances for both business people and workers as imports slumped and food prices rose.

Friends of the People

A number of Scottish politicians and middle-class activists associated themselves with the Whig Friends of the People Association which had been formed in London in April 1792. These included young aristocrats like James Maitland, Earl of Lauderdale, and his brother, Thomas, MP for Jedburgh, Lord Daer, the son of the Earl of Selkirk, Norman MacLeod of Macleod, recently-elected MP for Inverness, and the vain and eccentric Earl of Buchan. From Glasgow there was Professor John Millar and the president of the Glasgow Society for Burgh Reform, James Richardson, a merchant. These generally wanted some moderate measures of parliamentary reform. By early 1792 there were signs of the demands for reform widening. A Universal Liberty Club, with economic as well as political concerns, was established in Banff in January around Alexander Leith, a Portsoy distiller. It wanted parliamentary and burgh reform and supported abolition of the slave trade, and the Club was blamed for fomenting meal riots in Banff. In March 1792 the Glasgow Society of Burgh Reform, echoing the Declaration of the Rights of Man and the Citizen, was distributing medals with the inscription that 'Men are by nature free and equal in respect of their right; hence all civil and political distinctions and authority are derived from the people'. The right to resist the abuse of power or the deprivation of rights was justified, and sacred and inviolable rights were claimed to be 'Public justice, liberty of conscience, trial by jury, the freedom of the press, the equal freedom of election and equal representation'.[27]

The government proclamation in May against wicked and seditious writing, far from curbing interest, 'acted like an Electric shock' in the words of Norman MacLeod:

It set people of all ranks a-reading and as everybody in this Country can read,
the people are already astonishingly informed. Farmers, ploughmen, peasants,
manufacturers, artificers, shopkeepers, sailors, merchants are all employed in
studying and reasoning on the nature of Society and Government.[28]

Soon Thomas Paine's *Rights of Man* was circulating widely among those both
'with or without money'.[29] At the same time, the proclamation was part of a
government strategy to spread alarm among the better-off about the dangers
of French ideas. But, for a brief moment, a reform momentum was gathering.
A Dundee reformer, looking back from 1817, recalled 1790 until 1792 as a
period when there was an unprecedented collaboration by many from
different social classes: 'It drew the ranks of society closer together and
made them better acquainted with each other's manners and habits.'[30]

By 1792, however, there was a concern among the well-to-do that reform
movements were getting beyond their control and stirring up wider issues and
groups. Traditional boisterousness associated with the King's birthday celebrations took on a political dimension with attacks on the Dundas' home in
Edinburgh's George Square and the burning of effigies. One poor chaise
driver got fourteen years' transportation for his part in the riot, but the
authorities could not find evidence against those who were suspected of
having stirred up the protests with handbills. Among the reformers there was
growing anxiety that the government was leading the country into war and
was ready to encroach on basic rights, with the magistrates having been
ordered to enter houses to search out subversive literature.

The month of July 1792 saw Edinburgh alive with political activity to an
extent that had not been experienced in more than a century. A convention of
delegates and burgesses of Royal Burghs began with a declaration of loyalty to
the sovereign and his family and an assurance of 'the deepest sense of the
superior excellence of the British Constitution', but none the less it argued for
some measure of reform, although, as yet, refusing to extend the demands to
parliamentary reform. Another convention was of the campaigners for
county reform, which included people like Norman MacLeod and Lord
Daer, hopeful, thanks to court decisions which had removed many 'faggot
voters', that country reform was imminent.[31] The third was an altogether
more radical group, meeting in Fortune's tavern, who formed the Associated
Friends of the People specifically to campaign for reform of the electoral
system which would allow 'an equal representation of the people' and 'restore
the constitution to its original purity'. The leaders were the bookseller,
William Johnston, and the writer to the signet, James Campbell, but included
William Skirving, a tenant farmer, who had first got involved in politics in the
campaign against patronage and for repeal of the Test Acts.

Associated with these reformers was James Thomson Callender, who
under the pseudonym of 'Timothy Thunderproof' was publishing material
which became the influential pamphlet, *On the Political Progress of Britain*. In it,

he challenged the idea of there being a *British* constitution and attacked Parliament as 'a phalanx of mercenaries embattled against the reason, the happiness, and the liberty of mankind' and the constitution as 'in practice ... a conspiracy of the rich against the poor'. He lambasted the whole range of taxes being imposed, which he presented as an attempt by 'our southern masters' to destroy Scottish industry and as part of a wider English imperialism. Such a nationalist perception was perhaps more widespread than has generally been admitted. Lord Daer, while not himself opposed to the Union, claimed that 'the Friends of Liberty in Scotland have almost universally been enemies to union with England' and he tried to get across to Lord Grey the way in which the Scots saw themselves as 'a conquered province these two centuries' and 'always felt the degradation of artificial inferiority'. He himself questioned what had been gained by the Act of Union: 'You say we have gained emancipation from feudal tyranny. I believe that had no Union ever taken place we should in that respect have been more emancipated that we are.'[32]

The Edinburgh Friends of the People now took upon itself the task of linking the other reform societies which had appeared in various towns and mobilising public opinion behind a campaign for equal representation and shorter parliaments. A Glasgow Society for Constitutional Reform had also emerged in July with the approval of the Lord Provost and aimed at middle-class reformers. In Perth, in contrast, there were reputedly 1,200 members, mainly operative weavers and other workers, but led by the cloth merchants James and Moses Wylie, the surgeon William Bissett, a dissenting clergyman, the Revd Wilson, the Grant bothers, one a shoemaker the other a pig merchant, and the solicitor, David Lumsden, the secretary. There were soon societies in most other towns of any size.[33] According to Edinburgh's *Caledonian Mercury* political debate pervaded the length of the country and 'the peasant seems to be equally knowing of politics with the peer'.[34] In September Captain William Johnston proposed that the Friends of the People publish a journal, the *Edinburgh Gazetteer,* to counter hostile reports in the established press, and this eventually appeared in November. Robert Burns and his friends in Dumfries welcomed it:

> Go on, Sir! Lay bare, with undaunted heart and steady hand that horrid mass of corruption called Politics and State Craft! Dare to draw in their native colours those calm, thinking Villains whom no faith confines whatever the shibboleth of their Pretended Party.[35]

William Stewart, a Leith merchant, and John Elder, a bookseller, were issuing pamphlets on *The Rights of Man Delineated* and *The Origin of Government*, which among other things called for an end to regulation of wages and prices by magistrates: 'why are they [master tradesmen] not free to make their own bargain as the law-makers are to let their farms and houses at what they deem their value'.[36] The pamphlets were extensively distributed in the rapidly industrialising west of Scotland.

In October the Associated Friends of the Constitution and of the People was launched in Glasgow with Lt Colonel Dalrymple of Fordel as president. He had presided at the 14 July dinner to commemorate the outbreak of the French Revolution, which had toasted the natural rights of man and called, among other things, for the abolition of slavery. £1,200 had been raised in the city to send to the French National Assembly. A solicitor, George Crawford, was secretary and the advocate, Thomas Muir was vice-president. It quickly began to reveal rather more radical tendencies than previous groups, calling for universal suffrage, annual parliaments and an end to the war, while casting doubt on the value of petitioning. Another society in Partick called itself 'the Sons of Liberty and the Friends of Man' and seems to have consisted largely of young apprentices 'animated with a just indignation at the honour of the town being stained, by the erection of Burkified Society'. The members were to read and discuss Paine's works and link up with the Friends of the People in Glasgow and elsewhere.[37]

A group in Edinburgh around the chemist, pioneer balloonist, and 'obscure, tippling, but extraordinary body', James Tytler, also rejected petitioning and seemed to point to the need for more fundamental change. Tytler in a pamphlet attacked the House of Commons as 'a vile junto of aristocrats', the majority of whom were landowners, and 'it is the power of the landholders that the people must attack'. He challenged the significance of property with the declaration 'Let not money, or land, or houses, be thought to make a man fit for being an Elector or Representative, an honest and upright behaviour is the only qualification'.[38] The Perth reformers formed a branch and like many other places planted a tree of liberty, decorated with candles and apples. Dundee followed suit with at least two societies, the 'Friends of the Constitution' around Neil Douglas, a seceder clergyman, and the 'Friends of Liberty' around George Mealmaker, a weaver and seceder. The division was probably a class one with the latter consisting mainly of tradesmen and labourers. The Friends of Liberty met in the Berean Meeting House in the Overgate, and the pastor there, Donaldson, was an activist. The meeting house was near where the Unitarian clergyman, Thomas Fyshe Palmer, lived with his friend James Ellis, a cotton spinner, and he too was soon pulled in. The small number of Unitarians, with their links with English reformers like Dr Joseph Priestley and Dr Richard Price in England were an important focus of reform ideas. The Christie family in Montrose were responsible for bringing the Etonian Palmer to the north and, influenced by the writings of Price, they published and spoke on religious freedom. Such was Unitarian association with radicalism that the Lord Advocate, Robert Dundas, suggested that the authorities would wink at the conduct of the good people of Edinburgh should they decide to pull down the recently-erected Unitarian meeting house.[39]

Many of the leaders of the reform societies were businessmen, professionals and gentry. The Provost of Dundee still believed that brewers were behind much of of the trouble, stirring up hostility towards excise men. The reformers' aim, as Skirving told a colleague, was 'to prevent revolution ... by substantial reform' not to foment it.[40] But peat and coal shortages and the high price of food widened the unrest in many parts of the country. The government was also tightening up on revenue collection, insisting, for example, on the payment of a fee for registration of christenings and burials. Weavers and other small tradesmen began to join reform meetings as economic concerns joined political ones. The victories of the French army against the invading forces of reaction stirred enormous displays of enthusiasm. In the rural areas there was talk of dividing up landed property in the style of the French peasantry; in the towns as far afield as Stornoway, Inverness and Lerwick, there was talk everywhere of Paine's ideas and even of the republic. It was reported that a Gaelic version of *The Rights of Man* was circulating in the Highlands and that 'its damnable doctrines' were being 'eagerly embraced by the lower classes'.[41] In the playhouse in Dumfries the national anthem was met with groans and there were attempts to break into singing the revolutionary chorus, *Ça Ira* with its call for the hanging of all aristocrats. In East Kilbride, a young shoemaker had the *Rights of Man* 'pressed upon his attention, by acquaintances of all classes of religionists, even by the highest-toned Seceders'.[42]

As with Paine, radicalism called for a reduction in taxation and government expenditure. It stood for an end to the hated excise duties. It wanted the special protections given to the landed class swept away: the game laws, the corn laws, the restrictions on land sale through entail and the patronage act. Some of the reformers also wanted an end to the regulation of trade though guildry controls or through wage fixing, although in other cases the trade incorporations were a focus of discontent with the closed town councils. There was talk both of natural rights and also of restoring traditional rights, usually for the latter drawing upon English history. Most reformers essentially stood for a society where advancement would depend upon merit not on birth and connection. While prepared to talk of themselves at times as 'the people' or to present themselves as 'Friends of the People', almost to a man the leadership deplored the riots and disorder which had been unleashed. The Dundee Society, after witnessing five days of rioting involving as many as 500 people, rushed to declare that 'Liberty cannot be enjoyed without Law, and an exact obedience to the Law'.

Backlash

By November 1792 there was a general view among the political classes, both the supporters of Pitt's government and the opposition Whigs, that the popular movement had to be curbed. Many of the middle classes began to back away from their earlier support for reform. Archibald Fletcher told his wife that 'these violent reformers will create such alarm in the country as must strengthen the government'. George Dempster, wrote to his friend Sir Adam Fergusson that the 'horrors of this French Revolution ... have corrected a great deal of my democratical spirit'.[43] There was particular pressure from the industrialising west of Scotland, where crowds and organised protest among an industrial working class stirred greater fears than in Edinburgh. Dundas gloatingly pointed out that the manufacturers there now repented their earlier championing of reform. Glasgow soon had a Constitutional Association, which included leading millowners like Henry Monteith and John Dunlop, 'to check that unwarrantable levelling republicanism'.[44] As Home of Wedderburn wrote to his brother, 'the middle class ... foresee that any convulsion must produce unavoidable ruin to them, and are now doing everything in their power to check and restrain the Spirit of Sedition they have raised' [45] Another warned of the dangers of the talk of 'equality': 'If tradesmen think it fair that they should be equal to Lords ... their workmen will think themselves equally entitled to be on a par with them'.[46]

A few, like Thomas Muir, 'an honest enthusiast, but ... an ill-judging man', as Archibald Fletcher described him, failed to read the signs and, while deploring violence, continued to campaign among the weavers and craftsmen in the west. At the end of November delegates from various societies met in Glasgow and, at Muir's prompting, called a convention of Scottish delegates. One hundred and seventy assembled in Edinburgh between 11 and 13 December. The discussion was dominated by the issue of how to respond to the anti-reform backlash which was increasingly apparent. There were frequent reassertions of the constitutional nature of the reform movement and of its abhorrence of disorder. There was a debate also on whether what was aimed at was the safer 'restoration' of ancient rights or the more dangerous 'obtaining' of new rights. Did Scotland, as Muir suggested, have a freedom as ancient as that of England, or did it have to be created anew, as Skirving implied?[47]

The irrepressible Muir was keen to unite the Scottish movement with the much more active and militant reformers in the United Irishmen, which had been formed in 1791, largely by presbyterian business and professional people. The Irish movement was strongly nationalist and the address from the Irish which he sought to present to the Convention tried to tap into Scottish nationalist sentiment with references to Buchanan, Fletcher and Wallace and to 'an Embodied nation'. It was altogether too heady stuff for the majority of delegates and they declined to accept it. None the less, there was much rhetoric about living free or death and a vote against co-operating with the moderate burgh reformers.

As preparations for war with France increased, there was pressure on town councils and incorporations of trade to declare their loyalty. The Church, both the moderate and the evangelical wings of it, weighed in with considerable enthusiasm. They had never liked the presence of so many seceders among the reformers or the occasional references to the covenanting tradition.

Reformers, like the French, were increasingly preached at as evil and intent on undermining the Christian religion. The father of the future MP for Edinburgh, Adam Black, a stonemason and a dissenter, remembered the difficulty that a tradesman like himself, in sympathy with reform, had if they showed even the slightest desire to reform public abuses. They could be boycotted and harassed and 'many were afraid of their credit at the banks being affected by such a suspicion'.[48] Robert Burns hastened to assure his patron, Robert Graham, that he was not associated with reform movements, that he regarded the British Constitution 'to be the most glorious Constitution on earth' and that 'as to France, I was her enthusiastic votary in the beginning of the business – when she came to show her old avidity for conquest, in annexing Savoy etc. to her dominions and invading the rights of Holland, I altered my sentiments'.[49] None the less, he nearly lost his job. The Paisley businessman and reformer, William Carlile, found his credit at the Paisley Bank drying up until his friends threatened a run on the bank.[50] On the other hand, as Gallin points out, many of the loyalist addresses from trade incorporations, while deploring disorder and any threat of violence, still contained references to grievances which required reform.

The spotlight fell on the radical booksellers who distributed Paine's pamphlets and other reform writings, now declared seditious. A number of them fled, and those who did not ended in jail for three to six months. Johnston of the *Gazetteer* was summoned for contempt of court for impugning the partiality of the courts and Callender fled to America. Muir wisely decided to head for France, reputedly in a last-minute effort to save the King. The onslaught on Scottish reformers led to complaints that they were receiving little support from south of the border. Daer reacted with a strongly nationalist letter to Lord Grey,

> If this should go so far, or anything else should take a turn as to make the Tweed appear a boundary in political sentiment or action, it requires more confidence in the good sense of our countrymen than even I can reasonably have to believe that it is possible (though I do not think probable) that a fatal national jealousy may arise. Scotland has long groaned under the chains of England and knows that its connection there has been the cause of its greatest misfortunes.[51]

Against war

For many, the likelihood of war pointed to the prospect of yet higher taxation as well as the disruption of trade, and at a number of the radical societies at the beginning of 1793 there were resolutions against the war which were driven by such considerations as much as by any sympathy for France. But once war had broken out in February most of the reform leaders were keen to avoid such declarations and to narrow the focus to parliamentary reform. At the second convention held at the end of April 1793 many of the old 'respectable' names were markedly absent. While not wildly radical there were signs of a change of tone. There was to be no more petitioning and Skirving made the significant distinction that while earlier movements had been an aristocracy working for the good of the people 'we are the people themselves'.

In the west in particular, economic distress, financial panic and political demands were intermingled. A petition signed by 12,000 in Paisley attacked Pitt for having rejected reform and attacked the war for having brought about the 'ruin and distress of innumerable families'. A peace petition from Glasgow was organised by manufacturers and shopkeepers and there were worries on the part of the authorities that the forces to maintain order, the fencibles, consisted largely of 'discontented weavers'.[52]

Thomas Muir returned from France in July and was brought to court in the following month. He seemed to have decided that a political gesture with himself in the role of martyr was what was required. Vanity and obstinacy made him reject Henry Erskine as his defence lawyer. He can have been quite unprepared for the vituperation which spilled from Lord Braxfield on the bench. His crime in Braxfield's eyes was 'to go among ignorant country people, and among the lower classes of people, making them leave off work, and inducing them to believe that a reform was absolutely necessary to preserve their safety and liberty'. Not to have pressed for reform, but to have encouraged people to strike threatened social stability. Muir could reasonably have expected a period of banishment from Scotland. Indeed, after the sentences, a number of Whig lawyers suggested that that was all the law under which he was charged allowed. The fourteen years' transportation to Australia was the kind sentence given for crimes against people and property, not for political deviation. But Muir would not seek clemency and the Dundases, while fairly appalled at the sentence, would not undermine the standing of the legal establishment by acting without such an appeal.[53]

For reformers there was growing worry that the war was giving government the opportunity to restrict civil rights ever further. Dundee Friends of Liberty issued a paper, drafted by George Mealmaker and Fyshe Palmer, which warned that the House of Commons could no longer be seen as a guardian against the tyranny of the aristocracy, but was now part of that tyranny in a coalition against the people. As the executive every day increased its powers, so every day, it was argued, a new link was added to the people's chains. Again, the connection was made with economic grievances, with taxes and wars creating 'a list of bankruptcies, unequalled in any former time'. The implication was that petitioning to 'a wicked ministry and a compliant Parliament' was pointless.[54] Palmer paid the price in September in Perth when he received seven years' transportation for the sedition of pressing for universal suffrage. The judges rejected any idea that universal suffrage had ever existed in Scotland or, if it were to in the future, that it would lead to a freer society, pointing to the events of the Terror in France as giving 'no great encouragement to experiments of this kind'. As with Muir, Palmer's crime in the eyes of the judge, Lord Abercromby, was to have called together 'people ignorant altogether of the grievances which they are told they are loaded with, till they are assembled and taught that they are in a state of oppression'.[55]

Despite the increasingly hostile atmosphere, a third convention was held at the end of October. Only the most committed radicals were now left and they adopted unequivocal stances for universal suffrage and annual parliaments. This convention was to prepare the ground for an all British one to which representatives of the United Irishmen would also be invited, and Hamilton Rowan and Butler from the United Irishmen arrived in early November. The Government had introduced a Convention Act for Ireland which banned public meetings and one of the immediate concerns of the reformers was that a similar one would follow in Britain. Maurice Margarot and Joseph Gerrald of the London Corresponding Society liaised with Skirving and the Scottish delegates on the arrangements and brought a rhetoric into the proceedings which ignored the reality of the Scottish situation. John Brims writes of 'an irresponsible fondness for imitating French forms and styles' and R. G. Gallin argues that resolutions were being passed which indicated a readiness to defy Parliament and for the convention to offer itself as an alternative to Parliament should there be an attempt to ban meetings, suspend habeas corpus or to call in foreign troops, 'Hessians and Hanoverians'.[56] Charles Sinclair, one of the Edinburgh delegates, persuaded it to declare itself 'The British Convention of the Delegates of the People, associated to obtain Universal Suffrage and Annual Parliaments' and, since delegates elected to a convention had been Paine's proposed way of revolutionising society, it is little wonder that the authorities acted.

When the British Convention met early in December the well-prepared authorities, whose informers had infiltrated the proceedings, quickly moved to bring it to an end. Skirving from the Scottish delegates and Margarot and Gerrald from London were arrested. Like Muir, at their trials in the spring of 1794, they conducted their own defence with little understanding of the refinements of Scots law and paid the price with transportation. Only Maurice Margarot survived to return to Britain.

The Pikes' Plot

The chance discovery in May 1794 of about a dozen pikes, spearheads and battle axes in Edinburgh in the house of a bankrupt whose property was being seized led to what were probably quite genuine fears of armed insurrection. In Renfrew a crowd, calling for a national convention and appointing a 'citizen president' as spokesman, had forced the magistrates to release a reformer who had been taken into custody.[57] There was evidence of agitation and of discontent among the fencibles, many of whom were billeted in private houses and who, in some cases, had refused orders, particularly when faced with the prospect of being sent to England and even abroad. The

Scottish version of habeas corpus, the 1701 Act anent Wrongous Imprisonment was suspended and there were arrests. There is no doubt that Robert Watt, a merchant, who had until very recently been a government informer, David Downie, a jeweller and goldsmith and one of the tiny Roman Catholic community in the city, and a few associates had dreams of seizing the castle, the post office and various other public buildings as part of a wider British rising. There had been earlier loose talk among reformers that in the event of an uprising the troops would not fire on the people and of France sending troops to help.[58] George Mealmaker in Dundee was convinced that increasing government repression was closing the door to reform by constitutional means. On the government's part, Dundas believed that many of the Friends of the People outside Edinburgh had been arming and that Paisley in particular was on the verge of revolt. In fact no weapons were found in Perth, Dundee or Paisley where searches were made, 'though the intention of arming and holding regular nightly meetings, are perfectly ascertained'.[59] Watt was duly hanged in September although the elderly Downie's sentence was commuted to transportation, and there was mass detention of radicals in Paisley, Perth, Stirling, Dundee, Edinburgh and Glasgow.

With talk of arming coming from many different places, most of the better off were keen to display their loyalty by joining the Volunteers, which were intended 'to suppress domestic Tumult, and repel external invasion'. Even the most well-connected of moderate Whigs found life difficult. Henry Erskine, no supporter of an extended suffrage but a niggling critic of government over-reaction, found himself ousted from the deanship of the Faculty of Advocates. Most reformers kept their heads down. Thomas Hardy of the London Corresponding Society, recently triumphantly acquitted by a London jury, visited Scotland in 1795 but found a very quiescent situation. In England the acquittals of Hardy and Thelwell and the sharp rise in grain prices in 1795 led to an expansion of democratic reform activity, but not so in Scotland, despite the fact that in March something like an eighth of Edinburgh's population was receiving charitable handouts of food. The two 'Gagging Acts' at the end of of 1795 made political gatherings of more than fifty people without a previous application by seven householders illegal and made almost any statement treasonable which might imply the need for constitutional reform or contempt for the King. They confirmed the views of reformers that Parliament would no longer protect liberty because it was dominated by government placemen who 'pass any law Pitt chuses to propose'.

A Glasgow merchant writing to an American friend complained bitterly of 'the numberless additional taxes' and 'to crown the matter the progress our Ministers have made in Arbitrary government is infinitely beyond whatever could have been supposed to happen in this country formerly a land of liberty'.[60] It would be naive, therefore, to think that reformers did not continue to meet in secret places. It is doubtful, however, if there were at this time in Scotland, as some historians have suggested, extensive links between journeymen's trade societies and political reform activities. Trade societies continued to use the existing mechanism, often through the courts, for getting wages adjusted and the judiciary were careful not to do anything which would undermine that and add to the general unrest.[61] But there was popular discontent over a variety of issues. The army seems to have been universally unpopular, with various attempts to rescue convicted mutineers, and the reports from the Highlands were that it was becoming extremely difficult to persuade men to enlist.[62]

United Scotsmen

How extensive underground political activities were is obviously difficult to judge, but that they were there is in no doubt; what Charles Tilly calls a 'radical underworld of conspirators, confidence men, and zealots'.[63] There were links between the increasingly militant and conspiratorial United Irishmen and reformers in Scotland. As Elaine McFarland has skilfully shown these were not just links with Irish immigrants in Scotland, but educational and social links of long standing. William Drennan of the United Irishmen had learned his debating skills at the Edinburgh University Speculative Society. Thomas Muir had been there at the same time as Thomas Emmett, and Hamilton Rowan had been a fellow student of Fyshe Palmer at Cambridge.[64] In July 1796 the United Irishmen felt it worth their while to make their renewed effort at creating a union between Irish and British democrats through Glasgow, when two delegates from Belfast sought the approval of the Scots for their new draft Irish constitution.[65] By the spring of 1797 there was talk of the United Scotsmen, probably instigated by some Irish exiles, but spreading over the next few years into some twenty-six societies which have been identified, eight in Fife, five in Forfarshire, four in Ayrshire, two in Stirlingshire, one in Renfrewshire and the rest in Lanarkshire and Dunbartonshire.[66] The United Scotsmen was largely an organisation of small tradesmen and journeymen, originally formed in 1793. Weavers predominated and Catherine Burns has also found that it was strong in those areas where there was a seceder tradition. It was a tightly knit secret organisation consciously modelled on the United Irishmen, with no branch permitted more than sixteen members and with a national committee of delegates from local areas controlled by a small secret executive of seven based in Glasgow. Despite its composition, its demands were concentrated on political change, with annual parliaments and manhood suffrage, and it does not seem to have deviated into wider demands for social reform.[67]

George Mealmaker, disenchanted with constitutional methods, appears to have been the key figure. He had been briefly arrested during the pikes' affair, but released. However, his views on the futility of petitioning were well-known to the authorities. Early in 1797 he had published *The Moral and Political Catechism of Man*, which, as well as attacking the concept of hereditary privilege, defended the right of resistance to governmental oppression by the 'united wisdom and energy of a determined people'. The focus of the document was still on political reform and aimed largely at the small independent tradesman, not at some proletarianised working class. There was nothing in it that implied a redistribution of wealth, nothing of the second part of Paine's *Rights of Man* with its calls for greater state involvement. The enemies were aristocrats, monopolists and the vested interests of the old established merchant class, standing against the small producer and tenant farmer who wanted economic individualism.

Judging from the lack of surviving information about the United Scotsmen, the government was remarkably ineffective in penetrating its workings. The immediate worry was the unrest unleashed by the introduction of the Militia Act, which, for the first time, allowed the Scots to create a militia. This required the selection by ballot from young men between the ages of 18 and 23 of a quota from each county. Since it was possible to be exempted or to buy oneself out, the most vulnerable to this conscription were poorer labourers in the small towns and villages, but even some of the middle class could not afford substitutes. When it came into force in August 1797 'Scotland went stark mad as if it had been bit by Corsica', according to Sir George Elliot. There was resistance the length and breadth of the country, with extensive rioting in many small towns, the mobbing of the Duke of Montrose's house in Dumbarton, the Duke of Atholl's at Blair and of William Forbes's at Falkirk. In Ross-shire there was passive resistance and a refusal by the constables to carry out the Act. Some tried to widen the protest. Dalry rioters planted a tree of liberty and Lanarkshire protesters wanted the abolition of the taxes on horses. As radicals pointed out, here was further evidence of arbitrary government, while the authorities protested that the Act was being misrepresented as a kind of servitude. The killing of a dozen protesters, including women and a child, at Tranent, when troops opened fire to quell a riot, led to widespread protest and attempts to prosecute the soldierly. The Lord Advocate blocked these, but he in turn had to drop efforts to act against the rioters when he could not get the jury to convict.[68]

With the lack of any politically sophisticated leadership, the language of the United Scotsmen became increasingly defiant. It was a movement which specifically rejected leadership by the better off. They were to 'go by themselves'. There were reputedly toasts to the death of the King: 'The Old Dog's head cut off, the Bitch hanged and All the Whelps drowned'. But, as the discontent in Ireland turned into real rebellion and as government stirred up fears of French invasion, the movement began to fall apart. Just as in Ireland, there were divisions over both tactics and language. The authorities were convinced that the troops were being got at and there were tales of French emissaries (perhaps paroled French prisoners) spreading revolutionary messages among the radicals. Letters from the United Scotsmen were found among those seized in the naval mutiny at the Nore.[69]

Irish attempts to raise support for armed insurrection in Britain at the end of 1797 led to the arrest of Mealmaker and nine of his Dundee associates. In January 1798 he was sentenced to transportation to Australia where he died a decade later. Others, like the Glasgow leader, Archibald Gray, fled abroad to avoid arrest, while Robert Jaffray, David Black and James Paterson were transported for having 'most traitrously expressed sorrow for the success of His Majesty's arms and joy at the existing rebellion in Ireland'.[70] Despite the sentences and the arrest, or attempted arrest, of many others, the movement did not collapse and there were still hopes of a French invasion. There were also appeals to men and women in 'Ye Middle Ranks of Society':

> you must no longer devote your substance or services to the support of an iniquitous system, and a profligate ministry ... what have the middle ranks of society to expect from supporting the present system? their own degradation and final ruin.[71]

Activists continued to be blamed for undermining the discipline of troops being sent to crush the rebellion in Ulster and there was the persistent belief that others had penetrated the volunteers in order to learn the use of arms. From many parts of central Scotland there were reports of a 'spirit of Sedition and Democracy which abounds'.[72] It is impossible to separate in many cases what are the realities and what the terrors of those in authority. What we do know is that the executive committee of the United Scotsmen was still in existence in 1802, when there was again widespread talk of the possibility of insurrection in England. Talk of two thousand members in Auchtermuchty and Strathmiglo can have been little more than pipe dreams, but the evidence of scattered activity persists and the authorities certainly regarded some of the villages of Perthshire as 'a democratic nest'.

The uprising never came. Many of the potential leaders were picked up or fled. But also the worst of the economic distress was defused although discontents rumbled on. The *Caledonian Mercury* in May 1800, at a time of another round of widespread food riots, published a reward offer for a printer who had published a seditious handbill calling on the inhabitants to gather in the High Green 'under pretext of considering the High Price of provisions, and taking measures for remedying the evil'. But elements of the older paternalism remained, with food distribution, regulation of prices and wages still being practised to enough of an extent to remove the worst unrest. In a number of cases justices of the peace pushed up wages because of the high price of food, clothing and house rents.[73] Even the Militia Act, despite Tranent, was handled with a reasonable sensitivity, reflecting what Elaine McFarland calls the 'greater flexibility of power relationships in Scotland'.[74] Despite the harshness of some individual sentences there was only one execution and the majority of sentences were short and the acquittals many. Many of the Scottish ruling class, like the Earl of Lauderdale, believed that a 'friendly intercourse and relation ... between the wealthy and the indigent ... [was] the best cement to the stability of our constitution'.[75] The established Church played its part also with the General Assembly of 1800 welcoming the fact that

> the exertions of the virtuous, the writings of the wise, and the seasonable interposition of public authority, have served, by the blessings of Heaven to counteract the insidious acts of the disaffected.[76]

Also, as public orders for war supplies grew many of the merchants and manufacturers found their reform enthusiasm waning, and the more contracts there were then the more careful was the business community 'to shape their conduct, and trim their opinion, to please those who had the power of granting them'.[77] The last trial associated with the United Scotsmen was in 1802 when a Fife weaver, Thomas Wilson, received the relatively light sentence of one month's imprisonment and two years' banishment for seeking to overthrow the British constitution – a measure of the authorities' confidence. There was no Scottish equivalent of Colonel Despard's conspiracy of the United English or Robert Emmet's Irish rebellion. The crushing of both marked the end of insurrectionary dreams.

In twenty years many in Scotland had found a voice to call for political change. Enlightened aristocrats, discontented gentry, increasingly confident and assertive merchants and businessmen, had all good reason to be discontented with a political system which not only did not listen to them, but appeared to be becoming more repressive and more extorting. Alongside these, rising prices were pushing many of the less-well-off sections of the population to protest. Sometimes such protests took the form of a traditional riot, but for a few there was a linking of their economic condition with the failure of the political system. The middle ranks were learning to develop rational protest, but so too were the weavers and other workers.

Notes

1. R. A. Houston, 'Popular Politics in the Reign of George II: The Edinburgh Cordiners', *Scottish History Review*, 72 (1993), pp. 167–89; Alexander Murdoch, 'Politics and the people in the Burgh of Dumfries, 1758–1760', *Ibid.* 70 (1991), pp. 151–71.
2. Alexander Murdoch, 'The Importance of being Edinburgh. Management and opposition in Edinburgh Politics, 1746–1784', *Scottish Historical Review*, 62 (1983), pp. 9–10.
3. W. Hamish Fraser, *Conflict and Class. Scottish Workers 1700–1838* (Edinburgh, 1988).
4. J. G. Fyfe (ed.), *Scottish Diaries and Memoirs 1550–1746 Vol2* (Stirling, 1942), p. 405.
5. West Register House, CS 233/T2/18.
6. W. Knight, *Lord Monboddo and some of his Contemporaries* (1900), pp. 179–81.
7. Peter Stern, 'Law and Society in Eighteenth Century Scottish Thought' in N. T. Phillipson and R. Mitchison (eds), *Essays in Scottish History in the Eighteenth Century* (Edinburgh, 1970), pp. 164–5.

8. E. W. McFarland, *Ireland and Scotland in the Age of Revolution* (Edinburgh, 1994), pp. 21, 74.

9. Quoted in V. G. Kiernan, 'Sunrise in the West. American Independence and Europe' in O. D. Edwards and G. Shepperson, *Scotland, Europe and the American Revolution* (Edinburgh, 1976), p. 27.

10. D. Swinfen, 'The American Revolution in the Scottish Press', *ibid.* p. 68.

11. Andrew Hook, *Scotland and America. A Study on Cultural Relations 1750–1835* (Glasgow 1875), pp. 66–7.

12. *Chartist Circular*, No. 21, 15 February 1840.

13. Dundee Central Library, Lamb Collection, 17(5).

14. Murdoch, 'The Importance of being Edinburgh', pp. 14–15.

15. Ramsay of Ochtertyre quoted in Fyfe, *Scottish Diaries*, p. 201.

16. R. B. Sher, 'Moderates, Managers and Popular Politics in Mid-Eighteenth Century Edinburgh' in J. Dwyer, R. A. Mason and Alexander Murdoch, *New Perspectives on the Politics and Culture of Early Modern Scotland* (Edinburgh, 1982), pp. 202–3.

17. In theory, but not in practice, the saying of mass and any proselytising was forbidden. Michael Fry, *The Dundas Despotism* (Edinburgh, 1992), pp. 70–2.

18. See, for example, [Thomas Bannerman] *An Address to the People of Scotland, on Ecclesiastical and Civil Liberty* (Edinburgh, 1782).

19. Isaac Kramnick, *Republicanism and Bourgeois Radicalism* (Ithaca, 1990), pp. 9–10.

20. Ian Ross, 'Political themes in the Correspondence of Adam Smith', *Scottish Tradition*, V (1975), p. 19.

21. Dror, Wahrman, *Imagining the Middle Class. The Political Representation of Class in Britain c. 1740–1840* (Cambridge, 1995), pp. 140–1.

22. E. W. McFarland, *Ireland and Scotland in the Age of Revolution. Planting the Green Bough* (Edinburgh, 1994), p. 54, which contrasts the Scottish attitude with that of the Irish reformers.

23. *Caledonian Mercury*, 23, 28 December 1782, 6 January, 5 February 1783.

24. A. Fletcher, *An Inquiry into the Principles of Ecclesiastical Patronage and Presentation* (Edinburgh, 1783), p. 14; A Fletcher, *A Memoir of . . .* (Edinburgh 1819), pp. 34–5.

25. Philip Harling, *The Waning of 'Old Corruption'. The Politics of Economical Reform in Britain, 1779–1846* (Oxford, 1996), pp. 48–9.

26. J. D. Brims, 'The Scottish Democratic Movement in the Age of the French Revolution', PhD. Edinburgh, 1983, pp. 82–4.

27. *Caledonian Mercury*, 24 March 1792.

28. Edward Hughes, 'The Scottish Reform Movement and Charles Grey 1792–94: Some Fresh Correspondence', *Scottish Historical Review* , 35 (1956), p. 31.

29. *Edinburgh Advertiser,* 5 June 1792.

30. W. T. Baxter, *A Letter on Parliamentary Reform* (1817).

31. Fry, *Dundas Despotism*, pp.160–1.

32. Daer to Grey, 17 January 1793 in Hughes, ' Scottish Reform Movement and Charles Grey', pp. 34–6.

33. N[ational] A[rchives of] S[cotland] Home Office Papers RH 2/4/64.

34. *Caledonian Mercury*, 30 September 1792.

35. Burns to Johnston, 13 November 1792 in J. De Langley Ferguson, *The Letters of Robert Burns* , G. Ross Roy (ed.), Vol. II, p. 158.

36. R. G. Gallin, 'Scottish Radicalism 1792–1794', Ph.D. Columbia University, 1979, p. 114. Gallin sees this as a plea for the right of workers to organise. It is in fact a small tradesmen's demand against wage control.
37. Howell, *State Trials* XXIII.
38. Catherine M. Burns, 'Industrial Labour and Radical Movements in Scotland in the 1790s', MSc. thesis, University of Strathclyde, 1971, p. 129.
39. Laing Collection, Lord Advocate's Correspondence, 12 March 1792.
40. Brims, 'Scottish Democratic Movement', p. 174.
41. E. Richards, *History of the Highland Clearnaces, Vol. 2* (1988), p. 318.
42. *The Poetical Works of John Struthers, with Autobiography,* Vol. I (1850), p. LVI.
43. Dempster to Fergusson, 9 September 1792 in James Ferguson (ed.), *Letters of George Dempster to Sir Adam Fergusson 1756 - 1813 with some account of his life* (London, 1934), p. 22.
44. *Glasgow Journal,* 15 January 1793.
45. NAS Home of Wedderburn Mss. GD 267/1/16.
46. *Ten Minutes Reflection on the Late Events in France. Address by a Plain Man to his Fellow-Citizens,* (Edinburgh, 1793), p. 5.
47. Burns, 'Industrial Labour', p. 140.
48. Alexander Nicolson (ed.), *Memoirs of Adam Black* (Edinburgh, 1885), pp. 45–6.
49. Burns to Robert Graham of Fintry, 5 January 1793 in Ferguson, *The Letters of Robert Burns,* Vol. II, pp. 172–3.
50. Sylvia Clark, *Paisley. A History* (Edinburgh, 1988), p. 45.
51. Hughes, 'Scottish Reform Movement and Charles Grey', p. 35.
52. NAS, RH 2/4. 70.
53. Fry, *Dundas Despotism,* pp. 170–1.
54. Dundee Central Library, Lamb Collection, 17(5).
55. T. B. & T. J. Howell, *State Trials XXIII.* Palmer's friend Ellis went voluntarily to Australia with him.
56. Brims, 'Scottish Democratic Movements', p. 505; Gallin, 'Scottish Radicalism', pp. 195–8.
57. H. Dundas to Pitt, 23, 24 May 1894 printed in Report of the Committee of Secrecy, 1794.
58. Letter of William Peddie to his cousin, November 1792 quoted in Burns, p. 131.
59. *Second Report of the Committee of Secrecy of the House of Commons,* 1794.
60. H. W. Meikle, 'Two Glasgow Merchants in the French Revolution', *Scottish Historical Review,* 8 (1911), p. 150. Letter from John Sword to an American friend, December 1795.
61. For this see Fraser,*Conflict and Class,* pp. 70–1. R. Wells, *Insurrection. The British Experience 1795–1803* (Gloucester, 1986), p. 51 tries to show a link with political reform campaigns, but he misunderstands Scottish trade incorporations.
62. Hall, *British Radicalism,* p. 210.
63. C. Tilly, *Popular Contention in Great Britain* (Harvard 1995), p. 201.
64. McFarland, *Ireland and Scotland,* passim.
65. Wells, *Insurrection* p. 56.
66. Two delegates from the Glasgow United Scotsmen had attended the Convention of October 1793.
67. Burns, 'Industrial Labour', pp. 205–10.

68. Fry, *Dundas*, p. 234.
69. Wells, *Insurrection* p. 96.
70. Peter Berresford Ellis and Seumas Mac a'Ghobhainn, *The Scottish Insurrection of 1820* (1970), p. 83.
71. *Unite, or Be Ruined, Alias the Weavers' Budget. No. IV* (Edinburgh, 1798) quoted in Wahrman, *Imagining the Middle Class*, p. 151.
72. This from Denny in Stirlingshire in May 1799 quoted in Donald C. Smith, *Passive Obedience and Prophetic Protest. Social Criticism in the Scottish Church 1830–1945* (New York, 1987), p. 50.
73. For a more detailed examination of this see Fraser, *Conflict and Class*, pp. 74–80.
74. McFarland, *Ireland and Scotland*, p. 166.
75. *Letters to the Peers of Scotland* (London, 1794).
76. Smith, *Passive Obedience*, p. 21.
77. Baxter, *Letter on Parliamentary Reform*, p. 31.

CHAPTER TWO

Reform or Revolution 1802–32

The peace treaty in March 1802 was generally welcomed, particularly in the manufacturing areas which had found themselves cut off from important export markets. Reformers also generally welcomed the fall of the government, when Pitt resigned over the issue of Catholic Emancipation, although it made little change to the distribution of power in Scotland. Although he was slowly losing his tight grip on Scottish politics, Dundas lived up to his reputation as a clinger to the fruits of high office when he backed the new ministry, and the new Prime Minister, Addington, rewarded him with his viscountcy, as Lord Melville. He had, however, little time to revel in his new title when he unwittingly contributed to the revival of radicalism by his impeachment.

Old Corruption

Disquiet about the costs of the war, which was renewed on slim cause in 1803, had led to calls for the reduction in the emoluments that went with many of the offices of state and which were used for rewarding political insiders. Also, the intermingling of public and private monies, which was tolerated twenty years before, was now less and less acceptable. An inquiry into the navy which was Dundas's area of responsibility, revealed deep-seated mismanagement of government accounts which, while not proving it, pointed to corrupt use of naval money for speculation. It appeared to provide practical proof of radical assertions of corruption. Rumours abounded that Melville and his family were in receipt of more than £50,000 a year from public money, through various sinecures.[1] The radical journalist, William Cobbett, back from America, launched into attacks on a political system which lent itself to 'old corruption', and the government was forced to look again at administrative and economical reforms. Among middle-class reformers there was a sense of public life having been generally corrupted in the 1790s, first by Pitt's apostacy over the cause of parliamentary reform and then by what was seen as the general abandonment of principle, as most opposition politicians had rushed to join the ministerialists under the excuse of war with France. They believed that this lack of principle in turn had spread more widely 'and utterly destroyed everything like confidence in the professions or pledges of any man on public matters ... and every man was reckoned a fool or a wrong-headed enthusiast, who did not trim his political opinions to suit his interest'.[2]

In the repressive atmosphere which had been established by the turn of the century there were few signs of open reform activity, but familiar issues continued to stir popular disquiet. In Aberdeen, the King's Birthday celebrations in 1802 ended in a riot, when the Ross and Cromarty Rangers opened fire on a crowd of mainly boys and young men who had pelted them on their way back from celebratory drinks at the town house. Four of the young men were killed. The magistrates issued a warrant for the arrest of the regimental officers, but they were whipped off to Edinburgh and the Lord Advocate refused to prosecute. It led to much local agitation and money was raised locally to pursue the case, which ended in acquittal and not proven verdicts but left a residue of bitterness that justice had not been done.

The return of Charles James Fox to office in February 1806 in the Ministry of All the Talents cheered the Whigs, despite the fact that the ministry was forged from political expediency rather than by any principles. It did briefly hold out the prospect of peace with Napoleon, but little came of it. On the other hand, the abolition of the slave trade within the empire met a long-established radical demand although it gained the government little gratitude. Much more disquieting for many of the middle-class business community were the disruptions to trade occasioned by the increasingly extensive Orders in Council, which for East Coast merchants put obstacles in the way of trade with the Baltic and, much more seriously, for Glasgow merchants had a disastrous effect on the American trade.

For the middle class, the pattern of protest was becoming much more formalised. Wary of stirring street disturbances they preferred to argue their case through papers and journals. The *Edinburgh Review* became the voice of a younger generation of Whigs from 1802, with Francis Jeffrey as editor and Henry Brougham as a leading contributor, both students of Dugald Stewart. It sought to create and mould a middle-class public opinion in a manner that had never before been attempted. Its politics were critical of government and of Tory repression, but falling well short of calling for radical reform. It wanted to 'design political institutions suitable for modern commercial society'.[3] Another of the founders, Francis Horner, believed that 'the middling order', which he defined as those with 'the opinions, interests and habits of those numerous families who are characterised by moderate but increasing incomes, a careful education of their youth and a strict observance of the great common virtues', could be the foundation of a new political order.[4] But he and his colleagues were as yet some way from seeing themselves as spokesmen for the middle classes. Rather they still saw themselves as battling for control and influence within a fairly narrow élite, not as helping to overthrow that élite, and they preferred to use the traditional methods for getting at their opponents. In 1805, for example, Henry Erskine and his Whig colleagues threw themselves into a drawn out struggle to win John Leslie the chair of maths at Edinburgh University, despite the fact (or because of the fact) that at least some of his enemies regarded him as a 'democratic atheist'.[5] They also enthusiastically debated reform of the Court of Session.

But a bolder tone of criticism of government was increasingly apparent in some of the press. In Aberdeen John Booth's *Chronicle* from 1807 led the attacks on the renewed war, just at a time when there were signs of the stirring of a reform movement in London behind Sir Francis Burdett, and was publicly burned by loyalists for its pains. The *Berwick Advertiser* from 1808, the *Dumfries and Galloway Courier* from 1809 and, most of all, the *Montrose Review* from 1811 all had a mildly liberal tone critical of much of what went on. In 1809 the first *Glasgow Sentinel* appeared, after the *Glasgow Herald* would not publish an advertisement for a meeting to discuss the corruption in the selling of army commissions which had been revealed in the charges against the Duke of York and his mistress, Mrs Clarke. The *Sentinel* was critical of sinecures in general and called for electoral reform. It was also an admirer of William Cobbett, and Cobbett's twopenny *Political Register* circulated widely. Francis Jeffrey claimed that it had more influence than any paper ever had on ' that most important and most independent class of society, which stand just above the lowest'.[6] In was widely read and its attacks on excess and corruption in government chimed in with the discontents of small businessmen at the levels of taxation. On the other hand, worries about disorder and concern at anything which would undermine the value of the paper currency now in circulation made most business and tradesmen keen to maintain as much stability as possible and 'kept alive the terrors artfully excited of revolutionary plots and conspiracies'.

Further signs of discontent within the dominant classes emerged in October 1808 when Jeffrey and Brougham published a review of Don Cevallos' *On the French Usurpation in Spain*, which twinned the events in Spain and Portugal with the failures of the British political system. A system which failed to punish those responsible for the military disasters in Spain, Italy and Walcheren clearly required reform was the argument. Tories, like Walter Scott, were shocked by the piece and it was clearly seen as presaging a new movement which they felt had to be countered. But the Whig élite were not threatening some dramatic change. They were fairly appalled by the popular perception that 'great sums of public money are corruptly misemployed'.[7] What they wanted was strictly limited reform initiated from above. However, Jeffrey was beginning a process of trying to build links with moderate reformers, attacking the growth of government influence and control over the legislature. The role they played as advocates in court cases involving workers helped maintain their reputation as more radical reformers than they really were. They could even, on occasion, act as go-betweens between workers and their employers. When the Lanarkshire weavers in 1812 launched their campaign to get their wages reassessed by justices of the peace and the masters refused to accept, Jeffrey and Cockburn took up the weavers' case and tried to mediate.

Reform revives

The severe recession, particularly for exports, in 1811–12, as neutral countries resisted the British attempts to ban their trade with France and its allies, added to the stresses within the west of Scotland economy. War with the United States was imminent. It led to protests against the war and what was seen as an insensitivity on the part of government to the needs of commercial society. It also added to a perception that powerful metropolitan, shipping and colonial interests were being advantaged at the expense of those manufacturers who depended on the European and American markets. The well-established chamber of commerce in Glasgow led the criticism and backed Whigs, like Brougham, who were pressing for peace.[8]

Many manufacturers were frustrated also by the restrictions placed on their business by older regulations of trade. They resented the traditional restrictions imposed on business development by the trade incorporations and the fact that dues had to be paid to them. Even more they disliked the occasional fixing of wages by justices and the spread of trade unionism. If anything, this interference by the courts in industrial relations had been increasing at the end of the 1790s and in the early years of the new century as the gentry sought to restore social stability and maintain social peace. They had been relatively successful in preventing well-organised trade societies linking up with political movements. But as industry and trade expanded there were demands from business for the liberalisation of trade. The judiciary was beginning to show itself more aware of the arguments of Adam Smith and others that interference with trade would be kept to a minimum and more sympathetic to the demands of a commercial society. At the same time there was a hardening of attitude on poor relief which made it more difficult for the unemployed to receive support.[9] In the west, employers were collaborating to try to get the Combination Laws against trade societies applied to Scotland. Workers' societies of different trades responded by learning to collaborate and held delegate meetings to organise petitions against any such move.

The great strike of handloom weavers across much of central Scotland in 1812 to try to maintain court regulation of their wages brought matters to a head. The Lord Advocate and the Home Secretary were anxious lest these economic discontents would ignite political unrest. A correspondent warned the latter, Lord Sidmouth, that Parliament 'had nothing to *spare* of credit with the people, and *very little* would induce the body of weavers to join with the friends of parliamentary reform in England'.[10] They had wind of some sort of revolutionary movement, similar to the United Scotsmen, 'the Defenders', which had contacts in Ireland, England and Wales and there were recurring outbreaks of discontent among the militia.

There were other signs of increasing social tension. New Year riots in Edinburgh in 1811–12 ended in the death of a policeman and a clerk and, while probably just the result of youthful exuberance which got out of hand, none the less revealed simmering class antagonisms. The subsequent execution of three young men all under the age of eighteen caused a tremendous popular outcry. It was also difficult to keep up enthusiasm for a war in continental Europe which had dragged on for nearly twenty years and, even less, for a new war with the United States which was disrupting lucrative trade. There were concerns that French officer prisoners of war on parole were undoing the effects of war propaganda by being charitable and giving help to people: 'the common people ... have begun to consider the statements of the rapacity and cruelty of the French in Portugal and other countries they have devastated, as fabrications – and to believe them to be people by whom they would not be injured or oppressed, even were they their masters'. Also Maurice Margarot, undaunted by his fourteen years in Botany Bay, was back in Scotland renewing his old contacts. His every move was watched by government agents, but the discontents and the contacts were there to build on.

The revival in demands for political reform came quickly after the end of the wars with France. With Napoleon on Elba there was an expectation that the tax burden would be lightened. When this did not happen there were widespread protests against the income tax, which was particularly resented as an exposure of people's private affairs, and other property taxes. It was widely believed that it was needed not so much for defence purposes but to feed Tory extravagance. Public meetings of protest were held.[11] The celebration of Fox's birthday in Glasgow in January 1816 toasted the 'abolition of the British Inquisition – the Income Tax'. Even after the final defeat of Napoleon the tax issue continued to be uppermost. In Edinburgh there was an outcry when it was decreed that shops would be taxed in the same way as houses and therefore would be liable for the continuing window tax and the Whigs, Jeffrey and Moncreiff, associated themselves with the campaign against property taxes.

The English veteran, Major John Cartwright, who had been around advocating parliamentary reform since the 1770s, made his first tour of Scotland in July 1815, visiting Glasgow, Dundee and Aberdeen and a few of the smaller towns in central and west Scotland. Most of the newspapers ignored his presence. However, in October, Edinburgh reformers met in the fives-court in Rose Street to consider petitioning for reform of the House of Commons. Old reformers, like Captain Johnston in Edinburgh and Archibald Hastie in Paisley returned to the fray and stirred some action.[12] By early 1816 a petitioning movement was well under way on both sides of the border. There were different perceptions of the problems. The Whig position was still that it was too much executive power that was the problem and that that power needed to be reduced and controlled by a more critical parliament. An article in the *Edinburgh Review*, for example, suggested that another subject of complaint, rotten boroughs, were not the worst part of the system and could provide a base for men of 'the greatest talent and independence', while shorter parliaments might actually have the effect of increasing the power of the executive. It also argued that 'firmness to oppose the people, is some-times as necessary a quality, as independence to resist the Crown'.[13] The more radical position assumed that the whole political class with few excep-tions was largely corrupt and needed to be thoroughly reformed.

The abolition of the income tax in 1816 dealt with a major grievance of the better off, but it meant a higher burden of taxes placed on consumption, so that something like half the price of coffee, sugar, tea, soap, candles and tobacco was taxation. Taxes *per capita* had doubled between 1789 and 1815. Charles Tilly has calculated that about a third of average household income went on taxes in 1815 compared with only a seventh in 1801.[14] Unemploy-ment for many and the collapse of farming after years when a high demand for farm labour had helped keep rural discontents at bay, added to the general distress. There was serious rioting in Glasgow at the beginning of 1816 with attacks on a soup kitchen and a powerloom factory, which led to the intro-duction of the Malicious Damage Act for Scotland to deal summarily with such attacks on property. But there were still complaints also from the better off. In Aberdeen a meeting of the Incorporated Trades called for 'retrench-ment and economy', deploring the number of sinecures and pensions being handed out. They were also highly critical of the size of army which was still being maintained despite the fact that peace had come. It was viewed 'as dangerous to the liberty of the subject and highly unconstitutional', as well as expensive.[15]

Although Cartwright's Hampden clubs had initially attracted mainly mer-chants, tradesmen and shopkeepers, the general distress was causing support to widen. A letter in the *Glasgow Herald* in June 1816 referred to evidence of 'an extensive and widely-spread conspiracy for the avowed purpose of over-turning the Government'. With something like 300,000 being demobilised from the army in less than a year, the glut in the labour market was great. Handloom weavers were particularly badly affected and they began to look to parliamentary reform as the best hope of getting regulation of their trade re-introduced. Parliament in 1813 and 1814 had swept away all the restrictions on wages and on employment of apprentices which had existed since medi-eval times. This dealt with one of the major grievances of manufacturers, but left workers totally vulnerable to market forces. The political discontents remained, however. In Glasgow, on 29 October 1816, the largest political meeting yet held in the city had to be assembled outside the city boundaries at the estate of James Turner of Thrushgrove, a wealthy tobacco retailer, after permission to go to the Trades' Hall or the Green had been refused. Marching behind great banners, with bundles of rods, symbolising unanimity, large brooms, to sweep away corruption, and caps of liberty, the demonstrators showed how much had change since the 1790s. Here was a confident, well-organised assertion by ordinary people of their right to be heard by Parliament. It was claimed that 40,000 attended and the idea was to present a programme which would have the widest possible acceptance by all shades of reformer.

A striking feature was the bitterness about the war and its outcome which came out in many of the speeches. Archibald Gray, a reformer of the 1790s, spoke of all classes operating 'under an overwhelming load of indescribable calamity', with the middle classes 'galled by wants and debts' and tradesmen 'shutting up their shops or doing nothing in them'. It was the result of a war which seemed to have been fought, it was claimed, 'for no other object than the restoration of whatever was detestable, bigotted, and despotic ... the re-establishment of the despicable family of Bourbon, the restoration of the Pope in Italy and of the Jesuits, and the Inquisition in Spain'. Only 'retrench-ment and reform', the phrase that was to become the catch phrase of Liberalism for the next century, would change the situation, by removing 'those noble sturdy beggars ... who have fastened themselves like leeches upon the state'. This could only be done by the people having representatives of their own choosing.[16]

In the aftermath, the decision was made to send a delegate to make contact with the Hampden Club in London. Other meetings quickly followed in Calton and in Pollokshaws, and a Paisley one reputedly numbered 40,000 and attracted 'respectable persons'.[17] The themes were similar. The House of Commons had ceased to be a check on executive power and a defender of liberty, the war had been 'unjust and unnecessary' and expenditure on the army and the civil list had got out of hand. There were fears 'dangerous strides towards a Military Government'. At all the meetings the 'impolitic, unjust, iniquitous and calamitous Corn Bill' was condemned as having created two classes within the nation 'a neglected and wretched Populace, and a favoured and overgrown Landed Interest'.[18]

Radical reform

Popular discontent intensified as did official attempts to counter it, making use of a growing network of spies and informers. As economic conditions worsened, with the price of meal doubling in the last half of 1816, there were riots in Dundee first against mealsellers, but then directly against the provost and council. There were reports of secret conspiracies and arming in Linlithgow, Glasgow, Kilbarchan and Paisley and frantic efforts by the authorities to infiltrate the reform organisations. A militant, popular move-ment began to emerge, spreading like a contagion among the working classes, according to the sheriff substitute of Renfrewshire. In Glasgow it seems to have started in the cotton spinning mills and then spread to the handloom weavers, although the circumstances and the needs of the two groups were quite different. Cotton spinning was prospering, while the weavers, suffering from a catastrophic collapse in wages, wanted access to poor relief. According to the former paid informer, Alexander Richmond, there was a hardening of class divisions: 'a line of demarcation was drawn between the different ranks of society, and rooted antipathy and a ferocious spirit of retaliation was engendered in the minds of the labouring classes'.[19]

A Tradeston Society existed by the end of 1816 committed to a reform of Parliament 'by forcible means in the event of the Petitions of the People not being granted', while the Calton Society was committed to 'sane principles'. By January 1817 there was a central committee based in Calton but with contacts throughout Glasgow and the surrounding towns and villages, with Andrew Mackinlay, Hugh Dixon, John Buchanan and James MacLauchlan (who had been organising the weavers' campaign for poor relief) as leading figures. The aim was 'to obtain for all the people of Great Britain and Ireland, not disqualified by crimes or insanity the elective franchise at the age of 21 with free and equal representation and annual parliaments'.[20] Copies of Cobbett's *Political Register* circulated with a reading club to which people contributed a halfpenny a week to have a copy passed to them.[21] When Cobbett fled once again to America, it was replaced by Wooler's *Black Dwarf* with even more vigorous attacks on the aristocracy.

These societies were largely groups of workers and small tradesmen, but they were supposed to have been in contact with a 'Committee of Gentlemen' in Glasgow, and there were discussions about sending delegates to liaise with groups in England. According to press reports, delegates from Glasgow attended the huge meeting of representatives of Hampden Clubs and other reform bodies, called together by Cartwright in the Crown and Anchor in London in January 1817. The meeting was thrown into turmoil when Cartwright and Burdett came out in favour of a petition only for household suffrage, equal electoral districts and annual parliaments rather than universal suffrage.[22]

Early in 1817, the movement spread to Perth and Dundee. The *Dundee Advertiser* in 1816 had become the vehicle of reforming views thanks to its editor Robert Rintoul and two activists, the Forfar laird, George Kinloch and a teacher at the academy, Robert Mudie. Kinloch had come to public notice in 1810 when he took up the cause of harbour reform and succeeded in prising control away from the town council. In 1817 when Provost Riddoch refused to call a meeting on parliamentary reform, Kinloch presided over a great gathering on Magdalen Green attended by some 7,000. Another key figure was William Thomas Baxter, son of a factory owner, who issued letters on the need for parliamentary reform first to 'the tradesmen and labourers' and then to the inhabitants in general. These too asked what the war had been fought for. The distress, 'a scene of bankruptcy and ruin, among her

farmers, merchants, and manufacturers' was blamed on pensions and sinecures and the lack of effective control over Parliament which could only be
righted by annual parliaments and the ballot. He felt bold enough to quote
Thomas Paine, 'that for a nation to be free it is sufficient that it wills it'. The
problems stemmed from the Corn Laws and from the lack of universal
suffrage and annual parliaments.

The riots in London's Spa Fields and elsewhere and hair-raising reports of
events in Scotland from the Lord Advocate, led once again to the suspension
of habeas corpus and of the Scottish equivalent, a restriction on public
meetings and mass arrests of suspected activists. Those arrested and accused
of treason tended to be working men, mainly weavers and cotton spinners,
although with a smattering of teachers, a spirit merchant and the son of a
coalmaster. Judging from the direction of the questioning the authorities
were particularly concerned to try to unearth any Irish links. It seems to have
been a version of the United Irishmen's oath which was administered, and a
number of those arrested were of Irish extraction. Others were associated
with the Universalist Church in Glasgow, whose pastor, Neil Douglas, had
been an active reformer since his early years in Dundee.

Kilmarnock also seems to have been an area of considerable radical activity
at this time and Paine's *Age of Reason* circulated, playing 'sad havoc with the
settled opinion of a previously orthodox Kilmarnockian' and stimulating calls
for equal division of property.[23] In March 1817, two Kilmarnock men,
Andrew McLaren and Thomas Baird were charged with seditious libel. They
were representative of the different groups who were committed to reform.
McLaren was a poorly-paid weaver, who had seen his standard of living
plummet so that he was lucky to earn 5s a week. Baird, a shopkeeper and
former captain of the volunteers, was eminently respectable. Much to everyone's surprise, they received the relatively mild six months sentence, thanks
perhaps to an eloquent defence speech by Francis Jeffrey. In April, John
Keith, a mill manager, and William Edgar, a teacher, from Glasgow were
charged with administering unlawful oaths, but an inept Lord Advocate and
the uncertain nature of much Scottish law on sedition and treason led to the
collapse of the case. Their role in the trials further enhanced the reform
standing of Edinburgh Whigs. Cockburn, Jeffrey and others volunteered their
services to the accused free of charge. The next try by the authorities was
against the elderly Revd Neil Douglas, who in many of the fervent meetings of
his Universalist Church, usually in a hall of the Andersonian Institute, had
denounced both George III and the Prince Regent and declared that in the
House of Commons, 'seats were sold like bullocks in a market'. Many of the
more militant reformers were associated with his church. He too was
acquitted, as Francis Jeffrey again tore holes in the prosecution case. Finally
Andrew McKinlay, an Irish-born Calton weaver, and treasurer of the radicals'
inner committee, was hauled up in June 1817 charged with administering
unlawful oaths. From the authorities point of view the result was another

shambles. There were extensive legal arguments over whether a Scottish court could try anyone for treason and on the question of whether secret oath taking by itself was treasonable. When it was revealed by James Campbell, the chief witness, that he had received payment from the authorities the jury returned a verdict of not proven and McKinlay and his associates were released. At the same time there had been sensational revelations in the *Leeds Mercury* of the activities of W. J. Richards, 'Oliver the Spy', in acting as an *agent provocateur* in the unrest in Yorkshire and Derbyshire, which shocked moderate opinion. With the sedition trials, the suspension of habeas corpus and the tight control imposed on public meetings the parliamentary reform campaign waned. The working-class sections were rent with suspicion as accusations were tossed around about the presence of spies and *agents provocateurs* in the events of the last few months. Alexander Richmond, formerly active in the Weavers' Union, was publicly exposed as one such.

The authorities were also faced with renewed discontent among the better-off over the way in which their burghs were run. Henry Cockburn noticed that a younger generation of Edinburgh merchants had lost their subservience. In 1816 there were widespread protests in Paisley when the town council proposed to sell off the superiority of the town. Later that year, the burgesses in the Guildry of Montrose petitioned for the right to elect their own deacon, plus two councillors and for the right to see the annual accounts from the town. This was granted by the town council and ratified by the Convention of Royal Burghs, as was the decision to select magistrates by a secret ballot rather than by open voting, but when the result was a majority opposed to the dominant ruling clique on the council the matter was taken to the Court of Session, who declared the whole process illegal. However, a poll election of the burgesses was granted to appoint a new council and a new sett was approved. Dundee, which had been run by Provost Riddoch and his cronies for nearly forty years, and Brechin also managed to get changes which gave the burgesses the right to elect three of the twenty-one council members. Dundee and Annan petitioned for the yearly election of seven councillors, but their plea was rejected. A burgh reform movement revived with Archibald Fletcher, the old burgh reformer of 1782 making a reappearance.

Aberdeen's bankruptcy in early 1817 came after a mounting frustration at the lack of information on the town's finances emerging from the closed town council, run by the Hadden family and their business associates. The burgesses in the guildry blamed the 'secret junto' of the town council acting with responsibility to no one but themselves. The failure of the old council was so apparent that there were hopes that the campaign for burgh reform of thirty years previously might at last reach fruition and a new council elected by a poll of burgesses might be achieved. However, the old council was restored by the Privy Council and, despite claims that it was illegal and unconstitutional and contrary to the Claim of Right of 1689, it proceeded to self-select from the ranks of the old guard. Public feeling was vented on them by a stoning on their way to the kirkin of the council and a public meeting condemned the way in which the council persisted in pursuing measures contrary 'to the opinion of the great body of the inhabitants'.[24]

In Edinburgh, the incorporated trades and the merchant guildry also petitioned for change. Laurie, deacon of the dyers' incorporation, took the council to the Court of Session to try to get alterations to its procedures. The position in most of the royal burghs was now notorious and a parliamentary inquiry found that, as well as Aberdeen, Edinburgh, Dundee and Dunfermline were, to all intents, bankrupt. The reports (three of them in 1819, 1820 and 1821) on the Scottish burghs added to the demands for change, although as the government packed the committees with placemen the tone softened. Attempts to have the reports debated in the House were blocked and, although an 1823 Act allowed burgesses to complain of misuse of funds, there were petitions protesting at the inadequacy of such a measure.[25] Long before this it was apparent to many that parliamentary reform would have to come before effective burgh reform.

Middle-class demands may have switched back to burgh reform, but distress still persisted amongst handloom weavers and they continued to give a political edge to their protests. Debates on the best tactics continued among those who wanted reform. Some were convinced that the aid of 'enlightened and disinterested friends of liberty in a higher station' would be essential.[26] Others were prepared to talk of revolution. A Roman Catholic priest reported that his largely Irish population was so poor that they 'have nothing to lose in a revolution'.[27] Union Societies spread throughout the west of Scotland and increasingly seemed prepared to talk in terms of physical force. Links were developing with militant movements in the north of England. At the suggestion of the organiser of many of these Union Societies, Joseph Brayshaw of Yeadon, one of the many 'political entrepreneurs' (to use Charles Tilly's felicitous description) who were around at that time, there were boycotts of the heavily-taxed items of tea, beer, spirits and tobacco. A recurrence of unemployment during the summer of 1819 added to the tensions. In June, a large radical demonstration in Paisley, when the cap of liberty was once again on display, rejected the usual resolution for a petition to the Prince Regent, which it was claimed had been 'treated with contempt and insult' and agreed instead to issue an address directly to the nation. From different parts of the country north and south of the border there was talk of planned armed uprisings. Cockburn mused in his journal that 'the sedition of opinion . . . was [being] promoted by the sedition of the stomach'. Groups met to discuss the ideas of Cartwright, Hunt, Carlile and other English reformers and sported white hats to mark themselves as radicals. There was debate on equal division of property, but all were agreed 'that there should be no king, no lords, no gentry, no taxes'.[28] Others, particularly in Paisley, practised drilling and marching.

The cutting down of protesters at Manchester's St Peter's Field in August 1819 by local yeomanry and hussars shocked middle-class and working-class people alike and confirmed fears that the imposition of martial law was a possibility. Sixteen thousand protested on Paisley's Meikleriggs Moor and rioted when the Provost tried to prevent their carrying their banners through the town and when the band was locked up for playing 'Scots Wha Hae'.[29] In Dundee 10,000 gathered to hear George Kinloch denounce the authorities' actions in Manchester and call for annual elections, universal suffrage and vote by ballot. But it broadened into a wider protest. Sailors carried a union flag surmounted by a ships hull 'as emblematic of the ruined state of commerce', while other people carried a pole 'from which dangled a broken tea-kettle, and two broken teapots; and from another was suspended the fragments of a gill stoup of wine glasses, tobacco pipes and snuff boxes – memorials of luxuries once enjoyed by the poorest man in the kingdom'.[30]

At the end of September a large meeting of protest was organised in Glasgow. The men wore the green ribbons of the Union societies in their buttonholes, while young women marched bearing aloft caps of liberty. A new unstamped paper, the *Spirit of the Union,* which first appeared in October 1819 produced by two Glasgow printers, Gilbert MacLeod, a Unitarian, and Alexander Rodger, circulated among radical groups and denounced the 'farcical mummery of the house of corruption'. The government responded to the widespread unrest and criticism after Peterloo with the Six Acts, which made summary trial easier, increased the penalties for seditious libel, extended the newspaper tax to all periodicals carrying news, curtailed further the right of public meetings, banned training in arms and gave the magistrates extensive authority to search for arms. Among those arrested was George Kinloch. The last issue of the *Spirit of the Union* of 8 January 1820 announced the arrest of the editor and publisher, charged first with contempt of court for publishing a report on the arrest of George Kinloch and then for sedition. Kinloch and his family fled to Paris.[31] MacLeod ended with five year's transportation to Australia.

The Radical 'War'

The effect of the Six Acts was effectively to cut off the prospect of change by constitutional means and to leave the field to the more militant elements. A heady atmosphere of political rhetoric, social distress and fervent agitation among many groups of workers and reformers built up during the winter of 1819–20, while growing panic ensued among the authorities. How real the threats of armed insurrection were it is impossible to assess. Some of the talk of revolution was undoubtedly what John Bohstedt calls 'reveries of rebellion' performing 'a vital psychological function, leavening the more sober (but futile) movements with wistful fantasies and establishing a kind of emotional counter culture to the authority of the rulers'. None the less, the threats were taken seriously. Counter-revolutionary associations, like the 'Sharpshooters', came into being and anyone who had shown radical sympathies in 1793 was the object of suspicion. Troops found themselves pelted in the streets; the police in the west of Scotland were issued with cutlasses. Some activists had contacts with groups in Manchester, Nottingham and elsewhere and there was talk of a co-ordinated rising. Others had some loose links with Arthur Thistlewood and his Spencean associates in London, plotting in Cato Street the destruction of the Cabinet. Most protests meetings were in fact peaceful and orderly, but that in itself was reason for suspicion on the part of the Lord Advocate, who believed that that was 'contrary to the nature of Scotsmen' and therefore must 'denote some great but secret purpose on the part of the people'. He was convinced 'that revolution is the object'.[32]

In February 1820, the day after Thistlewood and his friends were arrested, a reform committee of some twenty-seven mainly weaver activists, meeting in Glasgow, were seized. They were still in prison in November 1820, although it is not clear what became of them. The movement clearly had been deprived of leadership, but troubles went on, with strikes, minor riots and even the burning down of a mill, all linked by the authorities to radical activities. By the end of March there were rumours circulating in Glasgow of a plan to set fire to the city. In Kilmarnock there was a demonstration with many of the marchers apparently carrying arms in fear of being attacked by the Edinburgh yeomanry stationed in the town. There is also evidence of a wider conspiracy to foment a rebellion linked to armed uprisings in Huddersfield and Barnsley.[33] But, in fact the main outbreaks in England were over before the Glasgow troubles exploded.

It was in this atmosphere that the *Address to the Inhabitants of Great Britain and Ireland* appeared on the walls of Glasgow, Paisley and Kilsyth on the morning of 2 April. Produced by three Parkhead weavers, Robert Craig, James Armstrong and James Brash, it called for a resort to arms and for a stoppage of all work until every man was 'in possession of those Rights which distinguish the FREEMAN from the SLAVE, viz: That of giving consent to the laws by which he is governed'. The call was not aimed specifically at the working class. 'The interests of all classes are the same', it declared:

> The protection of the Life and Property of the *Rich Man*, is the interest of the *Poor Man*, and in return, it is in the interest of the Rich, to protect the poor from the iron grasp of DESPOTISM; ... Equality of Rights (not Property) is the object for which we contend ... we think it indispensably necessary to DECLARE inviolable, all Public and Private Property.

The Address generated much activity in the villages and suburbs around Glasgow. There were parades and demonstrations, while many others kept away from work. Pikes and swords were taken out of hiding. Looking back from the vantage point of 1859 John McKinnon recalled the atmosphere in Anderston, an industrial village on the edge of Glasgow:

a considerable number of pike heads were made, and a number of poles were taken from the dye works which were standing, and they were used as shafts. Muskets and rifles with bayonets and powder and belts were exposed for sale in the windows of several gunsmiths, and everything portended the commencement of war.

In Paisley one of the radicals was shot when an attack was made on a house to try to seize guns, and cannon were mounted on the Clyde bridges after rumours of a march from Paisley. At a meeting mainly of weavers, on Glasgow Green, it was decided to march to Falkirk to the Carron Iron Works to get arms, the expectation being that by then Falkirk and Camelon workers would have seized the works. Andrew Hardie and a group of Anderston weavers joined up with Robert Baird and a group from Condorrat near Cumbernauld and, at a fairly leisurely pace, made their way towards Falkirk. There were probably not many more than fifty of them and when confronted by a troop of hussars at Bonnymuir they were easily rounded up. Four were wounded and forty-seven arrested. The following day in Strathaven, long a place of radical activity, the old reformer from the 1790s, James Wilson, a stocking weaver turned gunmaker, was given the honour of leading a march of reformers to Glasgow and to bitter disappointment on the Catkin Braes. Yet another group of about forty marched from Bridgeton to Kirkintilloch to help the expected uprising there. In Stewarton in Ayrshire, a radical shoemaker, sword in hand, proclaimed a new constitution. In Greenock, a crowd broke into the town jail and released some Paisley radicals who had been incarcerated there. Within a week it was all over.

We shall probably never know how far the events were triggered by the actions of *agents provocateurs* keen to bring the radicals out into the open. Certainly, given the ineptness with which the affair was handled there must be some credence in the arguments of Ellis and Mac A'Ghobhain that government agents played their part. After all, many of the key leaders were already arrested and large numbers of troops were in position in potentially sensitive areas, although, as Roach suggests, the thinness of much of the evidence at the subsequent trials suggests that spies were fewer than the authorities might have wished. On the other hand, others clearly genuinely believed that there was no alternative but to 'unfurl the red flag of defiance and trust to God and our own right arms for the salvation of ourselves, our families and our fatherland'.[34]

In the aftermath, house to house searches were carried out, mail was opened and arrests were widespread, including James Turner of Thrushgrove. Others fled to other parts of the country or abroad.[35] The *Glasgow Herald* noted that 'persons have disappeared not previously suspected of taking part in revolution'. Many of those seized were just locked up for a week or two and then bailed without further action. In all eighty-eight were indicted for treason, under the English law of treason, although only thirty actually appeared. Most were weavers, the rest nailers, smiths, shoemakers, tailors, a cabinetmaker, a schoolmaster, a grocer, a slater and a flesher. The death sentences on Baird, Hardie and Wilson – none of whom had been identified as leaders – and the rejection of the many appeals for clemency, plus the transportation of eighteen others, may have added to the sense of a government that was not listening. On the other hand, all eighteen of those who appeared at Stirling had been sentenced to be hanged, beheaded and quartered but had their sentences commuted. Elsewhere, the authorities found the juries unwilling to convict if there was the likelihood of its leading to the death penalty. The fact that only three were executed and that many others who had participated were released is perhaps another indication that the government had already crushed the radicals even before the uprising. Hardie went to his death asserting that he had come out to achieve his rights of 'annual Parliaments and Election by Ballot'. Asked why he should expect such rights, he replied, 'Because I think Government ought to grant whatever the majority of the nation requested'.[36]

Middle-class reform

It was effectively the end of revolutionary endeavours and it was the end of the largely working-class movement for political reform. Middle-class reformers had, on the whole, been at pains to distance themselves from the social unrest of 1819–20 and this gave some reassurance to the gentry. Once again, the Whig lawyers had maintained their credibility as reformers by acting for the defence in the trials and the whole affair convinced them that they had to reassert their leadership of the campaign for political reform. They liked to see themselves as standing somewhere between government and the extreme demands of the radicals. The campaign now would not be for anything approaching universal suffrage, but for the franchise for the middle class and, it was implied, a middle class 'so respectable and improving' that it could stand alongside the gentry in defence of property. Jeffrey in the period of radical unrest had noted 'the separation of the upper and middle classes of the community from the lower, which is now daily and visibly increasing' but also the division between the upper and the middle ranks, and he and Brougham began to argue strongly for a measure of middle-class enfranchisement.[37] Jeffrey and his associates called for a change of government at a meeting in the Edinburgh Pantheon, sensational for its novelty in Edinburgh. Where once the language had been people versus aristocracy, now it was of the capable, wealth making middle class who were the creators of social progress. The Whigs could 'occupy the middle ground, and ... show how a large proportion of the people are attracted to the constitution, while they lament its abuses'.[38] Other Scots, like the Benthamite James Mill, were putting forward similar arguments on 'a middling class' whose mission was 'to counterbalance the despotic tendencies engendered in other classes by the progress of improvement'.[39]

The affair of Queen Caroline, whom George IV was determined to divorce and to keep away from the coronation and which rumbled on between June 1820 and her death in August 1821 allowed Whigs to register protest by supporting her cause. Public meetings in Edinburgh and elsewhere allowed protest in a relative safe manner, which riled Tories but threatened no one. The Edinburgh one attracted 10,000 and when the bill of pains and penalties against her was thrown out, houses were illuminated in celebration in defiance of the magistrates. Elsewhere, addresses of congratulation were sent to the Queen from public meetings and some clergymen defied their presbytery by continuing to include the Queen in the usual prayers for the royal family. But the wider radical movement was now effectively moribund.

The prosperity of the early 1820s took the sting out of many of the working-class discontents. With the departure of Sidmouth and the suicide of Castlereagh, younger Tories came forward and began to adjust government politics to take account of the demands of middle-class businessmen. The royal jaunt to Edinburgh in 1822 no doubt provided an entertaining diversion, although the kilt did little to enhance the personal standing of the deeply unpopular incumbent of the throne.

The conclusion of the Whigs after 1820 was that reform was even more necessary if a recurrence of the more threatening revolutionary activities were to be avoided and, throughout the 1820s, they came forward as the moderate leaders of movements towards reform, linking up with middle-class reformers in various causes. One of these was the anti-slavery movement. Having achieved the banning of the slave trade in 1807, in the 1820s reformers moved on to campaigning for abolition. The Anti-Slavery Society appeared in 1823. Also the lesser gentry returned to attacks on the unfairness and corruptness of the county franchise, only to be told that any change in the franchise would breach the Act of Union.

The retirement of Lord Liverpool in 1827, however, after fifteen years in office was the harbinger of more dramatic changes. The resignation of Robert Dundas, the second Viscount Melville, was perhaps even more significant, finally bringing the era of tight political management in Scotland to an end. There was, however, only very limited interest in parliamentary reform at the end of the 1820s. One historian describes it as a 'virtually forgotten issue' as late as 1829.[40] Debates over Catholic relief gave encouragement to priest baiting even among those who were critical of Tory government, while most working-class activists were more concerned with building their trade unions in the aftermath of their partial legalisation in 1824–5 and as the economy began to pick up again. Nevertheless, there were significant changes in the 1820s. As Dror Wahrman has shown, it was in that decade that the concept of a middle class with specific political demands and capable of controlling and leading those lower down the social scale became firmly established.[41] It was the confidence drawn from this new perception that made such a wide section of middle-class reformers so ready to seize the opportunities presented in 1830.

The Reform Act

Three years of divided Tory rule as the party tore itself apart over Catholic emancipation came to an end in November 1830 when Wellington resigned and Grey, once an enthusiastic reformer but now much cooled on the issue, led the Whigs back into government. After all the years in the political wilderness the expectations were high that the new government would bring in constitutional change including an extended franchise. Reform Committees had already began to reappear in the aftermath of the French Revolution of July 1830 and before the Whigs came into office. Twenty-five thousand had signed a reform petition in Edinburgh in September 1830. A group of working-class reformers met in Alexander Tait's coffee house in the Trongate in Glasgow and flew the French tricolour.

By 1830 there was a very active trade-union movement in Glasgow, with a trades' committee and various co-operative groups which produced its own newspaper, *The Herald to the Trades Advocate*. The working-class reformers meeting at Tait's were largely the same people as those who ran the trades' committee. It was these who took the initiative in inviting the radical MP for Montrose Burghs, Joseph Hume, to visit the city in September 1830 to put the case for parliamentary reform. Hume's visit and the concern that the working class might act on its own led to the formation of a Reform Association. It was determinedly socially exclusive, consisting of leaders of the business élite – Dunlops, Tennants, James Oswald. The working-class reformers, on the other hand, were keen to see the campaign broadened and organised pro-reform meetings in which any idea of using violence to achieve their ends was deliberately eschewed. The co-operator and later Owenite missionary, Alexander Campbell, and John Tait, the brother of the coffee-house owner and 'the Moses of the Radical Camp',[42] took the lead in discouraging 'the idea entertained by the masses that physical force would ultimately be necessary to wrench a liberal measure of reform from the aristocracy'. It was a recurring theme in the *Herald to the Trades Advocate* that 'the style of 1817 and 1820' was no longer applicable: 'We prefer a gradual remodelling of the constitution to a violent and otherwise inevitable revolution'.[43]

Glasgow was unusual in the amount of working-class involvement in the campaign. Elsewhere it was gentry and businessmen and often the town councils and trade incorporations which were calling for reform. The press in the first two weeks of 1831 reported meetings in Dingwall, Hawick, Alloa, Bathgate, Cupar, Markinch, Inverkeithing, Leven, Kilmarnock, Renfrew, Inverary and Glasgow. In Dingwall the magistrates and town council called for burgh reform. The freeholders in Ross-shire and those in Clackmannan, where there were only six voters including the sitting member, demanded reform of the county franchise. The burgesses and householders of Hawick wanted 'full, free and equitable representation in the Commons House of parliament', the ballot and a franchise which would 'embrace a great proportion of the productive classes', while those in Kinross wanted 'to give a voice to the real property, wealth, industry and intelligence of the country'. In Bathgate it was declared that 'the people of Scotland have, in a great measure, lost confidence in their representatives, for during a long period of years they have attended more to the private interests of their own immediate constituents, than those of the public at large'.[44] An unprecedented level of political agitation was to continue throughout the rest of the year with petitions flooding in to Parliament and to the King. It was clear that despite the quiescence of the 1820s there was a mounting level of frustration which the return of the Whigs had unleashed.

It was quickly apparent that any reform offered by the new government would be a limited one well short of universal suffrage. Whigs and their supporters, 'proprietors and capitalists' as the *Scotsman* described them, were not going to support a system 'which would enable those who possess neither money nor lands, nor any ostensible community of interest with them, to tax them at pleasure, and in effect render those who have nothing, masters of the property of those who have much'.[45] The *Aberdeen Journal* was reassured that any changes would be in accordance with 'the wishes of the middle classes of society'.[46]

Initially, some working-class meetings, which were few in number, tried to get calls for universal suffrage, the ballot and annual parliaments or even for household suffrage and triennial parliaments, but arguments on what was practical politics and what was necessary to get middle-class support generally prevailed. When the details of the Whig proposals eventually emerged there was some expression of disappointment that the scheme did 'not embrace the whole of those who had a just and indisputable right to it'; none the less it deserved support, it was argued, since it would ultimately lead to a further extension.[47] The desire was to get any measure through in the first instance. The Glasgow Trades' Committee, following the example of a Paisley committee some weeks before, summoned a reform dinner in January 1831, inviting the other reform groups of the 'liberal landed classes' and the 'merchant princes'. It would prove the respectability and responsibility of the working class. The 'deluded brethren in the south' who had succumbed to violence and riot were condemned.[48] The trades' paper went out of its way to reject the idea that what was aimed at was 'equality of property'.[49] The hope was that the Whig reformers in the Reform Association could be persuaded to come into a Political Union on the model of Thomas Attwood's in Birmingham, 'embracing as far as possible the higher, middle and lower classes' and a Scottish Political Union was formed with Robert Wallace of Kelly, the MP for Greenock, as president. Although three of the twenty-seven executive were recognised working-class trade-union leaders, Daniel McAulay, James Nish, and Joseph Miller, membership was restricted by an entry fee of 6d and the leading figures were small business-men, like James Moir, a Gallowgate tea merchant, James Turner and John

Ure. This was a pattern repeated elsewhere, in Edinburgh, Dundee and Aberdeen, with middle-class associations and trades' political committees and limited attempts to unite middle class and working class through a political union.

Early in the morning of 23 March the Reform bill passed its second reading in the Commons by a majority of one vote. The news was greeted with illuminations in cities throughout the country. Glasgow and Edinburgh, with the approval of the the magistrates, were alight with transparencies, emblematic devices, variegated lamps, flags, bonfires, squibs, crackers and tar barrels. A few silhouettes of Thomas Muir appeared and at least some reformers saw it as the culmination of a movement which had begun in the 1790s. But the backlash started almost at once and anti-reform campaigns were launched. The effect was to do the Whigs work for them, since getting the bill through became the issue. When Edinburgh had its first working-class meeting for reform in April there was no talk of universal suffrage or annual parliaments or the ballot, only of the bill. An Edinburgh Political Union was firmly in the hands of lawyers and businessmen.

The government's defeat in committee in May and the subsequent general election unleashed another round of processions, meetings and petitions. The trade unions organised a great political demonstration in May 1831 on Glasgow Green which, according to Cockburn, attracted between 80,000 and 100,000, while the *Scotsman* estimated twice that. He concluded that 'the people of Scotland have probably never been in a state of greater excitement than now'.[50] When the town councils persisted in voting for anti-reformers there was an outcry. The election of R. A. Dundas in Edinburgh against Francis Jeffrey led to cries of 'Burn the Bailies' and 'a rope for Dundas', the smashing of the council-house windows and the mobbing of the provost. Elsewhere, the response was more serious, with riots in Ayr, Lanark, Dumbarton and Haddington when reformers went down to defeat. In Dundee a police office was stoned. English votes gave the Whigs a clear majority and the process of reform started again, with signs of growing impatience. The Edinburgh Political Union called for a speeding up of the whole procedure, while the *Scotsman* urged the middle class to push the measure through lest 'it ends, as it is sure to end, in revolution'.[51]

Once again, the bill passed the Commons only to be rejected again by the Lords in early October. In Nottingham and Derby there were serious riots, but in Aberdeen on 24 October 1831, despite of a day of wind and rain and the collapse of one of the platforms, between ten and fifteen thousand met in support of the bill in a quiet and orderly manner. Five days later a similar meeting in Bristol ended in the burning down of a sizable portion of the town, the mansion house, the customs' house and the bishop's palace. There was nothing comparable in Scotland, with the Glasgow Trades' Committee still urging moderation, although it did follow the lead of the Birmingham Union in discussing the formation of a national guard.[52] In Edinburgh, the council of the Political Union set out to 'discourage every attempt towards outrage, and to put down every attempt at unconstitutional insurrection'.

Worries about the determination of Grey's government to continue the struggle with both King and Lords led to renewed demonstrations. There was also particular concern that the £10 voting level might be altered or that the Scottish bill might be more limited than the English one. Sixty thousand turned out in April in Edinburgh's King's Park, with trade unionists alongside leading 'persons of eminence' such as Sir John Dalrymple, Sir James Gibson Craig and Sir Thomas Dick Lauder. Those who took the most active part tended to be those who had political ambitions in a reformed parliament. Continued obstruction by the Lords and the King's refusal to create peers led to the resignation of the government in May and Wellington's vain attempt to form a Tory one. The outcry was immense with suggestions, echoing old fears, that Wellington was planning a coup d'état and the establishment of military government.

Despite all the anxieties aroused by the cholera epidemic which was sweeping through the country, a second massive demonstration was held in Edinburgh's King's Park, where the tone was much angrier than that of three weeks before, with Adam Black calling for the Commons to refuse to agree supply until the bill was passed. Glasgow had its largest demonstration yet. Royal portraits were carried upside down, flags were dyed black, skulls were carried on staffs and death heads were painted on banners. Radical voices were heard condemning the Whigs as 'snakes basking in the sunshine of Reform, but ready to slink into their holes when the dark day comes' and Dr David Walker declared that 'It was now the Bill or the barricades. The Reform Bill must be passed or blood should flow'.[53] On the other hand, the meeting was chaired by Sir John Maxwell of Pollok. In Paisley the leading merchant, Archibald Spiers of Elderslie, denounced 'the minions of that curse of his country, Billy Pitt' and Wellington 'as no more worthy of attention than the gabble of a turkey cock on a leaping-on stone'. He hinted at withholding payment of taxes. For a week there were daily demonstrations in different parts of the country, with much singing of 'Scots wha hae' and banners threatening reform or else. Church bells were tolled in mourning and in Glasgow bars portraits of the King were turned to the wall or torn down.[54] Nine days later Grey was back in office. A number of further reform demonstrations were held, linking trade unions and middle-class reformers to strengthen the Whigs' backbone. One in Aberdeen attracted 20,000 and, in June, the Lords gave way and the English bill passed, with the Scots and Irish measures following in August.

Scottish reformers had shown themselves remarkably orderly in the campaigns for reform. Whigs and moderate middle-class reformers had most effectively kept control of the movement. If conclusions were drawn from the events of 1820 it was that there would be no repetition. Working-class leaders and middle-class reformers were determined to demonstrate a responsibility which they believed would win a first stage in parliamentary reform. What had emerged was a movement which spanned all classes from the gentry to the working class and which ensured that reform was persisted with against all the obstacles thrown its it way by King and Lords and which, while giving much less than many of the earlier reformers had hoped, was also more than the more moderate Whigs would have wished.

Notes

1. Harling, *The Waning of 'Old Corruption'*, p. 84.
2. W. T. Baxter, *A Letter on Parliamentary Reform addressed more particularly to the Inhabitants of Dundee and the East Coast of Scotland* (Dundee, 1817), pp. 23–4.
3. Biancamaria Fontana, *Rethinking the Politics of Commercial Society; the Edinburgh Review 1802–1832* (Cambridge, 1985), p. 10.
4. Horner to Francis Jeffrey September 1806 quoted in Anand C. Chitnis, *The Scottish Enlightenment and Early Victorian Society* (1986), p. 113.
5. J. B. Morrell, 'The Leslie Affair: careers, kirk and politics in Edinburgh in 1805', *Scottish Historical Review,* 54 (1975), pp. 63–82.
6. Harling, *The Waning of 'Old Corruption'*, p. 92.
7. *Ibid.* pp. 104–5.
8. J. E. Cookson, *The Friends of Peace. Anti-War liberalism in England 1793–1815* (Cambridge, 1982), p. 236.
9. R. Mitchison, 'The Creation of the Disablement Rule in the Scottish Poor Law' in *The Search for Wealth and Stability*, ed. T. Smout (1979), pp. 119–217.
10. NAS RH2/4/100 J. J. Dillon to Viscount Sidmouth, 31 December 1812.
11. *Glasgow Herald,* 6, 17 February 1815.
12. *Ibid.* 6 October 1815; Clark, *Paisley,* p. 56.
13. *Glasgow Herald,* 9 August 1816.
14. Charles Tilly, *Popular Contention in Great Britain 1758–1834,* (Harvard, 1995), p. 209.
15. *Aberdeen Journal,* 10 April 1816.
16. *Glasgow Herald,* 1 November 1816.
17. *Glasgow Chronicle,* 2 November 1816.
18. *Ibid.* 9, 12 November 1816.
19. A. B. Richmond, *Narrative of the the Condition of the Manufacturing Population* (1824), p. 54.
20. W. W. Roach, 'Alexander Richmond and the radical reform movements in Glasgow in 1816–17', *Scottish Historical Review,* Vol. 51 (1972), pp. 4–5.
21. The information on the 1816–17 activities comes mainly from Declarations of persons accused on treason in NAS AD 14/17/8.
22. *Glasgow Chronicle,* 28 January 1817.
23. James Paterson, *Autobiographical Reminiscences* (Glasgow, 1871), pp. 64–6.
24. *Aberdeen Journal,* 30 September 1818.
25. Theodora Keith, 'Municipal Elections in the Royal Burghs of Scotland', *Scottish Historical Review,* 13 (1916), pp. 266–78.
26. *Glasgow Chronicle,* 24 August 1819.

27. W. M. Roach, 'Radical Reform Movements in Scotland from 1815 to 1822', Ph.D. thesis, University of Glasgow, 1970, p. 188.

28. J. Paterson, *Autobiographical Reminiscences*,(Glasgow, 1871), pp. 64–7.

29. Glasgow District Archives TD 743. Autobiography of John Mackinnon.

30. James Thomson, *The History of Dundee*, (Dundee 1874), p. 381.

31. Kinloch was allowed to return after his daughter successfully petitioned George IV on his 1822 visit to Edinburgh.

32. quoted in Clark, *Paisley*, p. 58.

33. F. K. Donnelly, 'The Scottish Rising of 1820: A Re-interpretation', *Scottish Tradition*, VI (1976), p. 27.

34. Quoted in Roach, 'Radical Reform Movements', p. 231.

35. John McKinnon fled to Dundee.

36. *The Radical Revolt. A Description of the Glasgow Rising of 1820*, (Glasgow, n.d.).

37. Dror Wahrman, *Imagining the Middle Class . The Political Representation of Class in Britain*, (Cambridge, 1995), pp. 202–16.

38. *Ibid.* p. 255.

39. Quoted *Ibid.* p. 257.

40. John A. Phillips, *The Great Reform Bill in the Boroughs*, (Oxford, 1992), p. 17.

41. Wahrman, *Imagining the Middle Class*, chap. 7.

42. J. D. Burn, *Autobiography of a Beggar Boy*, (1978 edition), p. 139.

43. *Herald to the Trades Advocate*, 2 October 1830.

44. All from *Scotsman*, 1, 8, 18, 24 January 1831.

45. *Ibid.* 19 January 1831.

46. *Aberdeen Journal*, 1 December 1830.

47. *Herald to the Trades Advocate*, no. 25, 12 March 1831.

48. *Scots Times*, 8 January 1831.

49. *Herald to the Trades Advocate*, 26 March 1831.

50. Henry Cockburn, *Journal 1831–54, Vol. 1*, p. 76.

51. *Scotsman*, 6 August, 21 September 1831.

52. *Ibid.* 12 October 1831.

53. J. Fyfe (ed.), *Autobiography of John McAdam*, (Scottish History Society, 1980), pp. 7–9.

54. *Scotsman*, 16 May 1832.

CHAPTER THREE

The Chartist Years 1832–48

By its conclusion in 1832 the reform movement had become a movement of middle class and gentry with the working class providing the extras for the crowd scenes. The arguments, such as that of the evangelical *Scottish Guardian*, that a moderate reform measure would 'knit the hearts of the middle classes to the Constitution … and check popular excesses' had won the day.[1] No working-class figure emerged as particularly significant in the campaign. A few voices, like that of the Glasgow co-operator, Alexander Campbell, suggesting that the extension of the franchise would not solve the social problems faced by working people, were drowned by the pressure to get a bill of any kind through. Just as the gentry and middle class took the lead, so they were the gainers from the extended franchise. Alexander Bannerman, businessman with strong landed links, was returned in Aberdeen, Sir George Kinloch in Dundee, James Oswald in Glasgow, while in Edinburgh and its surrounding shires the knights and baronets who had come forward at the great rallies of 1831 and 1832 took their seats.

The Reform election

The popular enthusiasm for the new reform was soon muted when it became apparent just how limited the effect would be. Given the complete unrepresentativeness of the pre-1832 system in Scotland the addition of 60,000 voters was bound to be revolutionary, but 400,000 adult men still had no vote, and as Norman Gash pointed out a long time ago 'there was scarcely a feature of the old unreformed system that could not be found still in existence after 1832'.[2] The ambitious and rapidly-growing towns of Aberdeen, Dundee, Greenock, Paisley and Perth were each given their own member. Glasgow, now the largest city, was taken out of Clyde Burghs and given two members of its own. While Edinburgh, the only Scottish burgh with its own member before 1832, was given a second one. On the other hand, towns such as Airdrie, Falkirk, Hamilton, Kilmarnock, Cromarty, Oban, Peterhead and Port Glasgow were taken out of their counties and linked with often not very logical burgh groupings, effectively to remove urban (presumed Liberal) influence from the counties. The franchise was granted to ten-pound householders, both owners and occupiers, in burgh seats, but ten pounds was a high rental in Scotland and still excluded many of the lower middle class as well as nearly all wage earners. Thanks to careless drafting by Cockburn, the Solicitor General, the county franchise remained a mess, with little account being taken of the distinctiveness of the Scots law on land tenure. While some old abuses had been removed the room for new ones was ample. As William Ferguson showed, far from removing the possibility of creating nominal or fictitious voters, long a grievance with the lesser gentry, the effect was merely to make the price of purchasing a voter cheaper.[3] Tenants, in particular, had little protection from intimidation.

Although most of the emphasis during the reform campaign was on class collaboration, there were, at moments, signs of specific working-class demands. Alexander Campbell told a reform meeting in October 1830 that 'the working classes, on whom depend the whole fabric of society, should now begin to think more of themselves'.[4] He consistently argued that political reform was not enough in itself but had to bring about fundamental alterations in social relationships resulting in the working class retaining the whole produce of their labour. The *Herald to the Trades Advocate* listed seven reforms that they believed should follow parliamentary reform: free trade in corn, abolition of slavery, cultivation of waste land, reform of the law courts, yet wider representation of the people in parliament, proper use of charitable funds to provide education and the separation of church and state. The reform demonstration in Edinburgh in August 1832 came up with a very similar range of demands.

Campbell had also talked about the possibility of a specifically working-class parliamentary association, on the model of O'Connell's Catholic Association, which would collect money to fund an MP of their own class.[5] In the 1833 election there were tensions with middle-class reformers when attempts were made to organise exclusive dealing with those voters who had firmly declared themselves for popular candidates, and the cotton spinners' union was keen to pin down candidates to support factory legislation. In the end, reform candidates did well with Whigs winning 43 out of 53 Scottish seats. Some middle-class reform demands were immediately satisfied when the Lord Advocate, Jeffrey, brought in the long-awaited burgh reform act of 1833, which replaced the notorious closed corporations with councils elected by more or less the same electorate as for parliamentary elections. 1833 also saw the end of slavery within the British Empire, the culmination of a campaign instigated initially by members of the Society of Friends but closely associated with the political reform movement. Political reformers regularly mentioned the end of slavery as one of their demands, while pro-slavery people were generally on the side of anti-reformers. Many reform activists had seamlessly moved into the anti-slavery campaign after 1832.[6] Another irritant for the business community, however, exclusive trading privileges for members of incorporations, had to wait until 1839 before it was removed.

Disenchantment

Meanwhile, working-class radicals remained dissatisfied. In Aberdeen and elsewhere political unions remained in existence to continue to press for universal suffrage, annual parliaments and the ballot.[7] At the annual Thrushgrove meetings held each October to commemorate the 1816 gathering, the need for further reform was always raised. A monument to Hardie and Baird, the 'martyrs' of 1820, was unveiled at Thrushgrove in November 1832. A visit by the Liberal Lord Durham, one of the authors of 1832, brought similar demands for further reform. When Daniel O'Connell visited Glasgow in 1835, the Trades' Political Union organised its own demonstration and called for 'Household suffrage, triennial parliaments and vote by ballot'. In the little village of Fenwick in Ayrshire the 'Improvement of Knowledge Society' regularly debated political issues such as 'Whether Monarchical or Republican forms of Civil Government are best fitted for the People's Welfare' (concluding that it was the latter) and whether that change could best be achieved by moral or physical means. In April 1836 a debate on extending the franchise concluded that 'household suffrage in present exigencies is most expedient but universal is every man's right and most Beneficial'.[8] The *Workmen's Advocate*, which in turn gave way to John Tait's *Liberator* newspaper, kept up the demand for further reform.

Disenchantment with the Whig government was setting in rapidly, particularly after the harsh sentences on the Tolpuddle farm labourers, and there was increased polarisation between Whig-dominated local groups and more radical working-class organisations. The very lively trade-union movement also increasingly interested itself in politics, with both masons and ironmoulders in 1836 calling for franchise extension. The ever-active Alexander Campbell argued that unions 'must become *political* unions [and] agitate and petition, and demand, with one overpowering voice, relief from the burden of taxation'.[9] The extensive use of the stamp act against radical publications led to demands for repeal of 'taxes on knowledge', an issue which united working-class and middle-class political activists.[10] In 1836 a Radical Association of the West of Scotland welcomed the Irish radical, Feargus O'Connor to Glasgow.[11] The Association, chaired by the swarthy, Byronic figure of Dr John Taylor, a former naval surgeon who had come to notice with fiery speeches during the 1832 demonstrations, was for universal suffrage, annual parliaments and the ballot, and 'if members wished, a voluntary church'. Campbell was again a leading spokesman, arguing that the working class wanted their rights and that 'they had been taking instalments too long'. Now they wanted the whole.[12] There are numerous others signs of a continuing radical thread. In Aberdeen, for example, reformers pressed the local MP in

1835 to support annual parliaments, the ballot and repeal of the corn laws, while, in the election of 1837, an address to the working classes and non-electors called for the ballot, extension of the franchise, short parliaments, reform of the Lords and abolition of the corn laws.[13] Any expectation of getting more from the Whigs was dashed by Lord John Russell's assertion at the end of 1836 that he would never support the ballot and there would be no further political reform.

Against the Corn Laws

Hopes of reform of the Corn Laws were also rather quickly shattered by the new government. Since their reimposition in 1815 the Corn Laws had been seen as particular examples of an aristocratic ruling élite using Parliament largely for the defence of its own interests. With the price of grain tumbling in the early 1820s to less that half the 80s level at which the Corn Law allowed imports, the issue went off the agenda. However, in the second half of the 1820s prices began to rise again and, as the language of class became increasingly used in the 1820s, so the issue began to be painted even more sharply as one where middle-class interests were opposed to those of the landed class because of what the Corn Laws contributed to the stagnation of trade.[14] Joseph Hume regularly denounced them and talked of bringing in repeal motions. On the other hand, landowners like Sir John Sinclair rallied to their defence, blaming the inadequacy of protection for rural distress.

For the working class, the concern was that the laws artificially kept up the price of bread, and in 1826–7 Dundee factory workers had collected 7,000 signatures in favour of repeal. The *Herald to the Trades Advocate* found it easy to transfer its hostility to monopolies to positive support for free trade as 'a stimulus to exertion, [and] encouragement to the noblest energies of scientific genius'.[15] The laws were discussed during the reform campaign. At the great rally in Edinburgh in April 1832 the lawyer and editor of a literary journal, William Weir, who had also been one of the founders of the Edinburgh Political Union, had lambasted government's resistance to free trade and its 'absurd restrictions upon industry'.[16] The first repeal society, the Mechanics' Anti-Corn Law Association was set up by Edinburgh tradesmen in November 1833 with William Biggar, a printer, P. M. Knox, a teacher, James Alston, a joiner and George Fleming, a painter, as the leading members. They put forward the traditional argument that legislation which benefited a few at the expense of the many was wrong in principle, while complaining of the effect on food prices. But they also accepted what was the middle-class argument that the removal of the restrictions on imports would allow trade to grow and lead to an expansion of employment.[17]

Weir moved to Glasgow to become editor of the Whig *Glasgow Argus*. and a Glasgow Anti-Corn Law Society was formed at the end of 1833 by a number of middle-class businessmen. In contrast to Edinburgh, in the embittered

atmosphere of industrial relations in Glasgow in these years, there was little
encouragement given to working-class involvement. The Dundee situation
was something similar. A committee with at least ten working-class members
out of fifty was set up in 1833 which organised a demonstration in 1834, but
after a strike in which Edward Baxter tried to break the Dundee and Lochee
weavers' union the organisation began to fall apart and to divide on class
lines. With other issues on the agenda the movement against the corn laws
did not gather a great deal of momentum and there was difficulty in stirring
wide middle-class interest. Weir for one in 1835 questioned the value of
focusing on it. However, in the following year a number of Scottish radicals
attended the launching of the Anti-Corn Law Association (soon to be
League) in London. Among those linked with the new organisation were
Dr John Taylor, William Tait, Edinburgh bookseller and publisher, William
Weir and Patrick Chalmers of Auldbar.

Birth of Chartism

There are a few signs of remnants of political unions beginning to stir, but
there were also complaints from working-class radicals that those who ran
the reform campaigns were too exclusive and too limited in their demands. In
Edinburgh, after initial harmony with middle-class reformers over the corn
laws, some working-class radicals broke away to form their own 'Association
for a Further Improvement in the Representation of the People'. In 1836
John Taylor had taken over Tait's *Liberator* newspaper and re-launched it as
the *New Liberator*. The tone was now very different. While Tait had been
concerned to project a moderate image of the working class and to encourage
collaboration with middle-class radicals, Taylor adopted much more con-
frontational tones, which led to accusations that there was Tory money
behind it. Something of a romantic poseur, Taylor was seeking to unite the
trade-union movement, which had been expanding rapidly in the prosperity
of 1836, with political radicalism. Feargus O'Connor's tour at the end of 1836
gave a boost to the movement and encouraged some workers to turn away
from exclusive attention to trade-union building to reform of Parliament. A
National Radical Association for Scotland was formed.

The years 1836–7 brought a period of intense industrial unrest in the west
of Scotland among cotton workers, building workers, miners and ironwor-
kers. For some of the middle class it renewed fears about the dangers of
stirring up mass discontent and set back the hopes of those who had been
working to maintain an alliance between middle-class and working-class
reformers. The events culminated in the shooting to death of a strike breaker
and the arrest of eighteen spinners in July 1837. In October they had not yet
been brought to trial and public disquiet mounted with a petition of protest
signed by 20,000 being presented to Parliament. Eventually four of the
officials of the cotton spinners' association and another spinner were

brought to court at the last possible moment before the law required their release.[18] The obvious difficulties which the authorities were having in finding evidence and the way in which the indictment tried to link the events of 1837 to violent activities up to twenty years before immediately raised doubts about the procedures. The harsh sentences of seven years transportation on the spinners' leaders, respectable, self-improving working men, revived memories of Braxfield and the 1790s. The vendetta which Sheriff Alison, an old-fashioned Tory, launched against trade unionism in general and the manner in which the case was carried through stirred echoes of the repression of Pitt and Liverpool's governments. The result was that although there was no doubt that the cotton spinners' strike and trial aroused some class antagonisms and raised middle-class fears about any extensions of democracy, at the same time it also raised concerns about the impartiality of the system of justice.

The Scottish press initially accepted the authorities' case against the spinners and it took time for disquiet to mount. Taylor's *New Liberator* probably did little to help by reporting the speeches of the north of England Chartists, Augustus Beaumont and Joseph Rayner Stephens when they talked of going forth 'with dagger in one hand and torch in the other' to 'wrap in one awful sheet of devouring flame, which no army can resist, the manufactories of the Cotton tyrants'. On the other hand, Feargus O'Connor believed that their threats had saved the spinners from being hanged.[19] Taylor himself at a meeting in Leeds declared that 'the time for physical force had arrived ... It was high time to lay down the spade and take up the sword'. At the same time, a Committee of Trades' Delegates set up to campaign to get the sentences commuted and to counter the generalised attacks on trade unionism, found that they were getting support from the Chartist movement which was spreading throughout England. Indeed, Dorothy Thompson has argued that the sentences on the spinners gave a real stimulus to the nascent movement.

The beginning of the Chartist campaign proper in Scotland is usually dated from 10 April 1838 when a group, most of whom had been associated with the 1832 political unions, met in Glasgow to invite the Birmingham reformer, Thomas Attwood, to Scotland. They included the indomitable Turner of Thrushgrove, James Moir, and trade unionists such as James Proudfoot, a joiner, Pattison, an engineer and Thomas Gillespie, a printer. A similar gathering followed in Edinburgh.[20] The People's Charter was published by London reformers in May 1838 as the rallying standard for a new national movement for political reform. The aim was to unite the different reform organisations behind the single banner of the six points of the vote for all men over twenty-one; of more or less equal constituencies in terms of population; annual parliaments; the ballot; no property qualification for members of parliament and payment of members. Later in the month Scotland had its first mass Chartist rally when trade unions gathered on Glasgow Green to hear Thomas Attwood. Significantly, his message was

'Peace, Law, Order, Loyalty and Union' and the linking of working-class and middle-class reformers in a traditional petitioning campaign. On the other hand, the working-class spokesmen like Proudfoot, and Pattison went out of their way to comment on the fact that the meeting was largely organised by the working class alone. A letter from an Aberdeen working man to the Whig Lord Provost, who had refused permission for a reform meeting, brought out some of the sense of disenchantment with the middle-class reformers of 1832: 'Is it not wonderful then, that having allowed you and your friends to chalk out this alteration of the system, and having found it all chimera and humbug in its effects, we should try to lend a hand ourselves to repairing the ancient constitution of the country'.[21] Attwood's associates held meetings in Kilmarnock, Stirling, Dundee, Dunfermline, Cupar and Edinburgh. Other activists toured around in the summer successfully spreading the message of a new reform campaign for universal suffrage, and a Scotland-wide movement was launched.

Attwood and his colleagues preached class collaboration and reform through moral force. On the other hand, at the end of June 1838, forty radicals gathered in Glasgow with the republicans John Taylor and Thomas Gillespie, for an anti-coronation party, 'to show contempt for illuminations, and all the degraded foolery of coronations', and Taylor went on to denounce those who were calling for a firm rejection of violence as 'degraded cowards'.[22] But it was the moderates who set the tone for the future of Scottish Chartism. The leaders who came to the fore, John Fraser, a veteran of 1820, now based in Edinburgh and Abram Duncan, a pirn maker and lay preacher, with good Glasgow links, both pushed petitioning as the method and temperance as the most effective way of persuading Parliament to support working-class demands. There were, however, many different elements in Chartism each placing a slightly different emphasis on its objectives. The movement was a great deal less homogeneous and much more complex than is often implied. The debate over whether or not the use of physical force to obtain the charter was justified was only one of a number of issues of debate, and a relatively minor one.

Chartist discourse

Something of the flavour of the mainstream of the movement can be found in the Chartist press, which was the means by which a national movement was created. A number of radical booksellers had emerged as distributors of cheap publications aimed largely at the working class; Henry Robinson in Edinburgh, William Love, son-in-law of the Owenite, Alexander Campbell, in Glasgow, James Myles in Dundee and William Lindsay in Aberdeen. Through their agency the new Chartist press could be quickly distributed. While O'Connor's *Leeds Northern Star* circulated, it was mainly to their own papers that Scottish Chartists looked: the *Scottish Patriot* from July 1839 until early 1841 and the *Chartist Circular*, published between September 1839 and June 1842 by the Central Committee for Scotland of the Universal Suffrage Association and largely funded by the prosperous shoemaker, George Ross. Disappointment with the effects of 1832 were obvious. It had led to no change in the condition of the poor. Among the specific grievances were the imposition of military law in Ireland, the banishing of the Dorchester labourers, the reform of the poor law, the destruction of representative government in Canada, the enquiries into handloom weaving which had produced nothing, the failure to repeal the Corn Laws, and the increased use of spies and police. The explanations given for this state of affairs were a combination of class analysis and older views of the corruption of the system by a clique.

Working-class radical activists were struggling to find a discourse which made sense of the post-1832 situation. Blaming the aristocracy remained attractive: 'the mitred and titled vagabonds ... The cursed hereditary system', together with the game laws and the system of primogeniture were regularly attacked:

> Hereditary power corrupted the whole government, poisoned the press, demoralised society, prostituted the church, dissipated the resources of the nation, created monopolies, paralysed trade, ruined half the merchants, produced national bankruptcy – it could be overthrown if capitalocracy united with the people.[23]

The 'oppressive laws and iniquitous monopolies' maintained by the aristocracy affected employer and employed alike, claimed the *Scots Times* and 'compel masters to do what in other circumstances they would not think of'.

An alternative analysis was that a small group of corrupt politicians, the Whigs, having achieved power, had been corrupted by the system and were now abandoning the principles for which they seemed to have stood in 1832, and had 'a design to subvert the democratic principles of the constitution': 'A Whig is a political shuffler, without honour, integrity or patriotism'.[24] On the other hand, bitterness in industrial relations and a growing sense of betrayal by the middle class was also encouraging yet a different perspective. The poverty of a vast proportion of the working classes stemmed from the unjust distribution of the nation's wealth, 'because the lords of the middle class turn the power of their capital against the producers, and unite with the aristocracy in the wholesale plunder of the people'. 'A heterogeneous confederacy of wealth and title' was running the state for its own benefit.[25] Bronterre O'Brien wrote regularly for the *Circular*, and in his writing there are frequent references to the conflict of interest that existed between employers and workers. There was a growing sense of betrayal by the middle class, 'the real tyrants of society', until by 1841 the *Circular* was asserting that 'in countries where a few nobles and aristocrats constitute the ruling class, the condition of the producers is infinitely preferable to what it is under the *Liberals* of

France and England'.[26] On the other hand, at other times there was a direct appeal to the middle class, with the argument that 'the first effect of universal suffrage would be the repeal of the iniquitous Corn Law',[27] There was also resentment at the persistent attempts to demean working people. Scott's writings, for example, were condemned for presenting the noble born as 'generous, good and brave', while the people he 'contemptuously describes ... as cringing, fawning, creeping, half-crazed vermin, executing the despotic will of their master without compunction'.[28] The Chartists particularly resented an assumption that morality and social stratification were linked. It was suggested that the middle-class belief that 'wealth is a term somewhat synonymous with honesty and intelligence' made it difficult for them to conceive of how 'the hardworking man, who has nothing to subsist on but what he earns by the sweat of his brow' should have the same rights as themselves.[29]

The struggle for the Charter was set in the historical context of earlier struggles. The Covenanters were frequently cited who 'threw aside all personal considerations, and boldly defied the tyrant and his laws, when these infringed on the inherent rights which God had given men'.[30] The movement was linked to the struggles of the 1790s with sketches of Joseph Gerrald and others and much attention was paid to past Irish struggles, particularly that of the United Irishmen. There was a nationalistic element in some of the writing. William Wallace and William Tell are frequently cited and a great deal of attention was paid to George Washington and the American model of democracy. A usual implication was that what was needed was a great and enlightened leader, and it may be that this explains the persistent appeal of O'Connor to many. Past struggles were interpreted in terms of great leaders who had inspired their following. At the same time there was an implicit assumption that, because of the justice of the cause, victory was inevitable. The masthead of the *Chartist Circular* carried the Marquis de Lafayette's declaration that 'for a nation to love liberty it is sufficient that she knows it, and to be free, sufficient that she wills it'.

By 1840 there was a powerful anti-clerical tone in many of the pieces, reflecting the debates on church-state relations which were in the process of tearing apart the Kirk. The Christian element in the movement was strong, but there were also regular denunciations of the 'despotism of priestcraft' and of ministers as 'a time-serving sycophantic class'. Opposition was to establishment: 'Wherever an established priesthood has existed, the people have been mentally and physically enslaved ... and is designed to enslave the public mind, by exciting religious veneration for ecclesiastical establishment, and enforcing "passive obedience" to political iniquity'.[31] But dissenting ministers did not escape either, who had 'almost as one man ... set their face against the extension of the suffrage', and their attempts to evangelise would be fruitless until a man and his family had a supply of the necessaries of life: 'Fill the belly, cover the back, and the mind is open to receive impressions'.[32]

The *Scottish Patriot* addressed the clergy directly,

> You pretend to be the followers of Him who was, is, and shall continue to be
> the poor man's friend, even the meek and lowly Jesus. Yet, notwithstanding
> this, I find you constantly arrayed on the side of power, taking part with the
> oppressor, opposing every measure that would tend to enlighten the minds of
> your fellow men, or alleviate human suffering, and soften the pillow of
> distress … You ought to teach that all mankind are equal in the sight of God.[33]

Chartists were encouraged to return to 'pure Christianity', conducting their
own family worship without clergy.[34] The first Chartist Church in Scotland
opened in the spring of 1840.[35]

The debate over physical or moral force barely surfaced in the pages of the
Circular. As Dorothy Thompson has argued, 'Much of the violent language of
the Chartist leaders was a style of speech – a rhetorical device which both the
followers and the authorities recognised to be a form of bluff'.[36] And many of
those identified as 'physicals' were more moderate when it came to actually
deciding policy at the conventions than they were on the public platforms.
They were agreed that nothing could be gained from 'partial outbreaks', which
would just get them cut down by the military, and that success would depend
on 'the assistance and encouragement of those clear-headed, judicious men,
by whom every great movement amongst the people must be guided, if they
would expect to be successful'. On more than one occasion, however, there
were attacks on the doctrine of passive obedience taught by schools and
churches and, in April 1841, the *Circular* published a piece by Bronterrre
O'Brien on the question, 'Can Reform be obtained without Revolution?'
which did not rule out the idea of revolution. Another piece on John Knox
described him as 'a zealous Radical Reformer – a Democrat – a Republican,
and a physical-force Chartist'.[37] It was in John Fraser's *True Scotsman* that the
issue of tactics was most extensively discussed. Fraser had been a schoolmaster in Johnstone in Renfrewshire who had been arrested during the round
up of suspects in 1820 and held for four months before being called as a
witness in the Paisley treason trial. He, together with his friend, the Revd
Patrick Brewster, minister of Paisley Abbey Church since 1818, regarded any
return to the situation of 1820 as disastrous for the prospects of reform. Only
by disavowing violence could they hope to get the support of the radical
element of the middle class. On the other hand, Robert Malcolm's *Scottish
Patriot* which commenced publication in July 1839 was more equivocal and
refused to go along with resolutions completely rejecting physical force.

The Chartist press is full of history and literature, which usually although
not always has a political message, and full of poetry, the spell of which
caught many of the Chartist activists. All the Chartist press was also
concerned with self improvement, every bit as much as the mid-century
aristocrats of labour were to be. They felt that they had to respond to the
widely-held view that the working class was morally incapable of exercising

the franchise because they were too 'ignorant, too drunken and too improvident', by focusing on the 'improvements' which were occurring.[38] The *Circular* campaigned for a national system of education funded by the state and including education for women to produce 'a nation of philosophical, intelligent, and political mothers', 'the primary instructors of the rising race'.[39] Fraser's *True Scotsman* and the *Scottish Patriot* added temperance to the education and religion of the *Circular*. The *Patriot* claimed that Chartists were 'forming a character for the people which they had never before possessed – making them intelligent by instruction and moral by inculcating the principles of total abstinence'.[40] At the same time it continued with the traditional radical analysis that the danger to liberty came from tyrants in power and this could only be checked by the achievement of the Charter. The handful of those who seemed to be willing to talk about 'physical force if we must', people like Dr John Taylor, Thomas Gillespie and Alan Pinkerton linked the lack of the franchise with the fact that the working man was robbed 'of the fruits of his industry' and this had to be won back. But significantly Taylor always found much more receptive audiences in the north of England than he did in Scotland.

Moral force and physical force

There can be no doubt that Scottish Chartism, despite the odd outburst, was strongly attached to the moral force wing of the movement. Robert Lowery, Thomas Cooper and other moderates, always found Scottish audiences more congenial to their message of slow advancement and much moral improvement than some of their audiences in the south.[41] On the other hand, attempts to stifle debate and manipulate the movement did stir resentment. The determined effort by Abram Duncan and the radical minister of Paisley, Patrick Brewster, at a meeting on Edinburgh's Calton Hill at the end of December 1838, to keep the Scottish movement firmly identified with moderation, by rejecting 'physical force at any time, or any occasion whatever', backfired when it became an ill-concealed attack on Feargus O'Connor. O'Connor, who had toured Scotland on more than one occasion, had many admirers.

Despite the tensions the movement was clearly spreading and by the beginning of 1839 there were at least seventy-six Chartist or Radical Reform Associations.[42] Scots were well represented at the first convention held in London in February 1839. Hugh Craig, a Kilmarnock draper, chaired the opening meeting. The convention remained in session through until April, but differences quickly began to appear. When the issue of physical force was brought on to the agenda most of the Scottish delegates showed their unease. Hugh Craig returned home when the convention began to consider tactics, but, as a result, faced much criticism from his Ayrshire colleagues and soon pulled out of the movement. Patrick Matthew, a Perthshire laird, who was one of the Fife delegates, left because of 'the intemperate language and ultra character of the major party of the Convention', while the Edinburgh delegate Villiers Sankey believed that 'the people of Scotland were too calm, too prudent and too humane to imperil this cause upon bloodshed'.[43] Discussion of tactics continued at the convention and a series of 'ulterior measures' emerged, proposals for tactics to be adopted should the petition fail to move the government. These included exerting pressure on the middle class by dealing exclusively with those shopkeepers who supported reform, boycott of excisable goods, withdrawal of money from savings banks, strikes (a month long 'national holiday' was called for) and in the last resort armed resistance. These proposals triggered debates in the various Chartist localities and there seemed to be real danger of the movement breaking up in acrimony. Only in the linen weaving districts of Forfar, Kirriemuir and Dundee and among some in Ayrshire and Renfrewshire did there seem to be any support for the idea of a 'sacred month', but only when they were well-prepared. Most favoured continuing the peaceful agitation and spreading the message.

A conference called by the Glasgow Universal Suffrage Association in August to discuss a 'plan of organisation' met in Neil Douglas's old Universalist Church. The fifty-seven delegates revealed many of the tensions, but came out strongly in favour of avoiding violence, not necessarily because they believed that violence was wrong under all circumstances but because they believed that it was impractical.[44] There was widespread complaint of the lack of preparation for any kind of action and it was agreed to create a central committee to co-ordinate the Scottish movement which became increasingly self-contained. William C. Pattison, secretary of the steam-engine makers' union and William Thomson, the old-established champion of co-operative retailing and of the handloom weavers, were emerging as the most important leaders. In July, Robert Malcolm's *Scottish Patriot* was launched, backed by the unions and the Universal Suffrage Association. The attack by a force of Metropolitan police on the Chartists assembled in Birmingham's Bull Ring, the arrest of many English Chartist leaders and the disastrous Newport Rising at the end of 1839 confirmed most in their view of the hopelessness of directly confronting authority, particularly if the outbreaks were isolated ones. At the same time, arrests could help unite the movement in condemnation of the authorities and generally had the effect of boosting membership. But the death sentences on Frost and his associates gave a cause which could unite all shades of opinion sympathetic to the movement behind the demands for clemency. The campaigns bore fruit with the death sentences on Frost, Williams and Jones commuted and the Glasgow cotton spinners released from incarceration in the hulks at Greenwich.

The movement continued to spread throughout 1840 and 1841, although it was difficult to keep on repeating the same points without much sign of progress. Usually it required a visit from charismatic leaders from south of the border, like Peter McDouall or George Julian Harney, to revitalise a locality. Harney in the winter of 1840–1 had a very successful tour of the north-east and eastern Highlands. Patrick Brewster's condemnation by the presbytery for trying 'to excite the humbler against the higher classes of society' also stirred the movement. Divisions among the leadership remained common. Attitudes towards the demagogic O'Connor were particularly divisive. He was distrusted by many and his call for support for Tory candidates in the general election of 1841 temporarily drove some activists, like William Pattison, out of the movement.[45] One new tactic which was introduced, at the suggestion of James Moir, was to intervene in other public meetings to push through resolutions in favour of the Charter. It proved highly controversial and, therefore, immensely effective as a publicity tactic. Anti-patronage meetings, anti-slavery and poor-rate meetings were among those interrupted. There were also moves in Dundee to intervene in police commission elections where the franchise was based on household suffrage and candidates need only be ,10 householders.[46] Most controversially there was increased interruption of Anti-Corn Law meetings.

Chartism and the Corn Laws

Although beginning as a largely working-class movement in Scotland, the campaign against the Corn Laws, as it gathered momentum, became strongly identified as the movement of middle-class reformers. Unlike many of the leaders of the Anti-Corn Law League in England, most of the Scottish activists were concerned to emphasise that their aim was complete free trade not just free trade in grain. There had long been an assumption that repeal of the Corn Laws would be among the first decisions of a reformed parliament. Many of the Chartist activists had been active in the early stages of the anti-corn law campaign in the mid 1830s. Liberal newspapers like the *Herald* and the *Chronicle* in Dundee pressed the cause. However, both Fraser and Abram Duncan in 1838 had begun to attack the anti-corn law movement as a diversionary move by the Whigs to turn attention from the Charter. Fraser's *True Scotsman* declared 'away with the Corn Law agitation! To it we shall be no party. THE CHARTER THE CHARTER THE WHOLE CHARTER AND NOTHING BUT THE CHARTER'.[47] The *Scottish Patriot* criticised the corn-law repealers as short-sighted; 'they perceive but a single defect in a system whose entire constitution is rotten'.[48] At the end of 1839 the meeting which was to open a renewed Scottish campaign against the Corn Laws was disrupted by the Chartists and the tactic was followed elsewhere much to the indignation of the Liberal press. While no doubt there was some class antagonism between some of the Chartists and the middle-class businessmen who featured in the campaign against the Corn Laws, the disruption of meetings was as much about publicity as class conflict, and many of the active Chartists retained an involvement in the anti-corn law movement. In many cases it was middle-class political reformers with a good record from 1832 and earlier who were at the head of the anti-corn law campaign. On the other hand, scars of industrial battles in the 1830s could sometimes make it difficult for them to get working-class support. In Dundee, for example, there was suspicion of the Baxter brothers, active in parliamentary reform but with increasingly poor industrial relations in their mills.[49]

The Corn Laws, however, were only one of a number of middle-class grievances. In Edinburgh, merchants and tradesmen railed against a society whose political institutions continued to be dominated by lawyers who still retained their close links with the traditional landed ruling groups. Dissenters or voluntaries in Edinburgh and Montrose suffered from the particular grievance of an annuity tax levied to pay the cost of maintaining the established churches and, as a result, were very well organised protesters. Many were prepared to accept the stigma of imprisonment or forced sale of their goods rather than pay the tax. Many of those in the secession churches, such as the Peddie family, had a long tradition of support for political reform dating back to the 1790s and they continued to identify with the reform cause. Many of the early Chartist meetings were held in secession churches. The Voluntary Church Magazine in 1839 had actually declared support for universal suffrage, shorter parliaments and the ballot.[50] The draper, Duncan McLaren, who was chair of the Scottish Central Board of Dissenters, emerged as the key figure in this group in Edinburgh and he and his radical lieutenants led a persistent campaign against the Whigs who dominated local government in the city. In October 1837 there was even talk of trying to create a campaign of mass civil disobedience against the annuity tax and, although it came to nothing, one or two respected figures went to gaol.[51]

Complete suffrage

If Chartism had been mainly 'a knife and fork question', a response to distress, then the dire economic conditions of 1842 and the much weakened trade-union movement might have produced reasonably favourable conditions for it. The opposite seems to have been the case and mass unemployment largely led to the demise of Chartism in many places. With miners and handloom weavers both suffering the movement in Lanarkshire more or less collapsed. The most striking feature of 1842 in Scotland was the effect it had of persuading many middle-class reformers, who had hung back from support of the Charter, that a response to the working class was now necessary. The moves also reflected middle-class frustration at the parliamentary blocking of repeal attempts. Anti-corn law activists became increasingly convinced of the need to create a mass political campaign. The ousting of the Whigs in the 1841 general election made it easier to do this. Peel's Toryism, even in its new guise as Conservatism, unleashed all the bad memories of the 1820s. The proposals coming from Edward Miall of the *Nonconformist* newspaper and from the Birmingham Quaker philanthropist,

Joseph Sturge, in the winter of 1841–2 for a Complete Suffrage Movement, which would again unite working-class and middle-class reformers fell on fertile ground. While rejecting the name 'Chartist' the movement accepted the six points of the Charter as the ultimate goal.

Active anti-corn law campaigners identified with the new movement. At a soirée of the Anti-Corn Law Association in Aberdeen there were calls for 'a union of all classes' behind an extension of the franchise as the only way to get real change in the House of Commons. Meeting with local Chartists in Aberdeen, the Dean of Guild and leading shipowner, George Thompson, declared that 'he was one of those who refused to go on any longer with the [Anti-Corn Law] League unless it recognised the full right of people to equal representation'.[52] The leading Liberal newspaper, the *Aberdeen Herald*, began to take up the Chartist cause. Its irascible editor, James Adam, called to account by a bemused, rather Whiggish management committee, explained the change because the public mind was now 'ripe for the subject':

> The necessity for organic change has become daily more apparent! Not the working classes merely but the middle and some of the upper classes had been thoroughly awakened to the anomalies and the abuses and the glaring injustices of the existing system ... I believe there will be danger in the enfranchisement of the working classes, without the check of an educational test, but I am satisfied that there is a thousand fold more danger in keeping them as they are. Besides in excluding them we are acting unjustly – however we may excuse ourselves on the plan of expediency ... We should recollect that they have the same claim on us that we had on the Freeholders in 1830 ... Whatever we or others may do the Movement will go on: wisely and to some rational denouement if it be prudently guided – and foolishly and to fearful anarchy if it be neglected or mismanaged. I hold it to be the duty of every man of the middle class who can conscientiously agree to the demands of the reasonable portion of the unenfranchised to come forward now as in 1832 to prevent the popular agitation from being turned to bad purpose by wicked and designing demagogues. The torrent will roll on and it depends upon peaceable and well-disposed reformers whether it be turned into safe if not useful channels or allowed to overflow its banks carrying death and devastation in its course. In the disturbances in England we have a foretaste of what the masses may some day do if they are wholly left to themselves or to the direction of ignorant and dishonest leaders.[53]

Adam was able to carry with him a number of Liberal businessmen in Aberdeen and dissenters of various kinds.

Aberdeen may have been exceptional because the strong community links with the surrounding farming community made the anti-protectionist movement there relatively weak, but there were signs elsewhere of similar moves. In Edinburgh, Duncan McLaren and other voluntary church people called for collaboration between middle-class and working-class reformers and voluntarily introduced the issue at Anti-Corn Law League meetings. John

Henderson, editor of the *Glasgow Saturday Post and Renfrewshire Reformer*, took a very similar line, calling for individual views to be merged 'in the measure likely to be first successful and in the organisation which is the most complete and influential at the present time'. Elsewhere a few dissenting clergymen such as John Ritchie of Hope Park Church in Edinburgh and Andrew Marshall of Kirkintilloch and his son, William, in Leith, gave their support.[54] James Moir again led Glasgow Chartists back to co-operation with the middle-class corn law reformers. Sturge's visits early in 1842 won further converts. By the autumn, the Paisley Complete Suffrage Association had more than 570 members and Patrick Brewster was able to re-emerge as a leading spokesman. The Glasgow branch claimed a thousand members and Henry Vincent's lecture tour in the autumn on behalf of the Association packed huge meetings in Glasgow, Aberdeen and elsewhere. By the end of 1842 the dominant voices were all associated with the Complete Suffrage wing of the movement – Robert Lowery, the organising secretary, William Pattison, always an ardent corn-law repealer and regarded as the source of the most constructive ideas in Glasgow, William Thomson, and Robert Malcolm, editor of the *Patriot*.

There is no doubt that some Chartists viewed the new tone with considerable suspicion, but the rejection of yet another Chartist petition in May and a reaction against the violence of the riots in Lancashire gave the new movement considerable impetus. Not that all was tranquillity in Scotland. The sharp distress in the summer of 1842 which triggered the plug riots in Lancashire and the Black Country had its effects in Scotland. Dundee factory workers came out claiming they were for the Charter rather than for higher wages. Colliers and iron miners in Lanarkshire also struck and claimed that they would refuse to return until the Charter was granted. Events in Dundee came to a head with the attempts to generate a general strike and a march on Forfar to bring out the mills there. John Duncan, a shoemaker, who like his brother Abram was a lay preacher, spoke of rising 'with determination and power' to declare that they would no longer be slaves, and thoroughly alarmed the town council who began enrolling special constables. When fifty or so marchers from Dundee arrived in Forfar they were met by a large body of special constables and turned for home, where arrests had already started. But such activities strengthened the urgency for collaboration.

The new alliance with the middle class paid dividends in that in a number of places reformers managed to get returned to the police commission, where the franchise was slightly wider than that for parliamentary elections. But otherwise, the Chartist movement in Scotland in all its various segments was falling apart by the end of 1842. There was no national organisation and little effective leadership. The Chartist press was defunct. Only the Chartist churches kept a community of working-class Chartists in being and kept faith in the Charter, but they too were closely tied to the search for respectability. A religious aspect had always been important in Scottish Chartism. Fraser had talked of creating 'a golden age of harmony' based on 'love of God, love your neighbours and forgive your enemies'. In Aberdeen Robert Lowery preached on the need for teetotalism and moral and educational improvement. Despite the lack of organisation, however, it was claimed that 'a deep and firmly rooted conviction' existed that 'no proposed remedy short of the Charter is in any degree worth one moment's consideration' and that the movement would rouse again 'from a most refreshing slumber, which will be found to have invigorated, strengthened and given new energies to it'[55].

A symbol of the new spirit of conciliation was the raising of a monument to the political martyrs of 1793 in Calton cemetery in Edinburgh. Edinburgh Town Council, dominated by voluntaries who had their own resentments against the domination of a legal clique, had first accepted the idea of the monument in 1837 at the suggestion of Joseph Hume. The site was eventually agreed in 1842 and the foundation stone was laid by Hume in 1844. There was a long wrangle over what should go on the plinth and the families of the judges objected strongly to any direct reference to them. In the end, in May 1847, it was agreed to have a quotation from Skirving, ' I know what has been done these two days will be RE-JUDGED'. That same month the remains of Baird and Hardie were removed from Stirling and reburied in Sighthill Cemetery in Glasgow under a monument which reflected the new tone:

> But truth and right have better times brought round,
> Now no more traitors scorn by passing breath,
> For weeping Scotland hails this spot of ground
> And shrines, within all who fell for Freedom's faith,
> Those sons of her's now famed made glorious by their death.

Leading Chartists were working within the existing political system. In Glasgow, for example, Pattison, elected as a police commissioner, worked with Moir and Matthew Cullen on East End issues such as resisting encroachments in the public space of Glasgow Green. In 1844 Henry Vincent stood in Kilmarnock burghs on a programme supporting complete suffrage, abolition of the Corn Laws, church disestablishment and tax reduction and gained ninety-eight votes. In 1845, John McCrae, a schoolmaster, put his name forward as a Chartist, but withdrew before the poll. In 1847 Chartists came forward as candidates in Greenock, Aberdeen and Fife, while McCrae stood in Dundee. As Dorothy Thompson says, 'the Chartists had tried petitioning, they had tried the weapons of the strike, the mass demonstrations, even an attempted rising. As the decade proceeded, they were turning to self-help of various kinds'.[56] Some looked to co-operative production. The Aberdeen Association of Producers was begun by Chartist workers in 1844 with a store selling clothes and food. There and elsewhere there were Chartist savings banks. There was also some support for the Chartist land scheme during 1845–6, with a vision of peasant small holdings. Branches of the Land Society were formed in at least twenty-six places by the end of 1846, although, according to Wilson, support for the scheme in Scotland was slight compared with the response in England. Many more were caught up in the enthusiasm for teetotalism.

1848

The revolutions of 1848 in Europe and the unrest in Ireland stirred interest in Scotland but failed to re-ignite the Chartist movement. A meeting in Glasgow to congratulate the French on the success of their revolution heard the moderate Moir, soon to be elected to the city council, declare that the Whigs 'are looking forward with fear and trembling to the ultimate result of all this'. Unemployment and shortages plus the disquiet that the spread of cholera always occasioned led to food riots in Glasgow, Edinburgh and Aberdeen in the early months of 1848. There was a tendency, as always, to blame these on outside Chartist agitators, but, despite reports of 'Vive la Republique' being heard on Glasgow Green, the evidence for a political dimension in any of the riots is flimsy. Patrick Brewster in Paisley and Peter McDouall in Glasgow had both been addressing meeting of the unemployed, but neither was into stirring up disturbances. As *The Scotsman* said of them 'it is a mistake unjust itself . . . to call the disturbances "Chartist Riots". They had nothing political about them'. *Tait's Magazine* , now far from radical, blamed the trouble on 'the nervous officiousness of the authorities' and contrasted the moderation of Scotland, 'a democratic nation, calmly seeking and waiting for radical reform' with the excitement in England.[57] There was some comfort that of the 64 arrested, 36 were Irish. A month later, the Glasgow Chartist, James Adams, went out of his way at the convention to dissociate the Chartists from the riots.

Yet another national petition for the Charter stirred a new flurry of activity in the spring of 1848, but all the Scottish delegates to the national convention in London in early April were sceptical about the possibility of revitalising a mass movement. All were agreed that the way forward was in collaboration with the middle class. Outside the convention a few returned to more vigorous language. The introduction of the Crown and Government Security Bill to simplify the prosecution of political offenders reawakened memories of the six acts and fears of repression, as did the arrest of many of the Chartist leaders in England.

A few continued to believe that more vigorous language was necessary. While the Chartists were gathering on Kennington Common in London, a meeting of, reputedly, 10,000 on Calton Hill in Edinburgh was hearing John Grant declaring that 'the time was now come when it was the duty of every man, for his own individual safety, to arm himself'. Henry Ranken and Robert Hamilton added their voices, calling for everyone to get themselves a musket or a pike. Hamilton claimed that although he had always been a moral force man he was now prepared 'to talk sedition' and if everyone did so then the jails could not hold them.[58] Meetings and demonstrations continued into the summer of 1848, with talk in many places of trying to create what was described as a national guard. A heady atmosphere encouraged a tendency to exaggerate the numbers who were participating in such activities, such as the unlikely claim that in Aberdeen 6,000 Chartists were 'armed to the teeth and waiting for the fray'.

But the most significant events of 1848 were not the Chartist-inspired agitations, but the revival of middle-class radical movements. In Edinburgh, an alliance of Dissenters, Free Church, Anti-Corn Law League people and other middle-class radicals had succeeded in ousting the Whig Macaulay from his seat in the election of 1847. The campaign for repeal of the Corn Laws had been brought to a successful conclusion and Duncan McLaren and his associates in Edinburgh saw this as merely the first step in an attack on privilege across a broad front. The voluntaries, now united in the United Presbyterian Church, had a new strength and confidence. 1843 had seen the first voluntary, Adam Black, elected as Provost. McLaren's associate Bailie Stott, a congregationalist leather merchant, had proposed a universal suffrage resolution at the town council on 12 April 1848. It was defeated by twenty-one votes to eight, with the once-radical but now much mellowed Provost Adam Black warning that it 'would alarm the holders of capital and endanger the safety of property'.[59] Another dissenter, the veterinary specialist, William Dick, formed a branch of Lovett's People's League 'to effect a union of the working and middle class, and to combine all true reformers in one united and peaceful movement'. Local issues such as the collection of the annuity tax continued to shape Edinburgh politics. There were riots in July over annuity tax forced sales and Bailie Stott among others ended in jail for non-payment. In Glasgow, which also had its branch of the People's League, the city council agreed to petition in support of Joseph Hume's motion for extension of the franchise.

By the second half of 1848 the momentum had again lessened. The sentences of eighteen years' transportation on two of the Glasgow food rioters and ten years on another two were intended to be intimidatory. The arrest of Ranken, Hamilton and Grant and other Edinburgh Chartists in July curbed the more extreme statements. But, when Ranken, Hamilton and Grant were brought to trial in November the Edinburgh judiciary showed itself much changed from earlier decades. The prosecutor went out of his way to emphasise that 'this is not a prosecution for opinions', and the four months' sentences were in sharp contrast to the two years being handed out to Ernest Jones and other leading Chartists in England. James Moncrieff, the defence lawyer, could confidently declare that

There have been times when verdicts have been returned under circumstances of public prejudice, in which the voice, not of law merely, but reason and sense was drowned in one overpowering terror; verdicts which filled some, at least, who pronounced them with undying regret; and have stamped an indelible stigma on the times they characterise. I am under no apprehension of that kind today.[60]

Although O'Connor in his tour of Scotland still continued to stir considerable enthusiasm with his rhetoric, there were growing demands that any new reform movement be dissociated from him and others of the old guard.

There are various possible reasons for the nature of Scottish Chartism. One does not get the same sense of betrayal by the middle class after 1832, which was a factor in the class nature of some English Chartism – the idea that they had used working-class support, but had then abandoned the working class. There clearly were gains in Scotland as a result of the extension of the franchise in 1832 compared to the tiny electorate which had preceded it. There was no disenfranchisement of working-class voters such as happened in some of the more popular constituencies in England. On the other hand, because the £10 was a high franchise for Scottish burghs, many petit-bourgeois men still excluded. Also the reforms in the counties had not created the 40s freeholders that had long been sought, and the county franchise was so complex that it continued to lend itself to corruption by the creation of faggot votes, while excluding many small town middle-class people who in England had the vote. A great deal of the strength of Scottish Chartism lay in such Scottish small towns, like Montrose, Hawick, Dalkeith.

Another factor is that there is not a great deal of industrial unrest in Scotland in the 1840s after the break up of the cotton spinners' unions. There were certainly some bitter strikes, but nothing comparable to the plug riots which raged through the north of England, and new industries were beginning to gain in importance as textiles begin to lose their significance. As a result the kind of incidents which bring out class antagonism, while clearly not absent, were not all that common. Work on Paisley shows that textile workers there were readier to blame the problems of their industry on external forces – foreign trade or government policy – than on the action of their employers.[61] Even the issue of ten-hour factory legislation did not find a powerful group standing against it in Scotland. Clearly, many textile mill owners went to considerable lengths to circumvent the legislation, but there were few voices which actually spoke out against it. Ministers from the middle class's new Free Church were generally to be found in support of shorter hours.

Nor was there an 1834 Poor Law in Scotland, which provided the focus of a great deal of the working-class discontent in the north of England. Before 1845 the poor law in Scotland was in the hands of landed heritors and the Established Church clergy and helped add to anti-landowner and anti-clerical attitudes. There were plenty of complaints against the new poor rates, a belief that an inequitably heavy burden fell on the working class, and against the seven-year residency requirement before relief was granted. There were even calls for resistance, but the movement never gathered strength. The 1845 measure, while still harsh, was probably less arbitrary than the older system and had a measure of local control through the parochial boards. This allowed the focus of Scottish radicalism throughout the Chartist period to remain fixed largely on the aristocracy.

There was no popular Tory radical tradition in Scotland. There were no equivalents of William Cobbett, Richard Oastler, Joseph Rayner Stephens or even Ernest Jones, who attacked the middle classes, starting from a Tory perception that it was the middle classes and the changes they were bringing which were disrupting an acceptable social order. So the language is rarely that of conflict with the middle class. The middle classes were seen as equally exploited by an aristocratic system. At the same time, despite all that was said by Carlyle and others against the 'Scottish feelosophers' there is not a group of politicians who are firmly committed to the more extreme versions of the Manchester School. No Scottish MP stood out as a hard *laissez-faire* Liberal. Scottish Liberals still had a belief in the importance of the state, particularly the local one. It was still a society where paternalist attitudes prevailed and where there was a view that *laissez-faire* was inimical to social stability and that a little intervention was allowable. The elements and the attitudes which created Victorian liberalism were all in place in Scotland from the 1840s.

Notes

1. *Scottish Guardian*, 17 January 1832 quoted in Smith, *Passive Obedience*, pp. 73–4.
2. N. Gash, *Politics in the Age of Peel* (1952), p. x.
3. The average price before 1832 had been £500. W. Ferguson, 'The Reform Act (Scotland) of 1832: Intention and Effect', *Scottish Historical Review*, XLV, pp. 105–14.
4. *Herald to the Trades Advocate*, 2 October 1830.
5. *Saturday Post*, 4 August 1832.
6. Alexander Mitchell, *Political and Social Movements in Dalkeith from 1831 to 1882* (1882 Privately published), pp. 12–13.
7. *Aberdeen Pirate*, 4 July 1833.
8. 'The Fenwick Improvement of Knowledge Society 1834–42', *Scottish Historical Review*, 17 (1919–20), p. 123.
9. For Campbell, see W. Hamish Fraser, *Alexander Campbell and the Search for Socialism* (Manchester, 1996).
10. *Glasgow Argus*, 1,4 June 1835.
11. Fiona Montgomery, 'Glasgow Radicalism 1830–1848', Glasgow University, Ph.D. thesis, 1974, pp. 149–51.
12. *Scots Times*, 10 December 1836.
13. *Aberdeen Herald*, 3 January 1835, 22 July 1837.
14. Wahrman, *Imagining the Middle Class*, pp. 270–1.

15. *Herald to the Trades Advocate*, 27 November 1830.
16. *Scotsman*, 25 April 1832.
17. K. J. Cameron, 'William Weir and the Origins of the "Manchester League" in Scotland, 1833–39', *Scottish Historical Review,* 58 (1979), pp. 70–91.
18. McLean, the fifth person brought to trial, was not a leader of the union but may well have been responsible for some of the violence.
19. *New Liberator*, 6 January 1838.
20. *Northern Star*, 2 June 1838.
21. *Aberdeen Shaver*, LV, July 1838.
22. *Ibid.* 7 July 1838.
23. *Chartist Circular*, No. 4, 19 October 1839.
24. *Ibid.* No. 32, 2 May 1840; No. 34, 16 May 1840.
25. *Ibid.* No. 1, 28 September 1839.
26. *Ibid.*, No. 69, 16 January 1841.
27. *Ibid.* No. 10, 30 November 1839.
28. *Ibid.* No. 73, 13 February; No. 75, 27 February 1841.
29. *Ibid.* No. 32, 2 May 1840.
30. *Ibid.* No. 12, 14 December 1839.
31. *Ibid.* No. 18, 25 January 1840; No. 27 28 March 1840.
32. *Ibid.* No. 5, 26 October 1839.
33. *Scottish Patriot*, 15 February 1840.
34. *Chartist Circular*, No. 24, 7 March 1840.
35. *Ibid.* No. 32, 2 May 1840.
36. D. Thompson, *Outsiders, Class, Gender and Nation* (1993), p. 62.
37. *Chartist Circular*, No. 80, 3 April 1841.
38. *Ibid.* No. 6, 2 November 1839.
39. *Ibid.* No. 5, 26 October 1839, No. 9 23 November 1839, No. 25, 14 March 1840.
40. Quoted in A. Wilson, *The Chartist Movement in Scotland* (Manchester, 1970), p. 124.
41. Brian Harrison, 'Chartism, Liberalism and the life of Robert Lowery', *English Historical Review,* 82, 1967, p. 512.
42. A. Wilson, *The Chartist Movement in Scotland* (Manchester, 1970), p. 70.
43. J. T. Ward, *Chartism*, p. 118.
44. Tony Clarke, 'Early Chartism in Scotland: A "Moral Force" Movement?' in T. M. Devine (ed.), *Conflict and Stability in Scottish Society 1700–1850* (Edinburgh, 1990), p. 110.
45. *Scottish Patriot*, 10 April 1841.
46. *Northern Star*, 2 October 1841.
47. *True Scotsman*, 5 January 1839.
48. *Scottish Patriot*, 6 July 1839.
49. Cameron, 'William Weir', p. 76.
50. J. C. Williams, 'Edinburgh Politics 1832–52', Ph.D. thesis, Edinburgh University 1972, p. 42.
51. *Ibid.* pp. 150–1.
52. *Aberdeen Herald*, 26 February, 12 March 1842.
53. Aberdeen University Special Collections. Herald Collection. James Adam to Committee of Management, 24 August 1842.

54. W. H. Marwick, 'Social heretics in the Scottish Churches', *Records of the Scottish Church History Society*, XI, 1953.
55. *Northern Star,* 2, 9 September 1843 quoted in Wilson, *Chartist Movement,* p. 201.
56. Thompson, *The Chartists,* p. 306.
57. Wilson, *Chartist Movement,* p. 218; *Tait's Edinburgh Magazine,* XV, 1848, p. 577.
57. *Ibid.* p. 224.
59. *Scotsman,* 12 April 1848 quoted in Williams, 'Edinburgh Politics', p. 298.
60. John Saville, *The British State and the Chartist Movement* (Cambridge, 1987), p. 175.
61. T. Clark and T. Dickson, 'Class and Class Consciousness in Early Industrial Capitalism 1770–1850' in T. Dickson (ed.), *Capital and Class in Scotland* (Edinburgh, 1982), pp. 8–60.

CHAPTER FOUR

After Chartism 1848–68

Ian Hutchison has argued convincingly that 'politically the eighteenth century ended in 1847 with the defeat of the old Whig burgh clique' in Glasgow and Edinburgh. The 1832 Reform Act was finally beginning to have an impact on the electoral politics of the country. Scotland entered a period during which a broadly-based Liberal party, with a strong radical tinge, was able to unite a large swathe of the population. The election of James Moir to Glasgow town council in November 1848 symbolised what had happened, according to John McAdam: 'It was a test which quietly set aside the irreconcilables who would not unite and the mere "Whigs" who would not work for any real reform and harmonised the working elements of the old Radical and Chartist parties'.[1] Joseph Hume, as spokesman for the middle class, continued his relentless attacks on the aristocracy, in the language of the older radical tradition, arguing that cheap government was the most effective check on despotism. As a product of Montrose, he was immensely influential in Scotland. Hume introduced parliamentary reform proposals every year between 1848 and 1852, although he was only pushing for household suffrage, the ballot and triennial parliaments the 'little charter' of 1849. The call also for equal electoral districts had a strong appeal in Scotland, which claimed under-representation. Most Scottish working-class radicals after 1848 were prepared to go along with a step-by-step approach to reform. *Tait's Magazine* could confidently asserted that 'Ours are not a revolutionary people, and dislike changes accomplished by violence and intimidation'.[2]

Radical causes

A few attempted to keep the Chartist cause going. In June 1850 delegates from all corners of Scotland met in Edinburgh to hear O'Connor, but his demagogic skills were failing.[3] Paisley and Glasgow Chartists tried to organise to send delegates to a London Convention in February 1851 which sought to unite the various Chartist and social reform bodies, but it led to splits and acrimony between O'Connorites and others.[4] In the spring of 1852 delegates from different parts of Scotland met in Edinburgh 'to settle the policy of the

Scottish Advanced Liberal Party'. There was a reassertion of the commitment
to the six points of the Charter but a rejection of O'Connor's land scheme 'as
really nothing to do with them'.[5]

Delegates from various Glasgow trade societies associated with middle-
class reformers in Sir Joshua Walmsley's Parliamentary Reform Association,
which supported limited household suffrage, the ballot and triennial parliaments. There was considerable discussion over whether it was better to go
for manhood suffrage independently or to unite with Hume and Walmsley's
Association, 'which would rally round it a considerable portion of the middle
classes'. By a large majority they opted for the latter, while declaring that they
still adhered 'in the abstract to the principle of manhood suffrage'.[6]

Middle-class radicalism was still invigorated by the success of Corn Law
repeal. This was apparent even in Aberdeen. In the 1852 election seven
hopefuls put themselves forward as possible Liberal candidates. One identified himself as a Progressive Reformer, a second as an Anti-State Church
Campaigner, a third as a sabbatarian, total abstainer and against papal
aggression, a fourth as temperance and anti-French (this in the aftermath
of Napoleon's coup d'état). Another, the shipowner George Thompson, was
accused of 'climbing on the rock of Chartism'. In Edinburgh someone like
McLaren, John Bright's brother-in-law, like Bright himself, had a clear
programme of reform to follow repeal of the Corn Laws and, as he wrote
to George Combe in 1852, parliamentary reform was 'a means of promoting
many other reforms'.[7] The group of Independent Liberals, as they called
themselves, which formed round him, 'combining the various cohorts of
Dissenters, Free Traders and Social Reformers into one inviolable Legion',[8]
favoured vote by ballot and triennial parliaments, although vague on the
extent of franchise reform.

Anti Popery

Religious issues, so fraught in Scotland of the 1840s, also encouraged middle-
class and working-class collaboration. Evangelical fervour in the 1830s and
1840s affected working-class people every bit as much as the middle class.
According to Callum Brown, Sunday school attendance in Glasgow in the
1830s grew four times faster than population.[9] Anti-patronage riots had long
been a feature of popular Scottish politics and hostility to the established
clergy ran deep. But the establishment of the Free Church in 1843 was quickly
followed by the Maynooth affair in which the government agreed to provide
funding for Maynooth College in Ireland together with its catholic seminary.
The Maynooth grant stirred an anti-popery movement which was never far
beneath the surface in Scotland. Some historians of English Chartism have
seen the Maynooth affair as undermining the Complete Suffrage Association.
In Scotland it probably strengthened it, by further sealing the links between
voluntaries and many working-class leaders. Chartists, like the Duncan

brothers and Fraser, and many others were from Calvinist seceder groups, which could glide easily into anti-catholicism. Joseph Hume, once again returned as MP for Montrose Burghs, 'gave early warning of the surrender of both parties in the state to the demands of the Roman Catholic clergy'.[10] The Scottish Reformation Society was formed in Edinburgh in 1850, with the Protestant Alliance following soon afterwards. In Edinburgh, the Revd James Begg, noted for his concern with working-class living conditions, was a key figure in these. Glasgow had its own Protestant Laymen's Society and the Orange Order, drawing mainly on Ulster immigrants, revived in the 1850s. Anti-catholic sentiments could find a response among a working class growing increasingly concerned at the huge influx of Irish during the famine years. It perhaps strengthened the arguments for only a limited extension of the franchise which fell short of universal suffrage. The influential Hugh Miller used the Free Church's *Witness* to argue that universal suffrage would enfranchise the unskilled, shiftless, Roman Catholic, Irish while, with a limited extension, 'as opposed to Papists ... the Protestant party would gain in strength and that very considerably'.[11] As John Wolffe has shown, by the mid-century anti-catholicism had become well entrenched among the lower middle and upper working class and a desire 'to differentiate themselves from their poorer Catholic neighbours ... could become an logical extension of their aspirations to respectability'.[12]

Some of the better-educated and more sophisticated were wary about the cruder aspects of anti-catholicism and later Chartism had seen a considerable fund of sympathy with and involvement by Irish repealers.[13] Also many voluntaries had tended to see Roman Catholics as another group of dissenters from the establishment. But what gave them a 'respectable route' was the restoration of the catholic hierarchy in England in 1851, what Lord John Russell dubbed 'papal aggression'. Support for Mazzini and later Garibaldi and the Italian cause often became a cover for anti-catholicism. The Italian cause stirred considerable enthusiasm in Scotland in the 1850s among ex-Chartists. Mazzini was reasonably well known in that he had contributed articles to *Tait's Magazine* in the 1840s. Middle-class intellectuals, like Aberdeen-born David Masson, first secretary of the Friends of Italy in 1851, was motivated by what he saw as catholic expansionism. The Chartist James Adams was at the forefront of an anti-papal meeting in Glasgow in 1853.[14] Anti-catholicism could also bring in socialists and secularists. The *Reasoner* declared that 'every Protestant, every friend of religion and political reform is interested in the fall of Catholicism'. There has perhaps been a tendency to underplay the strength of anti-catholicsm outside the west of Scotland. It was not just anti-Irish sentiment which produced it, but it was very much part of Calvinism in all its various manifestations. Anti-papal lecturers, like Gavazzini, whose speeches were translated by young Henry Campbell who have not yet added Bannerman to his name, were assured of packed meetings. Kossuth was guaranteed to produce cheers when he talked of the evils of

Catholicism.[15] Many, sympathetic to political reform, were at meetings expressing sympathy with the 'oppressed and persecuted Protestants of Hungary'.[16] Glasgow was at the forefront of contributing to Garibaldi's rifle fund in the 1850s, when he 'still looked like an Italian sea captain and had poor prospects of political success'.[17]

Temperance

A second issue which acted as a powerful cement for middle-class and working-class radicals was the temperance movement. Chartism inherited an anti-drink tradition from the pre-1820 radical movements where the boycotting of excisable items like alcohol was used as a powerful political weapon. Working-class temperance and teetotalism pre-dates John Dunlop and the official founding of the temperance movement in 1828. It is not a question, as it is often presented, of the working class succumbing to essentially middle-class mores. Few working-class leaders were not aware of the devastating effects which drink could have on working-class families. It became a central part of Scottish Chartism. Robert Lowery was converted to teetotalism in an Aberdeen coffee house in 1841 and many saw teetotalism as the moral force which would finally transform society. It was always predominately a working-class movement and, by 1850, no significant Scottish trade union held its meetings in a public house. As elements, particularly of the evangelical middle class, took up the cause, more extensive cross-class links developed. With a readiness to accept communal regulation it is not surprising that many of the Scottish Chartists moved on to prohibition. Both John Fraser and Patrick Brewster were early supporters of a Maine Law in 1853 and the launching of a total abstinence society in Glasgow in the summer of 1853 after a visit by the temperance reformer J. E. Gough aroused a great deal of popular support, although it also led to divisions on whether the way forward was through legal or moral suasion. Again Duncan McLaren was a key linking figure largely responsible for the Forbes Mackenzie Act of 1853.

Education

Thirdly, there was education. A belief in the importance of education and the right to education was strong among Scottish radicals. Myths, if myths they were, about Scottish education were well-entrenched and an effective system of education was seen as the main route to general moral improvement. Chartists had called for a fully national system of education for boys and girls and effective training of teachers.[18] Campaigns in the early 1850s for secular schools attracted working-class radicals and further forged links with voluntaries. Throughout the 1850s there was a widespread belief that legislation to meet Scottish educational needs was being delayed in Parliament because of the sensitivity of the issue of education in England. The failure of the Lord Advocate's Education Bill in 1856 which would have allowed dissenters to become parochial schoolmasters was just one such example which seemed to prove the case.

Fourthly, and linked to the theme of education, there was support for the campaign against the so-called taxes on knowledge, the advertising and newspaper taxes which pushed up the cost of newspapers. It had long been seen by working-class radicals as a weapon of censorship against working-class papers. Many middle-class radicals saw it as yet another tax which needed to be eradicated. The Association for the Repeal of Taxes on Knowledge was formed in 1851.

Dividing issues

A number of middle-class radicals continued to argue that the working class needed to be conciliated so that 'neither Chartism nor Socialist demagogues will be able to obtain any considerable influence over them'.[19] And in the Scottish experience there is much support for Miles Taylor's argument that the the Chartist response to defeat and the end of the mass movement was 'rejoining and becoming reconciled to the mainstream of radical and liberal politics'.[20] There were, however, still many obstacles in the way of a cohesive middle-class/working-class radical alliance. There were still those among working-class leaders who wanted to bring about more fundamental social changes. There were some who wanted to create that democratic socialist programme which Margot Finn has identified in London, linking the aims of Chartism for political reform with the aims of Owenite socialists for social change. This line was pursued for a time by *The Glasgow Sentinel*, which claimed in the 1850s to be the second most popular newspaper in Scotland. Edited by the former Owenite missionary, Robert Buchanan, it was critical of those Chartists who separated social and political reform and who would not tackle the question 'what was to be done with the Charter when it was got?': 'A man cannot breakfast upon the suffrage – dine upon the ballot–nor sup upon electoral districts'.[21] It campaigned for what it called the 'Rights of Labour (Right to labour)', which at times seemed liked Louis Blanc's national workshops for the unemployed. It favoured home colonies, anticipating the demands of the late nineteenth-century socialists, co-operative production and emigration. The *Sentinel* consistently pushed the line that the suffrage was only a means to an end,

> the lever by which they must rouse themselves from the present state of degradation to comfort and intelligence. When the people, the real people, take the administration of their own affairs into their own hands, as they shortly will, let their first act be the enactment of a labour law which will secure for honest industry an asylum in the season of distress.

Small groups of Owenite socialists and secularists continued to discuss alternatives to capitalism in the Eclectic Society which met in a hall in Dunlop Street in Glasgow.

Crimea

A second dividing issue was the peace movement. Many of the middle-class radicals, following Cobden and Bright, saw the Anti-Corn Law League as merely the first step in a more universal campaign for peace. Cobden was campaigning for international arbitration. Bright had his Quaker pacifism. Many of the people associated with Duncan McLaren in Edinburgh were involved in the peace movement. An Edinburgh League of Universal Brotherhood had been formed in 1847 and there was a major peace conference in Edinburgh in 1853. McLaren himself was married to Bright's sister, Priscilla. Other associates like the Quaker Wighams in Edinburgh and Aberdeen and the Smeals in Glasgow, who had broadly been sympathetic to the demands for parliamentary reform, were now active in the peace movement as part of the extensive and influential Quaker network, which included the Peases in Darlington, the Carrs in Carlisle and the Frys in Bristol. But most of the working class did not go along that route.[22] Initially, it did appeal to a few who did not like interventionism in European affairs. But there was a long-established hostility to Russia and sympathy with the Poles. Russia's role in crushing the Hungarian uprising together with David Urquhart's campaigns added to the hostility and there was considerable support for Turkey.[23] Cobden bitterly complained to McLaren about the lack of much progress of the peace movement in Scotland suggesting that 'your heads are more combative than even the English, which is almost a phrenological miracle' and speculated that one of the reasons was that Scots had done particularly well out of the system of military rule in India.[24] Chartists seem to have gone along with G. J. Harney in regarding the peace movement as 'a weak washing flood of moral twaddle which involved condoning European despotism'. Lord Aberdeen's Peelite government was regularly attacked in the *Sentinel*: 'people are beginning to ask whether our government are accomplices of Russia or the allies of Turkey'. Just as Mazzini became a focus for anti-catholicism, so the Hungarian revolutionary, Kossuth, became a rallying point for anti-Russianism.

The Crimean War as much as anything marked a temporary parting of the ways between working class and middle class. Middle-class radicals, caught in the peace movement, lost faith in the working class as radical allies when they saw their enthusiasm for war. On the other hand, the enthusiasm for war quickly palled when the almost forgotten practice of billeting militiamen in private houses was revived.[25]

The attacks on the government did not stop with the fall of Aberdeen and the emergence of Palmerston. The attacks seem to go further than those of

J. A. Roebuck and the administrative reformers in England in their denunciation of nepotism and aristocratic government. It strengthened the demands
for parliamentary reform and the Administrative Reform Association was
criticised for assuming that you could reform the existing system without 'the
infusion of new and more wholesome blood into the legislature' by means of
an extended franchise. Only 'by taking the management of our own affairs
into our own hands' declared an Address from the Glasgow Democratic
Association, could the 'corrupt and incompetent rule … of this outworn
class' be removed. According to the *Sentinel*, 'If we had a Parliament really
representing the people, this absurd, wasteful, unjust and most iniquitous
system of conducting, or rather misconducting the business of the country
would not endure a single season.'[26]

Nationalism

Finally, there was some enthusiasm for European nationalism among Scottish radicals, but there is no great evidence of extensive working-class
support for Scottish nationalism. The National Association for the Vindication of Scottish Rights in 1853–4 caught the enthusiasm of many middle-
class radicals, including Begg and McLaren. Begg had good credentials with
the working class for taking up housing issues and campaigning for forty-
shilling freeholders to be admitted to the franchise in Scotland. He launched
the nationalist movement in a famous lecture to an Edinburgh UP Church in
1850 on 'National Education in Scotland Practically Considered', warning
that 'We are sinking in our national position every year, and simply living on
the credit of the past'. He linked it with denunciation of the aristocracy:

> The great national resources of our whole country locked up in the iron
> embrace of feudal despotism – little intelligence amongst the people to
> understand this far less to battle with it – the very passes of our mountains
> interdicted – the fishing on our rivers monopolised – our public grounds and
> gardens shut up – the Parliament of England despising us, our national
> guardians joining in the oppression.[27]

The Free Church *Witness* was sympathetic and Hugh Miller's assistant, Patrick
E. Dove, was particularly active.[28] Many town councils also declared their
support. But it attracted little working-class interest.[29]

It was not that there was no support for reform of the structure of
Parliament. There were frequent complaints of excessive centralisation of
power at Westminster, of the increased use of paid bureaucrats to direct
affairs and of the failure of Parliament to deal with pressing Scottish issues.
The *Sentinel* in 1853 favoured an American federal structure with the 'creation
of a local parliament in Scotland, England and Ireland – especially charged
with the consideration and enactment of all bills relating to railroads, docks,

harbours, canals, roads and their administration'.[30] But the agitation over heraldry and flying the right flags which obsessed the leadership of the National Association for the Vindication of Scottish Rights seemed far removed from working-class concerns. The Association had no radical programme. It was seen as attracting eccentric Tories, such as Lord Eglinton – he of the tournament – and was difficult to take seriously. Another element, those involved in campaigns for a Scottish national monument to Wallace, showed little sympathy with working-class aspirations and received little support in turn, although some ex-chartists such as John and William McAdam were active on the monument committee.[31]

Reform revives

A few radicals, however, did attempt to keep campaigns going. Duncan McLaren and the Revd James Begg combined to push forward the Scottish Freehold Movement. It was a long-running grievance that there was no 40–shilling freehold franchise in the Scottish counties and that burgh voters who had property in addition to their homes could not vote in the counties, as they could in England. The smallest of the English counties had a greater number of voters than any of the Scottish ones. There was also discontent that the Scottish counties were over-represented compared with the burghs. A conference in Edinburgh at the end of 1856 claimed that if the Scottish pattern followed that of England then Scotland should have 36 burgh and 17 county seats instead of the 30 and 23 which existed.[32] Small-town dwellers felt excluded from adequate representation. A Dalkeith activist complained, 'Our Members are not our representatives. They do not share our opinions, they do not sympathise with our feelings. They do not respect our rights'.[33] A meeting of the Freehold Movement in Perth, presided over by Laurence Pullar, called for the vote for all owners of property over £2 rateable value and all occupants who paid £10 rental or above to be given the vote in the counties, while the burgh vote should go to all who paid poor rates.[34]

Cheaper bread and an expanding economy in the aftermath of Corn Law repeal were removing some of the economic tensions, with Cobden complaining that 'the Big Loaf has choked Chartism and laid even Radicalism to sleep'.[35] Some working-class leaders argued that the first priority was to get the people 'well-fed, well-clothed, well-housed and well-educated' and then 'will the governing classes be compelled by necessity to yield to their demands'.[36] There was criticism of sectarianism and puritanism, 'free Churchmen, Forbes Mackenzieites, teetotallers and sabbatarians'.[37] It is possible also that many of the working class were losing their enthusiasm for the Free Church and the United Presbyterians as they tried to squeeze more resources from their members, and as both churches in their church-building programmes deliberately identified with middle-class areas. Bitterly fought debates within the churches over atonement and universal salvation

caused them to turn inwards. The Free Church also got caught up in sabbat-
arianism, while many of the voluntaries in Edinburgh found it difficult to see
beyond their battles over the annuity tax. There was a revival of industrial
activity with many trade unions beginning to reorganise and revitalise, and
renewed talk of the 'employer class' and the 'capitalist class' trying to break up
the trade unions.[38] The 1857 election seemed to confirm the view that with
Palmerston in office there was little hope for further significant reform. In
Glasgow and elsewhere old whiggish cliques seemed to be regaining control.
Among working-class activists there was talk of the working classes having to
deal with problems of unemployment themselves, of dealing with practical
questions not 'theoretical politics', and 'to work out their own emancipation
from idleness and consequent poverty'.[39] A writer in the *Sentinel* was complaining, The ministry is humbug; Parliament is a humbug; the public offices
are humbugs; and we are the most gullible, plundered, and humbugged people
in the world.[40] By the end of the 1850s many trade unionists regarded politics
as a source of dissension within trade unions and likely to weaken them in
their industrial activities, and there were moves to exclude political debate
from their meetings.

For others, faith in the essential validity of Chartist demands did not fade
and small groups of ex-Chartists continued to meet and to try to stir enthusiasm. Throughout the 1850s there existed a group of old and new radicals of
all social classes, many enthused by Mazzini and the struggles for Italian
independence. These were the people who were behind the renewed reform
effort launched as the Glasgow Reform Association in November 1858. John
McAdam in his autobiography lists about fifty people who were active either
as old radicals and reformers from 1832 onwards or who had supported free
trade and had been 'ever since in support of Parliamentary Reform and
Continental freedom'. Of those on whom information is known, eight had
been active in 1832 and in the Chartist period; half of them had actively shown
sympathy with Mazzini or Garibaldi; eleven of them showed evidence of anti-
papal sympathies; nine were or became involved in the anti-slavery movement, three were known temperance campaigners. There were business
people like Walter Buchanan and H. E. Crum Ewing, both merchants, John
Burt, a leather merchant, William Govan, a textile manufacturer, John
McGavin, a grain miller, and Hugh Tennent, a brewer. There were journalists
like Sam Bennett and George Troup, evangelical temperance activist and first
editor of the *North British Daily Mail*; academics like J. P. Nichol and his son
Professor John Nichol. There were trade unionists, including Alexander
Campbell who had returned from fifteen years as an Owenite missionary in
England. As so often with reform movements, the most active clergy were
Unitarians, Charles Clark and H. W. Crosskey. The latter was to be found in
most of the reform campaigns in Glasgow in the late 1850s and 1860s. He
advocated women's suffrage, acted as host to visitors like Louis Blanc and the
campaigner on behalf of the Italian cause, Jessie Mario White, on their lecture

tours. He was probably responsible for drafting the address from Glasgow
working men to Garibaldi in 1864. According to his biographer, his politics
were about 'the Establishment of the Kingdom of God upon Earth', a goal
which, despite his Unitarianism, would have appealed to many in mid-nineteenth century Scotland.[41]

It was John McAdam, who with his brother William, ran the Hyde Park
pottery, together with their Chartist associates, Moir and Matthew Cullen,
who were behind the formation of a Glasgow Reform Association in
November 1858. They were the group who had kept a Parliamentary Reform
Association alive during the 1850s, and who invited John Bright, now back in
Parliament after having lost his seat in Manchester, to come to Glasgow.[42]
Bright's call for a reform campaign was endorsed by the *Sentinel* with calls for
a new party. What was needed, it argued, was

> A courageous trust in the working people by those above them, and an
> intelligent confidence in the reformers of the middle and upper classes by the
> people, is what we want to realise progress that at no distant time, will secure
> rational liberty to every subject under the British Crown.[43]

Attempts to rouse mass support for a campaign, which did not go beyond
household suffrage however, made heavy weather and there were deep
divisions among reformers. Some ex-chartists saw the councils of trade delegates which were formed at the end of the 1850s as an obvious forum for
political discussion to rekindle interest in reform. Despite opposition, the
newly-formed Glasgow Trades Council at the end of 1858 agreed to associate
with Moir and McAdam's committee of 'advanced liberals', as they called
themselves, to press for manhood suffrage, vote by ballot, triennial parliaments and equitable electoral districts.[44] Others wanted to keep their trade
unions well clear of political controversy. Although a few trade unions organised special meetings on the issue in 1858–9, they found a fairly general apathy.

The Risorgimento, and particularly Garibaldi's adventures in 1859–60,
brought out much of the old enthusiasm for liberal nationalist movements
abroad and brought working-class and middle-class campaigners back together. Garibaldi was described as the 'Wallace of Italy' and some 260
volunteers (out of six to eight hundred British volunteers) left Glasgow to
fight in the British Legion alongside Garibaldi, although some Irish Catholics
also rallied to the defence of the Pope's territory.[45] Italy may have stimulated
the decision of the Glasgow Trades Council, driven on by its able young
president, George Newton, again to launch a campaign to get trade-union
support for parliamentary reform, arguing that 'he could not see how labour
[could] be treated without discussing politics'.[46] In an 'Address to the
Workingmen of the United Kingdom' they called for some evidence that
there was indeed a popular demand for reform. Only this would move the
present government. They made the novel proposal that trade unions were
'the best existing machinery for carrying out a successful movement of this

kind'. The demands were moderate, a five-pound franchise for boroughs and a ten-pound one in counties, as all that was practicable with the present Parliament, although pointing out that 'no measure of reform will be final that does not embrace manhood suffrage'. It also linked the demand for political reform to specific trade-union demands such as courts of conciliation and arbitration to settle industrial disputes.[47] It proved a disastrous move for the Glasgow Trades Council and many societies withdrew their affiliation. On the other hand, it stirred the Edinburgh Trades Council to contact the middle-class Reform Club and the Working Men's Association to see if they thought it advisable to launch an agitation, and it pushed London trade unionists into political activity.[48]

American Civil War

The embryonic reform movement was smothered by the growing agitation over the American Civil War. It was an issue which initially proved problematic for working-class radicals. There was no doubt about opposition to slavery. The draconian Fugitive Slave Law of 1851 had been widely condemned. The initial response of the *Sentinel* to the Southern secession in 1861 was to denounce slavery as a crime and to declare that it was better for the Republic to be destroyed than to be built on slavery.[49] The strongly prosouthern sentiment of much of the rest of the British press was attacked as a sign of a 'hatred of democracy'. However there were dissenting voices, including the Chartist John McAdam who saw the war as one of self-determination by the southern states and about a struggle for territorial ascendancy in the American West. By the summer of 1862, with the cotton famine hitting the Glasgow economy, there were signs of a change of attitude in the *Sentinel*, with calls for an end to the war. Soon the tone was even stronger and turned to denunciations of Federal despotism.[50] The war appeared not to be over slavery after all but over the right to secede so that 'it becomes impossible to regard either of the combatants as the champions of liberty'.[51] Even Lincoln's emancipation declaration in September failed to change attitudes, and the *Sentinel* lauded the south as 'united as one man, fighting for its homes and independence'.[52] Other radicals, however, such as Moir and Cullen, were supporters of the northern cause working with the Union and Emancipation Committee, with the former regularly being attacked as 'the Gallowgate tea dealer' in the pages of the *Sentinel*. In Edinburgh members of the Trades Council worked closely with the local Emancipation Committee, which included former Chartists and various clergymen, and a great meeting early in 1863 came out strongly in favour of Lincoln. Even here there were doubts expressed over whether the emancipation proclamation emanated from a desire to give freedom to the slaves or merely to attain political supremacy. In Dundee old reformers of middle class and upper class joined in denunciation of southern slavery.[53]

By the end of the war in May 1865 the *Sentinel*'s tone had altered again and it was full of praise for the USA.

The Second Reform Movement

Almost as soon as the war was over there was a revival of the campaign for parliamentary reform, with branches of the Reform Union, which favoured enfranchisement of male householders and lodgers, in both burghs and counties, who were rated for poor relief,[54] although, as always, there was the proviso that there could be no 'stipulation of finality short of manhood suffrage'. The idea was to attract as wide support as possible. The limited demands from Glasgow were scathingly condemned by George Howell, the secretary of the London-based Reform League, which was committed to nothing less than manhood suffrage: 'We are not surprised that the government should offer so little when the people are afraid to ask too much'.[55] Veterans of Chartism, like Moir, the chairman, and Matthew Cullen were well-represented, but so were new younger activists, such as the potter, George Newton, one of the joint secretaries. The language was different from that of the Chartist period. What was claimed was not some lost right, but the rights of 'citizenship', which would allow the mass of the population 'to look after their interests and advance their condition'. The focus, in particular, was on 'pauperism and social suffering', which it was claimed was worse than in any other civilised country, on the failure to provide a proper national educational system and on the failure to control public expenditure.[56] However, the debates on how far to push the reform demand continued. George Newton argued that they should only go for what was practical politics and that was household suffrage with a tight residential qualification. As he wrote reassuringly to the 'Adullamite', Lord Elcho, 'no scum would be entitled at any time; they do not live in one house long enough to qualify there'.[57] This cautious, restricted approach prevailed and, by the end of 1865, there was only one branch of the more radical Reform League in Scotland, at Burntisland in Fife.

Palmerston's death in October 1865 cleared a major barrier to further reform. Middle-class radicals seized the moment and there were rallies in both Edinburgh and Glasgow attended by Liberal MPs to back the reform proposals of the government. The Reform Union in Scotland, moderate as it was, was concerned by the very limited nature of Russell and Gladstone's 1866 bill with its £6 household franchise. Such a level, it was argued, would exclude many more in Scotland than in England. They also complained that by the proposals Scotland would continue to be under-represented at Westminster. The defeat of Gladstone's measure by a combination of Conservatives and dissident Liberals around Robert Lowe and Lord Elcho, Bright's 'Cave of Adullam', changed the mood. The Reform League demand for manhood suffrage and the ballot gathered momentum. By September 1866 supporters of both the Reform Union and the Reform League came together to form a Scottish National Reform League committed to press for manhood suffrage, under the chairmanship of Councillor John Burt, active temperance reformer, anti-slavery campaigner and vice-president of the pro-Lincoln, Union and Emancipation Society. Meanwhile George Newton had moved his position and proposed that the resolution should be for manhood suffrage and the ballot. His speech revealed how Bright and Cobden's criticism of war, which had lost them support in the 1850s, was now standing them in good stead:

> It had been said that if such a principle were adopted it would be handing over the government of the country to the mass to the detriment of the few. But he did not believe that the mass would always act together. Besides, these sections who governed the country had committed many blunders. They had led us into wars in which we had no interest, and had left our soldiers to perish in hospitals and trenches. He did not think that the mass would have done worse than that.

The joiner, George Ross, cited the support for southern slave owners and the suspension of habeas corpus in Ireland as further evidence of the failures of government. He called for justice 'to our Irish friends' and argued that Fenianism had arisen because of misgovernment: 'they have the right to cry out for good government as we have'.[58]

Forty thousand attended a Glasgow demonstration organised by the League and trade unions in October 1866, at which all the shades of reform opinion were present: Bright, Edmund Beales, president of the English Reform League, the former Chartist, Ernest Jones, and George Potter of the London Working Men's Association. John Bright, the great spokesman of Manchester *laissez-faire* Liberalism, argued that 'just laws ... would change the face of the country' and would be the means of eradicating 'this mass of misery ... this vast disorder', something which 'benevolence' (charity) could not do. According to Margot Finn, his analysis broke new ground by justifying democratic reform as an agent of social change. Class has failed, he declared, 'let us try the nation'.[59] The very active secretary of the Scottish League was a young Glasgow Unitarian watchmaker and jeweller, George Jackson. Jackson had come to the fore as a supporter of the North during the debates over the American Civil War. He spelled out his vision of what manhood suffrage would mean in a letter to the *Glasgow Herald*:

> Manhood suffrage means an educated people ... Manhood suffrage means important laws, the greatest good for the greatest number, increase in national prosperity, a greater demand for the products of the farmer and manufacturer, less paid for the support of State drones and blunderers, more money paid to the shopkeeper and sickness and old age provided for.[60]

It was precisely the kind of linking of political reform to social change which Owenite socialists like Alexander Campbell had been vainly calling for in the Chartist period.

By February 1867 more than 3,000 people had joined the central association of the Scottish Reform League and another 2,000 were members of its various branches in Aberdeen, Burntisland, Dumbarton, Dumfries, Edinburgh, Galashiels, Kilmarnock, Stirling, Selkirk and in most of the smaller towns around Glasgow. By the time of the first annual general meeting in September 1867 there were fifty active branches.

Edinburgh politics in the 1860s had, as always, been about the annuity tax, but to this was added a bitter dispute over the city's water supply. Working-class areas which were supplied from wells supported the campaign for investment in a better water supply, while well-supplied middle-class areas wanted to keep municipal expenditure to a minimum. Temperance also remained a powerful divider. David Lewis, a member of the Evangelical Union, who had experienced the humiliation of having his goods publicly sold to pay the annuity tax, was elected to the town council in 1863 and became the leader of a group of Independent Liberals bent on a reduction in the number of public house licences, on removing the annuity tax and, increasingly, on taking up working-class causes. To get the changes required they needed working-class support and, therefore joined the campaign for parliamentary reform.

Edinburgh trade unionists began to move, forming a Working Men's Political Union to press for residential manhood suffrage although with the qualification that 'it was not to be understood that, while they had adopted the principle of manhood suffrage, they would refuse to have anything less'.[61] An Edinburgh trades' demonstration for reform was held in November 1866 and leading trade unionists gave strong backing to the Reform League, although the Trades Council at this time was in considerable disarray. The Working Men's Political Union, whose president was William Troup, a tailor and chair of the Trades Council, became a branch of the League. It forged links with the middle-class radicals in Edinburgh, the Independent Liberals, who had put up the money to cover the costs of the demonstration, and meetings were almost always chaired by Lewis or some other Liberal Radical town councillor.[62]

The League's national leadership in Scotland tended to be dominated by petty bourgeois figures such as the councillors Burt and Moir from Glasgow, Lewis from Edinburgh, Cochrane from Paisley and all of these were committed to maintaining links with the radical wing of the Liberal Party. A reform conference in Glasgow in March 1867 heard an Aberdeen delegate declare that they would have to go as near to revolution as in 1832 in order to get a bill, and the Chartist, John MacAdam, declared that no reform bill 'was ever granted without the dread of brute force', but such sentiments caused horror to Councillor Burt and the League leadership.[63] They did, however, set out to woo the trade unionists by linking the cause of reform to working-class demands for reform of legislation governing relations between employers and employed. But there were soon tensions, with some of the trade-union leaders in Glasgow and, by the autumn of 1867, there were rival organisations.

The election of 1868

Although the English Reform Bill was passed in August 1867, it was not until February 1868 that the Scottish measure got through. With the bill passed, the next issue was the election. Alexander Campbell and the *Sentinel* had, like George Potter in London, been calling for candidates 'practically acquainted with the habits and wants of the working class' and who would support curbs on the power of capital.[64] The League was determined to back Liberal radicals and, in Glasgow, approached various notable radicals before eventually settling on a local Liberal activist, George Anderson, who had shown some interest in social questions. His nomination was pushed through, despite considerable opposition from those, like the miners' leader Alexander McDonald, who wanted a working man to be selected.[65] The League also agreed to support the sitting members Robert Dalglish, who was a member of the tea-room group in the Commons, Liberals who had supported Disraeli's reform measure, and the very right-wing William Graham.

Critics of the League, led by James Adams, formed an Association of Advanced Social and Political Reformers, which 'would seek to secure working men to represent the interests of labour in parliament', and only if that proved impossible would they look 'to get men to represent them whose interests were opposed to their own'.[66] They took up the cause of those who still remained disenfranchised and condemned the failure of the Reform Act 'to remove the barriers which stand in the way of labour being represented by men of its own order', calling for payment of members of parliament and of election expenses.[67] The people in this group had been members of a loosely-organised Democratic Society which had kept the ideals of Chartism alive through the 1860s. They were all small businessmen and shopkeepers mainly from the east end of the city. As well as Adams there was James Martin, a tailor and draper in the Gallowgate, Moir, a Gallowgate grocer, John Burt who was in the leather trade and the recently-arrived John Ferguson, a publisher, who was to carry the ideas into the Irish Nationalist movement.[68] In Edinburgh too a group, led by the Chartist upholster Henry Ranken, wanted a declaration of independence from all political parties and wanted the 'working classes of Edinburgh to have one member of parliament to themselves'. But the momentum of the Reform League was impossible to stop.

The League's message was that all reformers should unite behind a common policy, accepting household suffrage as an instalment.[69] The Edinburgh trade unionists, however, went further than any other group of unionists in Britain in trying to draft a working-class political programme. The Trades Council compiled a list of questions to candidates on social and industrial issues. These dealt with the protection of trade-union funds threatened by legal decisions in England, the extension of factory legislation, repeal of master and servant acts, the establishment of courts of arbitration, nationalisation of the railways, the establishment of a national library for Scotland, a 'national, compulsory, unsectarian system of education', restrictions on the deck-loading of ships and 'a system of legislation which shall make it compulsory to provide full house accommodation for those of the working classes who may be evicted from their dwellings in consequence of civic improvements, railway acquisition, or similar causes, previous to such eviction taking place'.[70] When John Bright visited the city in November 1868 they pressed these demands on him.[71] They wanted to ensure that reform resulted in social change, even if some of what they were proposing was unpalatable to middle-class radical allies. However, in the end no candidate emerged to oppose the radical sitting MP, Duncan McLaren, in harness with the very moderate John Miller, and their return could be welcomed as 'the end of Whiggery in Edinburgh'.[72]

The only working-class candidate to stand in Scotland was the Scottish miners' leader, Alexander McDonald in Kilmarnock Burghs, a constituency which embraced Dumbarton, Rutherglen, Renfrew and Port Glasgow, as well as Kilmarnock. While offering himself as the 'people's candidate' against the Whig, Edward Bouverie, and supported by contributions from working people, as a critic of too close entanglement with middle-class radicals he received no backing from the Reform League, which put up Edwin Chadwick. McDonald was denounced as a Tory trying to split the Liberal vote, which he denied, but 'neither was he a Liberal in the ordinary sense of the term; and he would be political hack to no man. He remained content to be one of the friends of labour'.[73] The only leading figure to support his cause was the Positivist, E. S. Beesly, who had been warning English unionists against placing too much reliance on middle-class radicals to solve their social problems.

Women's suffrage

The Reform Bill of 1868 briefly raised the issue of women's suffrage. John Stuart Mill had unsuccessfully sought to have the word 'person' substituted for the word 'man' in the bill. In the 1830s there had been those who advocated the right of women to the vote, but received little response.[74] In the Chartist years there were groups of women activists and a powerful letter from a woman weaver in Glasgow published in the *Northern Star* suggested a strong latent demand:[75]

> It is the right of every woman to have a vote in the legislation of her country, and doubly more so now that we have got a woman at the head of the government. Arouse ye women of Scotland, and demand your liberties and your rights; join heart and soul with the men in the great radical agitation - it is the cause of the suffering many.

But, as Anna Clark has shown, Scottish Chartists had come to accept the powerful concept of separate spheres of activity for men and women.[76] According to the *True Scotsman*, 'nature has not, in general bestowed upon them [women] those mental and physical attributes which qualify for the discharge of political duties'.[77]

The defeat of John Stuart Mill's amendment to replace the word 'man' in the Reform Act with the word 'person' acted as stimulus to action, with the formation of an Edinburgh branch of the National Society of Women's Suffrage in November 1867, with Priscilla McLaren as president and her step-daughter Agnes McLaren as secretary, along with their Quaker friend Eliza Wigham.[78] The Reform Act of 1868 presented new opportunities. A number of women, led by Ella Burton in Edinburgh and inspired by the activities of Lydia Becker in Manchester, tried to get their names included on the electoral register. John McLaren, son of Duncan, argued the case in Edinburgh that women occupiers had once been allowed to vote for commissioners of police, but the registration court rejected the claim.[79] In Aberdeen the assessor, responsible for compiling the electoral register, was a leading feminist, John Duguid Milne, through his friend Alexander Bain a correspondent of John Stuart Mill. Milne had written a pamphlet on the need for middle-class women to get into the world of work. Only by participating in work and business, he argued, could women 'take a part or feel an interest in political and social movements, or to influence public opinion, national virtue, or national progress'.[80] He duly agreed to enter the names of 1,088 women householders in the electoral register. His arguments were that according to the dictionary the word 'Man' included the whole human race and that an Act of 1850, the Romilly Act, had decreed that in all acts the word male be taken to include female unless the contrary was specifically stated and also that, in the past, women had voted until the seventeenth century. Finally, he had argued that the Scottish Reform Act of 1832 had only used the word 'persons' without the adjective male. The sheriff, however, overthrew the decision.[81]

Conservative working men

Not all radicals opted for Liberal candidates. In Glasgow, both James Adams and James Martin of the Democratic Society, disenchanted by the failure of the Reform League to back a working man as a candidate, encouraged their supporters to vote Conservative. Adams argued that the Conservative Party was the party which had brought Catholic Emancipation, repeal of the Corn Laws, the Reform Bill and ten-hours' factory legislation and were likely to bring the nine-hours' day; and a Conservative Working Men's Association appeared.[82] In Edinburgh, one or two leading unionists objected to the Reform League's identification with the Liberal Party and criticised the attacks on the Conservative government.[83] In addition, leading unionists

from Glasgow, Edinburgh, Aberdeen and Paisley signed a declaration of
support for Lord Elcho, in East Lothian, who had been a leading opponent
of the extension of the franchise, but who had worked with trade unions to
get reform of the master and servant legislation.[84] In other words, politics
and the need for social reform were still often separated. Liberals tended to
scoff at the idea that working men could be Conservative, with John Stuart
Mill famously suggesting that a Conservative working man was such a *rara
avis* that could one be found then he should be kept in a glass case. But
Working Men's Conservative Associations spread in the aftermath of 1868.
The Glasgow one, formed in January 1869, soon had branches in every ward
and its own office by 1872. It claimed 2,800 new members in 1873–4 alone.[85]
Like those who joined in Dundee the stimulus may have been what were seen
as Gladstone's concessions to Irish Catholicism, with much talk of the need
'to resist all attempts to subvert our Protestant faith'.[86]

Just as in 1832, parliamentary reform in 1867 and 1868 had been carried
through by means of a broadly-based alliance of working-class and middle-
class reformers. It had taken time to arouse much enthusiasm among the
working class for a renewed campaign of reform, but the threats to trade-
union funds, the hints of legislation to restrict the activities of trade unions
and the attacks on the character of the working class by figures such as
Robert Lowe had caused great offence and stirred the trade unions to
support the reform campaign. Middle-class radicals had come to recognise
that they needed the support of sections of the working class if they were to
win their campaigns for reform. Working-class leaders had seen the need for
middle-class support and acceptance if they were to make advances. Both
groups saw reform not just as a recognition of the rights of citizenship but
also as a means to achieving very specific goals.

Notes

1. Fyfe, *Autobiography of John McAdam*, p. 16.
2. *Glasgow Sentinel*, 4 October 1851.
3. *Northern Star*, 25 May, 15 June 1850.
4. *Glasgow Sentinel*, 8, 29 March 1851.
5. William Lindsay, *Some Notes: Personal and Public*, (Aberdeen 1898), p. 3.
6. *Glasgow Sentinel*, 13 March 1852.
7. J. C. Williams, 'Edinburgh Politics', p. 68.
8. J. D. Mackie, *Life of Duncan McLaren*, Vol. II,(1888), p. 27.
9. Callum Brown, *A Social History of Religion in Scotland since 1730* (1987).
10. Mackie, *Life of Duncan McLaren*, II, p. 3.
11. *Witness*, 16 February 1856, p. 2 quoted in Smith, *Passive Obedience*, p. 205.
12. John Wolffe, *The Protestant Crusade in Great Britain 1829–1860*, p. 301.
13. For this see Mitchell, *The Irish in the West of Scotland*, chaps 7, 8.
14. *Glasgow Saturday Post*, 19 February 1853.

15. J. Handley, *The Irish in Scotland* (Cork, 1945), pp. 96–9; *North British Daily Mail*, 27 January 1860; Dundee Central Library, Lamb Collection 119(2).

16. *Glasgow Sentinel*, 30 January 1860.

17. W. Hammond, *Recollections of a Handloom Weaver*, (Glasgow, 1904), p. 64.

18. *Chartist Circular*, No. 5, 26 October 1839.

19. *British Quarterly Review*, XVIII, 1953, pp. 187–202.

20. Miles Taylor, 'The Decline of British Radicalism 1847–1860' (Oxford, 1995), p. 111.

21. *Glasgow Sentinel*, 29 March 1851.

22. *Ibid.* 12 November 1853.

23. *Ibid.* 22 April 1854.

24. Mackie, *Life of Duncan McLaren*, II, p. 10.

25. A. Mitchell, *Political and Social Movements in Dalkeith* (1882), pp. 58–65.

26. *Glasgow Sentinel*, 6, 13 January 1855.

27. H. J. Hanham, *Scottish Nationalism* (1969), p. 72. A recent case had involved the Duke of Atholl trying to shut off the right of way from Blair Atholl to Braemar through Glen Tilt.

28. H. J. Hanham, 'Mid-Century Scottish nationalism, Romantic and Radical' in R. Robson (ed), *Ideas and Institutions of Victorian Britain* (1967), p. 151.

29. *Glasgow Sentinel*, 12 November 1853.

30. *Ibid.* 20 August 1853.

31. *Ibid.* 13 December 1856.

32. *Scotsman*, 26 December 1856.

33. Mitchell, *Politicial and Social Movements*, p. 73.

34. Mackie, *Duncan McLaren*, II, p. 146.

35. Taylor, *Decline of British Radicalism*, p. 158.

36. Beaton, secretary of the Edinburgh Trades Council, *Glasgow Sentinel*, 30 November 1861.

37. *Glasgow Sentinel*, 2 December 1853.

38. *Ibid.* 4 October 1856.

39. *Ibid.* 22 May 1858.

40. *Scotsman*, 26 May 1855.

41. R. A. Armstrong, *Henry William Crosskey, Ll.D., FGS. His Life and Work* (Birmingham, 1895), passim.

42. *Glasgow Sentinel* 18 September, 27 November 1858.

43. *Ibid.* 25 December 1858.

44. *Ibid.* 20 November 1858.

45. Iain Hutchison, 'Politics and Society in Mid-Victorian Glasgow 1846–1886', Ph.D. thesis, University of Edinburgh, 1974.

46. *Glasgow Sentinel*, 30 October 1858.

47. *Ibid.* 2 November 1861.

48. *Ibid.* 30 November 1861.

49. *Ibid.* 5 January 1861.

50. *Ibid.* 14, 28 June 1862.

51. *Ibid.* 5 July 1862.

52. *Ibid.* 3 January 1863.

53. *Dundee Advertiser*, 25 April 1863.

54. *Ibid.* 1 July 1865.

55. Bishopsgate Institute, Howell Collection, Howell to G. Newton, 27 November 1865.

56. Howell Collection, Glasgow Reform Union, 6 June 1865.

57. NAS, Wemyss Papers, Newton to Elcho, 10 July 1866.

58. *Glasgow Sentinel*, 22 September 1866.

59. Margot Finn, *After Chartism. Class and nation in English radical politics, 1848–1874* (Cambridge, 1993) p. 251.

60. *Glasgow Herald*, 30 January 1867 quoted in Hutchison, 'Politics and Society', p. 236.

61. *Scotsman*, 15 October 1866. John Hodge in his memoirs, *Workmen's Cottage to Windsor Castle* remembered seeing an ermine clad 'peer' in a cage in this procession with the the the label 'what the people would do to the peers'.

62. *Scotsman*, 15 March 1867.

63. *Ibid.* 22 March 1867.

64. *Glasgow Sentinel*, 16 November 1867.

65. A detailed examination of the divisions can be found in W. Hamish Fraser, 'Trade Unions, reform and the election of 1868 in Scotland', *Scottish Historical Review*, L, (1971), pp. 138–57.

66. *North British Daily Mail*, 22 July 1868.

67. *Ibid.* 17 July 1868.

68. G. B. Clark, 'Rambling Recollections of an Agitator' in *Forward*, 11 June 1910.

69. James Moir at Scottish National Reform League, *Glasgow Sentinel*, 21 September 1867.

70. I. MacDougall (ed.), *The Minutes of the Edinburgh Trades Council 1859–1873*, (Scottish History Society, 1968), pp. 225, 228, 231–2.

71. *Scotsman*, 6 November, 1868.

72. *Reformer*, 21 November 1868.

73. *Scotsman*, 18 September 1868.

74. *Herald to the Trades Advocate*, no. 25, 12 March 1831.

75. *Northern Star*, 23 June 1838.

76. Anna Clark, *'The Battle for the Breeches': Gender and the Making of the British Working Class* (1995).

77. *True Scotsman*, 10 November 1838.

78. Leah Leneman, *A Guid Cause. The Women's Suffrage Movement in Scotland* (1995 edit.), p. 12.

79. *The Reformer*, 3 October 1868.

80. *Industrial and Social Position of Women in the Middle and Lower Ranks* (1857), p. 36.

81. *Aberdeen Journal*, 7 October 1868.

82. *North British Daily Mail*, 14 November 1868.

83. *Edinburgh Evening Courant*, 30 January, 6 February 1868.

84. *Glasgow Sentinel*, 14 November 1868.

85. J. T. Ward, 'Working-Class Conservatism in Nineteenth Century Scotland', J. Butt and J. T Ward (eds), *Scottish Themes*, (1976).

86. Dundee Central Library, Lamb Collection 17 (3).

Chapter Five

Liberal Scotland 1868–86

It was quickly realised after 1868 that working men had failed to grasp the opportunities presented by the extended franchise. No working-class candidate had been elected anywhere in Britain. Many of the new electors had failed to vote. The Reform League had ensured that working-class votes were largely delivered to Liberal candidates. Before 1868 there had been little thought given to the practical problems of getting working men elected. Almost immediately there were calls to rectify that. George Potter, the London unionist, who had a regular column in the Edinburgh Independent Liberal paper, *The Reformer*, spelled it out:

> Working men, as a body, were not sufficiently alive to the great importance of a direct representation of labour, and of the incalculable influence it would have upon their condition. They have permitted themselves to be used as instruments of ambitious politicians, and allowed their cause to go by default. The mistake must not be repeated. Working men now have the vote. Let them lose no time in organising and preparing for the next election – which may not be so distant as some persons expect – and the blunder committed at the late election may be abundantly rectified at the next.[1]

An 'Old Radical' claimed that the lesson to be drawn is the 'the working class will never get political and municipal power from the middle class *unless they take it*. They have – if they will only organise themselves and stand loyally together – the means of taking it now', and if they do not they 'will find the possession of votes a mere barren privilege not worth having'.[2] The death of the former Chartist leader, Ernest Jones, just after the election was taken as an opportunity to recall his remarks on his recent visit to Scotland when he had counselled working men 'to exercise faith in no party, but to trust to themselves'.[3]

Attempts to exert some influence in municipal elections were only slightly more successful. In Glasgow, George Jackson failed to win in a largely working-class ward. In Aberdeen, where political controversy over local issues was intense in 1869, it was regarded as 'impracticable to put forward bona fide working men, this year as candidates', and trade union leaders backed the Liberal radical 'Party of Progress'.[4] The Dundee Trades Council co-operated with other groups in supporting particular candidates, none of whom was a working man.[5] The Edinburgh trade unionists were highly critical of the Town Council over its refusal to increase the wages of scavengers and to appoint an inspector under the Workshops' Act and the Trades Council came to the decision 'to use its best endeavours to secure the direct representation of labour in the Edinburgh Town Council'.[6] A decision to contest the Canongate ward was altered when the Independent Liberal Party offered to support a working man in Broughton ward, in opposition to the retiring councillor, who had deserted the Independent Liberals. Less than a fortnight before the election, however, the renegade councillor returned to the Liberal fold and was accepted. The Trades Council tried to transfer its effort back to the Canongate ward, but had little time available to make an impact. The episode, not untypical of many such incidents over the succeeding decades, left a residue of bitterness and a determination by the Council in future not to associate with any of the political parties 'but confine itself to the representation of labour'.[7] Two trade-union candidates were put forward in the following year, unopposed by the Liberals. Both were convincingly defeated, but out of the Municipal Election Committee there emerged a permanent body calling itself 'the Scottish Reform Union' to 'advocate the political rights of labour' and to 'embrace every opportunity of securing a more extended representation of labour in civic bodies'.[8]

The women issue

There was also much discontent with a reform measure which still fell well short of manhood suffrage and had done nothing to reduce the cost of elections. There was still no secret ballot, the county franchise had not been touched and only twenty-four MPs in 1871 supported a motion for payment of MPs. The issue of women's suffrage also remained unsatisfied.

The Scottish Reform League had been critical of the exclusion of women from the 1868 Act, particularly since the right of women ratepayers in England to have the vote in municipal elections had been recognised.[9] Leading middle-class radicals again took up the cause. Duncan McLaren chaired a meeting, organised by his wife and daughter, in Edinburgh's Queen's Hall, where middle-class sympathisers such a Professor David Masson, Jacob Bright (brother of Priscilla McLaren), Sir David Wedderburn, MP for South Ayrshire, and the Revd Dr Wallace, minister of Greyfriars, called for a bill to confer the electoral franchise on women who were qualified as owners or occupiers in their own right.[10] The following year an even larger meeting heard John Stuart Mill on the issue, and the platform party included women associated with Edinburgh's best-known reforming families – Mrs and Miss McLaren, Mrs and Miss Wigham, Mrs Masson, Miss Dick Lauder and Miss Craig among others.[11] Immediately after that meeting Agnes McLaren and Jane Taylor, the secretary of Galloway Women's Suffrage Association, toured the Highlands and the North-East on behalf of the cause and received some support from local clergy across the denominations among others.[12] Even old Chartists succumbed, with the Paisley shopkeeper, Robert Cochrane announcing his conversion because 'when he saw men like John Stuart Mill leading in this movement, it was time to ask ourselves why we are in opposition'. There were signs of gathering momentum, with some ninety-five public meetings reported in 1872 and women's committees in existence from Lerwick to Haddington. The movement was predominantly a middle-class one, but there were indications of working-class interest when Jessie Craigen, an activist from the north of England, addressed various open-air meetings in Scotland. At least one working man chair at one of her meetings saw the suffrage issue as 'a working-class question, for the bad laws by which women were oppressed would never be got rid of till they gave women a fair share of representation, and those bad laws came keenest on working women'.[13]

Activists like Priscilla McLaren, Ella Burton and Flora Masson, daughter of David Masson, continued to campaign during the 1870s. There were deputations to the government in 1877 to seek support for a women's suffrage bill, but the bill was talked out. Some success came in 1882 when Scottish women householders were brought into line with their English sisters and granted the vote in municipal elections. More than 5,000 celebrated the victory in Glasgow's St Andrew's Hall.

Working-class radicals

There was disenchantment on the part of many working-class leaders when their erstwhile middle-class allies showed little sympathy with trade-union demands. Duncan McLaren, like many other radicals, supported the Criminal Law Amendment Act of 1872 which put tight restrictions on picketing during strikes, and resolutely set his face against the campaign for its repeal. But, despite class tensions, there was still considerable room for co-operation between working-class and middle-class political activists. The temperance movement remained a particularly powerful link, with campaigns for a permissive bill to allow local option to exclude public houses from particular areas and for restrictions on licensing hours. Among the working class it was given a boost by the introduction of the dynamic Independent Order of Good Templars from the USA in 1869. The organisation grew rapidly and, by 1876, could claim over 62,000 mainly working-class members and more than 800 branches. The evangelical revival occasioned by the visit of the American evangelists Moody and Sankey also reinvigorated the temperance movement. Divisions over tactics between different sections were papered over and the Permissive Bill Association took the lead in turning the movement into a powerful political force in all the main Scottish towns. Huge meetings at the end of the 1870s gathered to hear itinerant temperance reformers like Canon Ferrer and others.

The campaign for educational reform to provide an adequate state-funded system of schools also linked some middle-class and some working-class reformers. In Edinburgh the Independent Liberal Party had an 'extensive, liberal and unsectarian system of education' as a leading demand. What was wanted were schools under the management of parents, more schools and compulsory education.[14] A Scottish National Education League was formed in Glasgow in January 1870 with political reformers like Jackson and James Moir and leading trade unionists such as the veteran John MacCalman and the up-and-coming president of the Trades Council and founder of Kinning Park Co-operative Society, Andrew Boa. It differed from the movement in Edinburgh and in England in that it contained hardly any non-establishment churchmen and did not lay emphasis on the need for education to be non-sectarian. There was considerable disappointment for some radicals with the 1872 measure, which allowed religion to continue to have a place in education, but they failed to arouse a working-class agitation. Education League candidates fared badly in the first school board elections of 1873 where the bulk of the working-class vote went to those Iain Hutchison describes as 'crypto-Conservatives running on the "use and wont" ticket'.[15] The clergy of all denominations continued to retain a tight hold on education.

A few working men took up the republican cause, following Dilke and Chamberlain, a cause which stirred considerable enthusiasm in 1871. It stemmed from growing criticism of the Queen for her failure to participate in public life other than when pressing Parliament for increases in the civil list. Arthur Ponsonby's pamphlet, *What does she do with it?*, made a powerful impact. Charles Dilworth, calling for the setting up of a Republican Club in Edinburgh, claimed that the Queen had done nothing for the last ten years other than collect her salary. It was launched in July with a visit of the London trade-union leader and republican, George Odger, and with a Dr Williams in the chair.[16] A Dundee Republican club was inaugurated in May 1871, quickly garnering about 130 members. The leading figures were socially mixed, a slater, an emigration agent, a hairdresser, a mill overseer, a labourer, a shoe-maker and an auctioneer. The last, Constantine McCaffrey, was secretary.[17] In Glasgow, John Ferguson was chairman of the local club.[18] The terrors of red revolution stirred by the events associated with the Commune in Paris were used as a stick to beat the nascent movement in Britain. But, as a writer in the *Reformer* noted, the movement was considerably stronger than many believed even if 'some of those who are pushing to the front of the movement in England are atheistic communists more that Republicans'.[19] Some linked it to demands for abolition of the House of Lords.

Land reform

The third issue which could, as always, unite working-class and middle-class radicals was the issue of land reform with its accompanying assaults on the aristocracy. Early reformers like Paine, Ogilvie and Spence had all called for land reform. The Anti-Corn Law League people had linked 'free trade in land' to the demand for free trade in corn, but then the issue had languished. The Aberdeenshire-born barrister, James Morrison Davidson in 1868 had embarked on a campaign, which was to last for nearly thirty years, calling for the ousting of the landed class from the ranks of Liberals, 'whatever their professions of Liberalism might be'.[20] Letters in the radical press regularly denounced 'aristocratic jobbery' and the restrictions placed on land sales. There was vocal criticism of the game laws and Duncan McLaren was associated with Mill's Land Tenure Reform Association which was formed in London in 1869. The former Chartist, Ernest Jones, who attracted a great deal of support in Scotland in the 1860s, spoke on land nationalisation, influencing among others Professor J. Stuart Blackie, professor of Greek at Edinburgh University.[21]

There were also signs of growing discontent in the Highlands, with John Murdoch's *Highlander* newspaper from 1873 until 1882 forming a focus for both land-reform campaigns and a Gaelic language movement. The Gaelic Society of Inverness formed in 1871 reflected a revival of interest in Gaelic language and culture. J. Stuart Blackie, a romantic enthusiast for all things Celtic, gave the movement a high profile with his campaign for the establishment of a chair of Gaelic at Edinburgh University, and for the right of children in Highland schools to use Gaelic. It was, however, John Murdoch who most effectively succeeded in linking this romantic interest in Gaelic with a campaign for land reform. Brought up in Islay, Murdoch had been on the edges of various radical movements: Chartism in the north of England and Young Ireland in 1848 in Dublin, before retiring to Inverness in 1873 to publish *The Highlander*.[22]

A number of land issues caused particular discontent in both Highlands and Lowlands. The game laws, with the right to hunt across tenants' land and the special protection given to game was becoming especially provocative. In the north-east and in the Lothians, William McCombie of Tillyfour on Donside, and George Hope of Fenton Barns in East Lothian had campaigned for reform in the 1860s, to allow control of game to protect their crops. McCombie's cousin, also William, editor and owner of *The Aberdeen Free Press*, vigorously took up the tenant farmers' cause in the north-east. In the Highlands, as whole areas became playgrounds for the rich, game preservation was imposed even more ruthlessly and intensified crofters' grievances at exclusion from access to land. Secondly, the law of hypothec in Scotland meant that landlords had the first call on a debtor's assets, making it very difficult for a tenant farmer to get credit. Attempts to reform the law of hypothec, while supported in Scotland, had been regularly frustrated by English MPs.

During the 1870s John Stuart Mill and the Land Tenure Reform Association discussed issues such as land nationalisation or, at the very least, the public administration of waste land. He argued that 'the appropriation of land by private individuals had gone far enough' and suggested that rather then individual allotments there should be co-operative experiments.[23] Although Mill himself died in 1873 his radical step-daughter, Helen Taylor, published some of his late essays posthumously in the *Fortnightly Review* of 1879. Their impact was powerful as the great philosopher of Liberalism was seen to be challenging the central concept of the sacrosanctity of private property.

Amid the relative prosperity of the early 1870s, coming after the hard years of cattle fever in the late 1860s, the land reform movement made only limited headway. But the increasing flood of cheap imports from the United States as the mid-Western prairies were opened up brought renewed problems for many farmers. Also the general economic depression of the late 1870s and especially the widespread unemployment in 1879 stimulated renewed examination of the causes of unemployment. The lack of access to land and the relentless driving of people off the land into the cities was the favoured explanation. The Aberdeenshire businessman and small landowner, J. W. Barclay, MP for Forfarshire, presided at a meeting in London in July 1879 to form the Tenant Farmers' Alliance. Its original aim was to get better farmer representation in Parliament to campaign for a bill which would give Scotland something like what in Ireland was known as the three Fs, fair rents, fixity of tenure and free sale.[24] In the end the Alliance contented itself with a programme which sought to get compensation for improvements, the reform of the game laws and of the laws of distress and hypothec, to obtain a fairer division of local taxation between landlord and tenant and to get an elective system of county government. At the founding meeting of the Scottish area of the Alliance many of the familiar reformers were present. As well as Barclay, there was David Wedderburn MP, John McLaren, J. B. Blackie, Charles Cowan.[25]

Bulgarian atrocities

The election of 1874 was the first to take place where the full effects of the extended franchise could be felt and the first where there was a secret ballot. It resulted, for the first time since the 1840s, in an overall Conservative majority and revealed a clear disenchantment with the Liberal government on the part of many working men. This disenchantment stemmed from many issues. It included the slowness to implement a trade-union act to protect union funds and, when it did come, its accompaniment by a draconian Criminal Law Amendment Act. The Edinburgh trade unionists abandoned McLaren because of this. There was also discontent with the shape of the Education Act of 1872. What the defeat also exposed was a marked Liberal failure, compared with the Conservatives, to get to grips with organising the new electorate. The extent of the defeat of both radical and Whig sections of the Liberal Party, however, came as a shock and there was an immediate search for issues which could revive the radical cause.

Gladstone's re-emergence from retirement and his denunciation of the Turkish government's bloody repression of a Bulgarian uprising in 1876, which the Liberal *Daily News* had brought to public attention, proved a suitable emotional cause. It responded to mounting frustration among radicals that Disraeli and the Conservatives were making the running on all fronts. The Liberal leadership was seen as offering only negative opposition in parliament rather than putting forward progressive new policies.[26] Now, middle-class radicals the length of the country found a 'safe' cause around which they could unite, but also one which was able to attract considerable working-class support. A number of Workmen's Peace Associations were in existence, including one in Aberdeen, which had the support of the Trades Council. The radical newsagent, William Lindsay, was sent as a delegate to the peace movement conference in Paris, financed by the Association and the Trades Council. Mass meetings were held to denounce the Turkish atrocities and to condemn Disraeli's government for neither exposing what had gone on nor condemning it. Disraeli's cynical argument that such was the nature of Oriental regimes was seen as particularly offensive.[27] The possibility, which seemed a likelihood in 1877 and 1878, that the events might lead to the country being pulled into a war with Russia on behalf of the Ottoman Empire fuelled even more fervent agitation. Liberal Associations, intended to generate a radical voice within the Liberal Party, began to appear. They led the demand for neutrality in the the event of a Russo-Turkish war. Town councils across the country began to pass resolutions supporting this. Meetings were held in cities and towns throughout the country. Provost William Collins presided at a great meeting in Glasgow city hall. Aberdeen had its largest meeting in decades, denouncing what was described as 'mischievous meddling' in foreign affairs.[28] Meetings in Edinburgh and elsewhere condemned the press for trying to stir up the new 'jingoism'. Old radicals made their appearance. James Moir was there in Glasgow and George Thompson in Aberdeen. But it aroused small towns as well as activists in the cities. In Elgin, Provost Culbard, generated a particularly vigorous campaign.

Anti-Imperialism

The fact that the British gained Cyprus from the Berlin Congress which sought to settle Balkan tensions linked it to the wider issue of imperialism which was coming to the fore as a result of the invasion of the Transvaal, the invasion of Afghanistan and the Zulu Wars. The former Liberal Chancellor, Robert Lowe, brought the word 'Imperialism' into common use with his denunciation of what he defined as 'the assertion of absolute force over others … the oppression of the weak by the strong, and the triumph of power over justice'.[29] The young Lord Rosebery rejected Cyprus as a 'white elephant', pulling the country into the politics of Asia Minor and suggested that 'even India might be held at too dear a price'.[30] The Liberal radical press denounced the Disraelian argument that 'territorial aggrandisement and the accumulation of a multitude of interests abroad ... [were] proof of national greatness and well-being'.[31] From the Highlands, an area producing many of the troops of Empire, *The Highlander* called for the churches to raise their voices against expansionism.[32] There was a concern about the corrupting effects which expansionist policies were having, of 'the indifference to suffering, the positive relish for the wholesale murder which the masses are acquiring day by day as they read of the struggle going on for conquest and military glory'.[33] There were calls for 'a protest from the hearths of the toiling millions'.[34]

Gladstone arrived in Scotland in November 1879 for his Midlothian campaign in an atmosphere which was more than ready to hear his denunciations of Disraeli's imperialism. 'The dominant passion of England,' he declaimed, 'is extended Empire', kept in check until now 'by the integrity and sagacity of her statesmen'.[35] What was need was a restoration of morality in politics. In 1879–80 Gladstonian popular liberalism was at its peak in Scotland. John Bright had acted as the John the Baptist of the movement[36] in the 1850s and it had found a response in Scotland. Bright's argument was that there was the possibility of a cross-class alliance which could bring about moral radical reform. It was an idea taken up with some enthusiasm by many in Scotland, strengthened by the notion that there were distinctly Scottish issues which were above those of class. Duncan McLaren was confident that the newly enfranchised 'will consider the freedom they have gained as a trust, by the exercise of which they can help in a very large degree the extension of righteous legislation'.[37] Gladstone, who could always play up his Scottish roots very effectively, was able to take over Bright's mantle in the 1870s, although Bright himself continued to be widely admired.[38] Gladstone could flatter the Scots, as he did in Midlothian, by implying that they could be treated to a higher standard of political discourse than was usual south of the border. The moral earnestness appealed to a nation reared on preaching. Both Gladstone and Bright were able very effectively to tap into older radical language by playing with the concept of 'the people', where wisdom and morality resided, as opposed to the implied effete and corrupt class interests of their opponents; the 'masses' against the 'classes'. Liberalism was presented as the natural successor to the traditions of Chartism. The argument that politics should be based on principle was presented as having a particular appeal to a nation which reputedly had ever been ready to take a stance based on first principles.

Disappointed hopes

With the Liberals swept back into power in 1880 on the strength of Gladstone's stirring rhetoric, radical hopes were high, but were soon disappointed. W. H. Russell's exposé of atrocities by the army in southern Africa intensified the criticisms. For some the Boers could be compared to the Scots Covenanters and the annexation of their territory was seen as an act of gross betrayal. Donald Currie of the Castle shipping line, with its route to the Cape, had worked in the 1870s to get compensation for the Orange Free State for British annexation of the Kimberley diamond fields and regularly spoke up for the Boer cause.[39] The excesses of Lord Roberts in Afghanistan had echoes of Glencoe, with 'women and old driven from burned villages into the hills in winter'.[40] John Murdoch addressed the 'Noble Afghan Highlanders':

> our sympathies are with you. *We* claim the same patriotism also, and yet, sorry are we to have to lament this day the inglorious mission of our noble Scottish Highland Regiments – to make war on the noble Highlanders of Afghanistan.[41]

The enthusiasm for Beaconsfield's imperialism, just like the earlier jingoism for war with Russia, was seen as a peculiarly English phenomenon reflecting an alliance between the Conservatives and 'the baser portion of the populace'.[42]

The problem with the high moral tone is that it had created expectations of a new morality in foreign policy which were unlikely to be satisfied. Frere and Shepstone in southern Africa were perceived as being in the hands of land speculators, but, far from pulling out, Gladstone's government, dominated by aristocratic Whigs, got more involved.[43] The annexation of the Boer Republics unleashed widespread protest. Sir David Wedderburn wrote to *The Scotsman* condemning the 'iniquitous seizure … of a free community composed of Christian whites' as 'a national crime'. Follow-up letters by others once again drew parallels between Dutch presbyterians and Scotch presbyterians and warned that 'we are sowing the seeds of hereditary animosity in the hearts of people vastly more formidable than the Irish'.[44] Wedderburn and a number of radicals formed the Transvaal Independence Committee set up in 1881. The secretary was Gavin Brown Clark, editor of the Good Templar magazine, a former member of Marx's International Working Men's Association and gradually emerging as an ubiquitous figure in radical movements.

Clark, who had spent time in southern Africa, produced numerous pamphlets in support of the Boer cause. His *British Policy Towards the Boers: A Historical Sketch* (1881) went through some six editions and he was later reputed to have been in the Boer camp when they defeated the British force at Majuba Hill in 1882. In Glasgow, the *Weekly Mail*, owned by the city's radical MP, Dr Charles Cameron, called for the restoration of the Zulu leader Cetawayo and declared that there were no British interests to protect in Zululand. Anti-War meetings were held in Glasgow and Edinburgh, although at the Glasgow one a motion in support of the government was carried 'by the Home Rulers and Tories' according to the *Mail*.[45] The recently-ousted editor of *The Scotsman*, Robert Wallace,[46] writing on the 'Philosophy of Liberalism' saw imperialism as 'the revival of the old instinct of conquest' which was against everything that Liberalism stood for. To Wallace the history of Liberalism was the history of the struggle of the subjugated community to emancipate itself from the bondage imposed on it by the conquering oligarchy, both lay and priestly, whether in the form of striking the fetters from its own liberties or abolishing the privileges with which the dominating class has sought to fortify its position.[47]

Cameron's *North British Daily Mail* opposed every territorial expansion or informal extension of British power in these years, relentlessly questioning the motives of those who were pressing for expansion and generally condemning them as in pursuit of greedy economic interests. The anti-war agitations also brought John Bright back into the public eye and he was elected rector of Glasgow University.[48]

Matters only got worse with the bombardment of Alexandria and the invasion of Egypt. G. B. Clark co-ordinated the calls to get out of Egypt. At the founding of the Aberdeen Radical Association at the end of 1884 there was denunciation of entanglements in Egypt 'for the benefit of bondholders and Jews', with the hope that the newly expanded electorate 'would exercise a counterbalancing influence on the Government'.[49] Gordon's expedition to Khartoum, despite his Scottish connections, stirred little enthusiasm in the Liberal press. Just as in the 1870s, the English were blamed for jingoism. 'Cockneydom and the nation are once more at variance', pronounced the Aberdeen liberal organ, and 'it will be a happy day of deliverance when the last British soldier plants his last footstep on that portion of the African continent'.[50] As Bernard Porter points out, Jingoism and imperialism were linked by anti-imperialists as a particular state of mind, bringing out – exactly as Gladstone had argued – the vulgar, the aggressive and the immoral which it was statesmen's duty to curb.[51]

Land Wars

Land reform, however, still remained the most crucial issue. Bad harvests in 1881 and the accompanying difficulties which this presented for farmers rekindled the tenant farmers' alliance. There were rent strikes and protests throughout north-east Scotland and elsewhere. The farmers called for re-form of the land laws, revaluation of their farms, security of tenure and tenants' rights. Six thousand attended a meeting in Aberdeen in December 1881 and constituted themselves into the Scottish Farmers' Alliance, with branches throughout the main farming areas. The main base of the campaigns remained the North-East where the Alliance leadership retained close links with the radical wing of the Liberal Party. It contained elements whose views were often difficult to reconcile and the alliance was always an uneasy one. As Ian Carter shows, there were subtle differences of aim between the capitalist farmers in the larger, fertile holdings and the small peasant farmers living on marginal hill farms. Bigger farmers were principally concerned with getting rid of hypothec, reform of the game laws and compensation for any investments they made as tenants.[52] A more radical group, led by Quentin Kerr of Patna in Ayrshire and some smaller West Aberdeenshire farmers, tried to protect the smaller tenants, to push for all the provisions of the Irish Land Act to be extended to Scotland and to get a court set up in each county to regulate the conditions of occupancy and to support the judicial fixing of rents. There was a running battle within the Alliance's executive over where to place the emphasis which reflected very different class interests.[53]

It was not only those who worked on the land who felt the effects of restrictions imposed by landowners. The mountains were being discovered and artists and walkers were regularly subject to harassment by gamekeepers as long-established rights of way were being closed off. When James Bryce, MP for Tower Hamlets, an enthusiast for the Cairngorms, introduced his Access to the Mountains (Scotland) Bill in 1884, which would have specified that 'no owner of uncultivated mountain or moorland shall be entitled to exclude any person from walking on such land for purposes of recreation or scientific or artistic study' his mail bag was full of accounts of confrontations in the Scottish mountains. He and his son were to battle vainly for years to get legal recognition of the 'right to roam'.[54]

In Ireland the land agitations of 1879–80 had adopted an altogether more aggressive stance and the effects of this began to be felt. The activities of Michael Davitt's Irish Land League spread to Scotland. There had long been political activity among the shopkeepers and publicans who were the more prosperous elements of the Irish community in the west of Scotland. Many had been active campaigners for repeal of the Irish Act of Union and a few, in the 1850s and 1860s, dabbled in Fenianism. In 1871, thanks to the Antrim-born Protestant, John Ferguson, who had arrived in Glasgow at the end of the 1850s, the first branch of the Irish Home Government Association on the mainland was formed in 1871. It later became the Home Rule Confederation. In 1879 Ferguson, Edward McHugh, Michael Clarke and other leading members of the Home Rule campaign formed a branch of the Irish Land League. When Michael Davitt addressed a great rally which they organised in Glasgow's city hall in 1879 he called for land nationalisation, and many early Scottish socialists dated their first political awareness from that meeting. Branches of the Land League spread among the Irish community, as protests against Forster's Coercion Act intensified. John Ferguson remained the key figure, linking Irish and Scottish grievances and, at this stage, regularly advising Irish voters to vote Tory.[55] But it was Davitt who set out to broaden the appeal to the working class. He more than anyone made the link between the Irish national question and social issues, arguing that only a home-rule parliament would effectively tackle social problems. His arguments for nationalisation of land and of the mining royalties paid to landowners appealed to the anti-aristocratic tradition of the Scottish radicals.

Henry George

It was in this atmosphere that the ideas of the American writer Henry George began to percolate from the United States. In some ways his ideas had been anticipated by the Ayrshire farmer, writer and early nationalist Patrick Edward Dove, who had edited the *Commonwealth* newspaper in Glasgow in the early 1850s. Dove had argued that the landowners' appropriation of rent was a root cause of poverty. It has even been suggested that George's ideas were plagiarised from Dove's *The Theory of Human Progression*.[56] Whatever the source, George brought to the fore ideas which challenged that widely-held view that it was individual failings, and particularly intemperance, which explained the plight of the poor. G. B. Clark was one of the first to make contact with George and he ensured that *Progress and Poverty* was widely reviewed in the British press. George's book was a powerful assault on orthodox political economy. He challenged the acceptance of a society in which poverty could still exist alongside progress, what he called 'the increase of want side-by-side with the increase of wealth'. He proposed that the first step to any fundamental elimination of poverty depended upon the monopoly on land being destroyed. His solution was to have a single tax on land values which would make all other taxation unnecessary.

George made his first visit to Scotland in 1882 and his oratorical skills stirred considerable enthusiasm, particularly in the Highlands where there was already a wide unrest over crofters' rights of access to land. Continuing land clearances such as that recently carried out by the Aberdeen paper-maker, Pirie, in Leckmelm in Rosshire, and by the dreadful W. L. Winans in Kintail, who had pursued Murdo Macrae, a Morvich cottar, in the notorious pet lamb affair, built on resentments. A mass meeting in Inverness at the end of 1880 heard the minister of Leckmelm, John MacMillan, denounce a policy which converted 'Highland glens into vast wastes untenanted by human being', and call for an agitation against it. On Skye the crofters of Brae, near Portree had tried to reassert their grazing rights on land owned by Lord MacDonald and brought about the first major direct confrontation between authorities and the crofters. It at last got the movement wider attention. Two and a half thousand people attended a meeting in Edinburgh to hear the Revd James Begg call for a commission of enquiry. Elsewhere religious sensibilities were offended and economic discontents sharpened by the landing of steamers at Strome ferry on the sabbath and by the prosecution and hefty sentences on the protesters.[57]

Angus Sutherland, a school teacher at Glasgow Academy and president of the Glasgow Sutherland Association, founded the Highland Land League in Edinburgh in 1882. He favoured creating small holdings for a system of peasant proprietorship.[58] G. B. Clark, on the other hand, seems to have favoured a measure of land nationalisation, with land being taken over by the state as the present holders died, something similar to the ideas being propounded in England by the naturalist Alfred Russel Wallace, who in 1881 founded the Land Nationalization Society.[59] Clark and George together formed the Land Restoration Society.[60] It quickly linked with the land reform movement in Scotland in the Scottish Land Restoration League, 'to restore the Soil of Scotland to the people for whom it was intended, and to remove this great shame and crime from the land we love'. Alexander Mackenzie's *History of the Highland Clearances*, published in Inverness in 1883 and well-publicised in the *North British Daily Mail*, brought the story of the clearances to a wider public for the first time. Cameron, the publisher of the *Mail*, was president of the Federation of Celtic Societies which Blackie and Murdoch had brought into being in 1878, and was determined on making Highland land reform a political issue.

In response to the agitation, the Home Secretary, Sir William Harcourt conceded in 1883 a Royal Commission under Lord Napier. In spite of the almost exclusively landlord representation on the Commission the evidence which it heard and published was a damning indictment of 150 years of landowner exploitation of the Highlands. In the end the Commission's recommendations were cautious in the extreme and the Crofters' Act did nothing to encourage the break up of big estates to make more land available, although it did provide a substantial measure of security for some Highland crofters. None the less to many it was evidence that the power of property could be successfully challenged. In six Highland counties crofters were given fixity of tenure, the right to a fair rent and compensation for improvement when they gave up their holding. Despite the fact that the land court had no crofters' representative most rents were halved by the court, although it made little use of the provision to extend the size of holdings and deer forests continued to increase in size.

It was to keep up the pressure on the Royal Commission that the Highland Land Law Reform Association was launched in March 1883 with G. B. Clark in the chair.[61] The Association spread the campaign for reform, prepared the possible witnesses for the Commission and made the issue a national one. The Association now prepared to contest the coming election in what the Duke of Argyll called 'a Scotch Parnellite Party'.[62]

The campaign in the Highlands culminated with the success of the Crofters' Party in the election of 1885. G. B. Clark had a stunning victory in Caithness by a majority of 892, despite accusations that he had been with the Boers at Majuba Hill. Dr R. Macdonald defeated the Scottish Liberal whip, Munro-Ferguson, a Ross-shire landowner; D. H. Macfarlane, a former Irish MP, who had switched his interest to his homeland, and the first Roman Catholic MP to be returned in Scotland, won Argyll, J. McDonald Cameron Wick Burghs and Fraser Mackintosh, landowning former member for Inverness Burghs took Inverness-shire. Only Angus Sutherland failed to break ducal influence in his native county.

The debates over land reform continued after the crofters' legislation of 1886. In the non-Highland counties between 1882 and 1886 some gains were made. Hypothec was abolished, the game laws had been modified to allow shooting of game on his land by the farmer and some tenant rights had been secured by the Agricultural Holdings Act. But the hopes of the radical element in the Scottish Farmers' Alliance, which, significantly, in 1886 had taken the more all-embracing title of the Scottish Land Reform Alliance, of getting the crofting legislation extended to other parts of Scotland were disappointed. As Ian Carter concludes in his pioneering study of farm life in the north-east of Scotland concluded:

> Northeast peasants could not mobilise sufficient political muscle to force the Liberal government to give them the same legislative protection that Highland peasants were to enjoy. The reason for this inability was not lack of numbers. It was the failure of northeast peasants clearly to realise and represent their own class interest ... Capitalist farmers were allowed to present themselves as the representatives of all farmers, to pursue their sectional interest under the guise of pursuing farmers' general interest.[63]

Land reform and the cities

Henry George's second tour of 1884 set out to rouse the city population. In Glasgow he lectured on 'Scotland and Scotsmen', in Aberdeen on 'The Cause of Commercial Depressions and of increase of Want with Increase of Wealth' and in Edinburgh he declared that the depression was not due to over-production but to unjust distribution.[64] Branches of the Land Law Reform Association spread, distinguishing themselves from the tenant farmers' campaign by insisting that any reform of the land laws had to be 'in favour of the people'.[65] But even more significantly a new organisation was formed in Glasgow, the Scottish Land Restoration League, at a meeting chaired by John Murdoch. The aim was 'for the purpose of restoring the land to the people on the lines laid down by the author of *Progress and Poverty*' or, as William Forsyth said, 'a society to impeach landlordism'.[66] The Irish were represented by John Ferguson and Richard McGhee and it was the latter who suggested the name. George drew up a 'Proclamation to the People of Scotland' and nearly 2,000 quickly enrolled in the new League. Within a month, 150,000 adherents were being claimed. The SLRL focused on George's solution of the single tax on land, which they proposed should be four shillings in the pound, but they also broadened the campaign into an attack on mining royalties thus linking it with Davitt's arguments. Michael Davitt had been around a fortnight before George and was broadening his assault. He likened the position of labour to that of slavery and declared that 'until the existing labour system was merged into co-operation and the power of capital to regulate the price of labour was reduced to a minimum slavery would not be eradicated from civilized society'.[67]

The land issue generated interest in the urban west of Scotland because there were large numbers of Irish and Highlanders around, who had quickly romanticised their rural past into simple black and white terms of wicked landowners clearing simple peasant folk. But it also found a resonance because the unemployment problems of the cities tended to be explained in terms of people being pushed off the land and into the cities. The League's manifesto declared:

> We hold that the fact that the Land of Scotland – the rightful heritage of the whole people of Scotland – having, by a long course of usurpation and fraud, been made the private and exclusive property of a few of their number is the reason why more than two-thirds of Scottish families are compelled to live in houses of one or two rooms; why wages are so pitifully low in every department of industry; ... and why Scotsmen are compelled to emigrate, while great tracts of their native land, from which men have been driven, are given up to beasts and sport.

There is no doubt that the campaigns of George and Davitt broke the mould of conventional politics and, as Alexander Webster, Unitarian minister and chair of the League noted 'men began to associate for heretical aggressive-ness'.[68] The Henry George Institute in Glasgow provided a base for serious economic study, with J. Morrison Davidson producing a stream of pamphlets for it from a tenement in Montrose Street. For others it 'widened their social vision'. Although Henry George was soon to become violently anti-socialist, in 1884 he was posing questions which were challenging capitalism. 'Plutoc-racy,' he claimed, 'is quite as harmful as aristocracy. The capitalist who makes a vast pile out of material derived from the land may as reasonably be robbed as the landowner whose property produces the material'.[69] Aberdeen Land Law Reform Association published a circular which condemned private property in land and landowners who

> first rob the labourer, then evict him; hence the congested, miserable state of honest working men, who are now confined to small rooms in town, or com-pelled to live in hovels on the seashore ... Is man therefore to starve in order that a 'landlord' may use God's earth as a playground? Honest Labouring Men, now is your time to say, No. Lift up your voice, and further God's intention with regard to your right to labour and live, and 'His will be done on earth as in heaven'. Submit no longer to slavery and starvation.[70]

For many George's critique was to be a stepping stone to socialism.

Five Scottish Land Restoration League candidates stood in the election of 1885. J. Shaw Maxwell, the future secretary of the Independent Labour Party, stood in one of the new Glasgow seats as did William Forsyth and R. Wallace Greaves. John Murdoch offered himself for the Partick Division of Lanark-shire and J. Morrison Davidson in Greenock. James Martin, a campaigning eastender not in the League, offered himself as an Independent Labour candidate. They polled only a handful of votes, but symbolically the rejection of Liberalism was important.

Within five years of what was the highpoint of Liberal radicalism disenchantment had set in. There was much life left in radicalism and few as yet seriously questioned its basic tenets. There were attempts by the left of the party to win back the initiative. Radical associations were formed, like that in Aberdeen, that called for the abolition of the House of Lords, payment of MPs, nationalisation of land, progressive taxation, disestablishment, a land tax, international arbitration, and 'A Scotch Department for the furtherance of national business, free education, free justice, woman [sic] suffrage, and amendment to the poor laws'.[71] Such a body could incorporate most of the demands coming from labour. None the less, the failure of whole sections of Scottish liberalism to break free from Whig, landowner influence, the disastrous abandonment of hopes of a moral foreign policy and the failure to address some of the main social problems were all contributing to a new stirring outside the ranks of Liberal radicalism.

Notes

1. *Reformer*, 26 December 1868.
2. *Ibid.* 12 November 1870.
3. *Ibid.* 30 January 1869.
4. *Aberdeen Herald*, 6 March 1869.
5. *Ibid.* 28 November 1868, 4 September 1869.
6. Edinburgh Trades Council Minutes, 5 October 1869.
7. *Ibid.* 5–26 October 1869.
8. *Ibid.* 27 December 1870; *Reformer*, 22 October, 5 November, 17 December 1870
9. *Aberdeen Herald*, 14 November 1868.
10. *Reformer*, 22 January 1870.
11. *Ibid.* 14 January 1871.
12. *Ibid.* 30 September 1871.
13. L. Leneman, *'A Guid Cause'. The Women's Suffrage Movement in Scotland* (1995 edition, Edinburgh), pp. 2–6.
14. *Reformer*, 29 August 1868.
15. Hutchison, *Political History*, p. 133.
16. *Ibid.* 8 April, 1 July 1871.
17. Dundee Public Library, Lamb Collection 17 (13).
18. *Forward*, 18 June 1910.
19. *Reformer*, 1 April 1871.
20. *Ibid.* 18 December 1868.
21. G. B. Clark, 'Rambling Recollections' in *Forward*, 18 June 1910.
22. James Hunter, 'The Politics of Highland Land Reform', *Scottish Historical Review*, 53, 1974, p. 76.
23. W. Wolfe, *From Radicalism to Socialism. Men and ideas in the formation of Fabian Socialist Doctrines 1881–1889* (Yale, 1975), pp. 58–60.
24. *The Highlander*, 30 May 1879.
25. *Glasgow Herald*, 13 November 1879.
26. *People's Journal*, 10 November 1877.

27. *Elgin Courant*, 12 September 1876.

28. *Daily Free Press*, 8 January 1878.

29. R. Lowe, 'Imperialism', *Fortnightly Review*, October 1878.

30. *Daily Free Press*, 10 July 1878.

31. *Ibid.* 31 August 1878.

32. *The Highlander*, 7, 14 March 1879.

33. *Ibid.* 25 April 1879.

34. *Ibid.* 30 March 1878.

35. W. E. Gladstone, 'England's Mission', *Nineteenth Century* (September 1878), p. 584.

36. The image is Patrick Joyce's in *Visions of the People. Industrial England and the Question of Class* (Cambridge, 1994), p. 47.

37. Mackie, *Duncan McLaren*, Vol. II, p. 162.

38. see, for example, *Aberdeen Daily Free Press*, 14 January 1878.

39. A. Davey, *The British Pro-Boers 1877–1902* (Tafelberg, Cape Town, 1978), pp. 12–13.

40. *Aberdeen Daily Free Press*, 2, 3 December 1879.

41. *The Highlander*, 2 January 1880.

42. *Aberdeen Daily Free Press*, 24 November 1879.

43. *North British Daily Mail*, 30 December 1882.

44. *Scotsman*, 1, 3 January 1881.

45. *Glasgow Weekly Mail*, 2, 9 September 1882.

46. Wallace, formerly minister of Greyfriars' Church in Edinburgh, abandoned the ministry and became editor of *The Scotsman* before becoming a lawyer and later MP for Central Edinburgh.

47. J. Campbell Smith and William Wallace (eds), *Robert Wallace. Life and Last Leaves* (1903), p. 293.

48. *Glasgow Weekly Mail*, 24 March 1883.

49. *Aberdeen Daily Free Press*, 23 December 1884.

50. *Ibid.* 7, 14 February 1885.

51. B. Porter, *Critics of Empire: British Radical attitudes to colonialism in Africa 1896–1914* (1968), p. 90.

52. Ian Carter, *Farm Life in Northeast Scotland 1840–1914. The Poor Man's Country* (Edinburgh, 1979), pp. 165–75.

53. *Aberdeen Journal*, 26 January 1884; *Aberdeen Daily Free Press*, 15 December 1884.

54. Tom Stephenson, *Forbidden Land. The Struggle for Access to Mountain and Moorland* (Manchester, 1989), passim.

55. *Glasgow Herald*, 12 November 1879; *Dundee Advertiser*, 11 April 1882.

56. J. D. Wood, 'Transatlantic Land Reform, America and the Crofters' Revolt 1878–1888', *Scottish Historical Review*, 63, (1984), p. 95.

57. The coming of steam trawling was undermining the fishing side of crofters' activities. The rioters were released after half their sentences was served. *Glasgow Weekly Mail*, 29 September 1883.

58. D. W. Crowley, 'The "Crofters' Party", 1885–1892', *Scottish Historical Review*, 25, (1956), p. 112.

59. G. B. Clark, *A Plea for Nationalisation of the Land*, (1882).

60. *Forward*, 13 August 1910.

61. Hunter, 'Politics of Highland Land Reform', p. 50.
62. *Ibid.* p. 54.
63. Carter, *Farm Life in Northeast Scotland*, p. 172.
64. *Glasgow Herald,* 20 February 1884; *Aberdeen Daily Free Press*, 21 February 1884.
65. *Aberdeen Journal*, 22 February 1884.
66. *Glasgow Herald*, 26 February 1884.
67. *Ibid.* 5 February 1884.
68. Alex Webster, *Memories of the Ministry* (1913), p. 23.
69. *Aberdeen Journal*, 16 December 1884.
70. *Inverness Courier*, 24 January 1885.
71. *Daily Free Press*, 6 February 1885.

CHAPTER SIX

Roads to Socialism

The turn of the 1880s was a period of extraordinary cultural ferment. The old ideas and values were under challenge. Church and chapel were no longer held in the high esteem they once were. Evangelical moral certainties were under attack from Darwinian ideas and German biblical criticism. Churches could no longer enforce conformity and a questioning of orthodox doctrines was in the air. There were few prosecutions after the Bradlaugh/Besant trial of 1877 for putting forward unpopular ideas. There were also signs of growing disquiet with the shibboleths of old Liberalism and new theoretical positions stemming from the spread of idealist philosophy and from the rediscovery of socialism.

Idealism

Scottish philosophers and many churchmen embraced the philosophy of idealism which T. H. Green had been propagating at Balliol College, Oxford, to which many Glasgow students went as Snell scholars. The idealists argued that in order to provide all with the opportunity for what Green called 'positive freedom' it was necessary on occasion for the state to intervene and perhaps even to limit individual freedom for a greater community good. While still seeing the individual as central, idealists were concerned to place the individual firmly within a community and to reject the atomistic assumptions of utilitarianism, that suggested that society was merely the sum of its individual parts. Idealist philosophy was spread in church and university by the immensely influential Edward and John Caird at Glasgow and by Henry Jones at St Andrews and then at Glasgow. As Donald Withrington has argued, by drawing on aspects of the Scottish past which accepted the need for regulation and for the subordination of the individual to the common good, Scottish idealists could very readily embrace the idea that a democratic government had a role to play in creating the good society.[1] As early as 1875 John Caird had argued that:

> religion needs to ally itself with political and social wisdom. To enquire and
> discover if there be any mechanisms of society which shall remedy or prevent

such a state of things; any deeper conception of the rights and duties of property, any modification of the conditions that affect the distribution of wealth or the relations of capital and labour.[2]

In 1881, Donald Macleod, minister of the very influential Park Church in Glasgow, was arguing that 'the spirit of Christianity is essentially socialistic – not the socialism of the Nihilist assassin or the communist petroleuse, but the socialism of the New Testament'.[3]

Socialism

There were many ways in which new political ideas were spread. The London monthly journal, *Modern Thought*, established in February 1879 'for the free discussion of all subjects ... of interest to humanity' was read in Scotland. A number of articles on Marx's ideas were published there in 1881, by Ernest Belfort Bax. The ideas were further picked up by Archdeacon Cunningham that same year in an article in the *Contemporary Review*. Bax wrote, 'We are passing through a revolutionary epoch, the most severe crisis of which is yet to come, and ... to prepare for this inevitable crisis is the real task of the true friend of progress in the present day'. In debating societies, radical associations and Land League meetings socialist ideas were beginning to be discussed.[4]

Elsewhere there were those who were influenced by the ideas of the American, Henry Thoreau, with his message of 'simplify, simplify' and by Walt Whitman, who linked this with perceptions from eastern religions. Yet others sought a new life of fellowship inspired by the elusive scholar Thomas Davidson, the brother of the ever prolific pamphleteer, J. Morrison Davidson. Thomas Davidson had arrived in London in 1881, emanating what William James called an 'inward glory' and attracting to him a small group of those who wanted moral reformation in the Fellowship of the New Life. Yet others sought change through reformed eating and reformed dress. As Stephen Yeo has pointed out, the idea of socialism as an alternative religion was a powerful one, particularly at a time when orthodox belief was being challenged.[5] Doubt, guilt and concern that industrial society was not bringing the progress that it was supposed to, or just personal crisis, could turn people to socialism. In Scotland, in particular, socialism as an extension of Christianity and socialism and as alternative faith to Christianity were both tremendously powerful forces.

It was in this atmosphere that the London stockbroker, H. M. Hyndman appeared on the scene. He was different from many other radicals in that he was coming from the right in politics, rather than from Liberal radicalism. He sympathised with Randolph Churchill's ideas of Tory Democracy, but came to the conclusion that vested interests were unlikely to allow the Conservative party to adapt quickly enough to respond to the needs of the masses. He began to see himself as a kind of English Lasalle who could unite socialist aspirations with patriotism. He also seems to have had hopes of putting himself at the head of a new Chartist movement for universal suffrage, and there are echoes of earlier radical views in some of his writings where he sees the state being corrupted by power being concentrated in the hands of a small effete ruling class.

Hyndman, along with Helen Taylor, Herbert Burrows and the ever-present G. B. Clark, had been behind the formation of the Democratic Federation in London in 1881, whose aim was to link various small radical associations. There was the odd branch of it in Scotland. In the summer of 1881 a group of 'Social Democrats' meeting in Hamilton, perhaps influenced by Engels' calls in the *Labour Standard* for the creation of a political workers' party, resolved to form a Scottish Labour Party with a programme that included nationalisation of industry.[6] Hyndman, who was always treated with considerable suspicion in Scotland, perhaps because of his Tory links, made his first appearance in Scotland with Henry George in 1882. In June 1883 the Federation published *Socialism Made Plain*, written by Hyndman and a new recruit William Morris, which argued that social and political power was monopolised by landlords and capitalists, who lived off the workers. The poverty of the workers could only be eradicated by replacing capitalism with a collective system of ownership. Radicalism, from roots within Liberalism, had always focused attention on the monopoly of land. Hyndman's radicalism from the right was readier to attack capitalism. *Socialism Made Plain* expounded the theory of surplus value, the extra hours which workers were forced to toil in order to create the wealth by which the idle live. In January 1884, the Democratic Federation declared itself socialist, and, as well as universal suffrage, proportional representation and payment of MPs, called for the 'socialisation of the means of production, and the organisation of Society' and launched one of the most influential socialist papers, *Justice*.

Engels regarded it as the initiative of '"educated" elements sprung from the bourgeoisie'[7] and premature before the working class had been won round. But it attracted some exceptional young men, such as John Lincoln Mahon, an Edinburgh engineer, and Robert Banner, a bookbinder, both of whom had been active in the local republican club. It also probably lost some radicals, but, it was in the summer of 1884 that John Bruce Glasier, William J. Nairn, Robert Hutchison and Moses McGibbon founded a branch of the Social Democratic Federation in Glasgow. Most of them had been associated with an earlier Democratic Club. Their diversity was not untypical. Glasier was a young draughtsman with poetic ambitions, illegitimate son of a farmer and cattle-dealer. He had first been enthused by Davitt's 1879 address in the Glasgow City Hall and, for a time, had been active in Irish Land League politics. Nairn was a stonemason from Brechin, now living in Glasgow, and moved by the plight of the Highlands. McGibbon was a stockbroker, who put up the money for the branch, and Hutchison, Nairn's brother-in-law, a hard-drinking shoemaker. Dundee had a branch soon afterwards, with James Duncan, a calenderer, and a few associates who preached the message of socialism in the open at week-ends.

Hyndman was in Glasgow in October to address the first public meeting, but the tensions were already there within the organisation. Thanks to Hyndman's authoritarian attitudes, the unity of the new movement did not last long and a group led by William Morris broke away to form the Socialist League. Morris offered a different view of socialism. Not for him the regulatory state. He saw conventional politics as having little point any more than did the search for what he called 'palliatives'. The League aimed at 'the realisation of complete revolutionary socialism, and well knows that this can never happen in any country without the help of the workers of all civilisation'.[8] The emphasis, therefore, was to be on educating the working class to an adequate level of consciousness rather than, as Hyndman was pointing, towards participation in parliamentary elections. There was a similar split in Scotland with Socialist League branches appearing in Glasgow, Paisley, Hamilton, Blantyre, Coatbridge, Rutherglen and other towns in 1885–6.

The League attracted, in particular, disenchanted artists and intellectuals who, like Morris himself, had had their eyes opened by Ruskin to the ugliness and moral degeneracy of the modern age. Its 'single hearted devotion to the religion of Socialism, the only religion which the Socialist League professes', as the manifesto declared, appealed to such. James Mavor, the professor of Political Economy at St Mungo College, was secretary of the League in Glasgow and the activists included R. F. Muirhead, assistant professor of Greek at the university. Among sympathisers was Henry Dyer, another academic and editor of the *Scottish Co-operator*, and the wealthy coal exporter, Daniel Macaulay Stevenson and his artist brother, Macaulay Stevenson, grandsons of the working-men's leader in the 1830s, Daniel Macaulay. There were a few working men but Morris noted in 1887 that the members of the Glasgow branch were mainly 'clerks, designers and the like'.[9] Bruce Glasier was immediately converted by the appeal of Morris:

> There he was, a sun-god, truly in his ever afterwards familiar dark-blue serge jacket and lighter blue cotton shirt and collar, without scarf or tie – a kind of glow seemed to be about him, such as we see lighting up the faces in a room when a beautiful child comes in . . . As we listened our minds seemed to gain a new sense of sight, or a new way of seeing and understanding why we lived in the world, and how important to our own selves was the wellbeing of our fellows.[10]

No such address had been heard in Glasgow before, he claimed, 'no such single-minded and noble appeal to man's inherent sense of rightness and fellowship towards man'.

In Edinburgh socialist ideas had been brought from France by the ex-mayor of Paris, Leo Mélliet, an exile in the aftermath of the Paris Commune, who lectured in French at the university. An Edinburgh University Socialist

Society was formed in the Spring of 1884 with William Morris giving the opening lecture. A key figure in Edinburgh was the dynamic Andreas Scheu, an Austrian socialist exile, a cabinetmaker, 'filled to overwhelming with energy and enthusiasm'.[11] Scheu had been in Edinburgh at the start of the 1880s before moving to London. He had been spreading socialist ideas among the young men like Banner associated with the republican club and the secularist societies, and to John Rae and John Leslie, who like many had come by way of the Irish movement. He had returned to Edinburgh in the summer of 1884, after quarrelling bitterly with Hyndman because of his racism and jingoism. As well as his furniture work he was also agent for Dr Jaeger's Sanitary Wool System and, reputedly, had converted George Bernard Shaw to the reformed clothing cause. There was also a distinct Christian Socialist element focused on the Revd John Glasse of Greyfriars' Church, who gathered round him 'a band of brilliant and talented young men – lawyers, doctors, students, and a very select few of the elite of the working classes – and inspired them with his own zeal to go forth to work for the New Cause'. In that setting they absorbed an eclectic mixture of Proudhon, Marx, Morris and Kropotkin.[12] According to David Lowe,

> The Scottish Labour Movement was not founded on materialism. The instinct for freedom and justice which animated the Covenanters and the Chartists also inspired the Nineteenth century pioneers. Their teachers and prophets were Jesus, Shelley, Mazzini, Whitman, Ruskin, Carlyle and Morris. The Economists took second place. The crusade was to dethrone Mammon and to restore the spirit and to insist that the welfare of the community take precedence of the enrichment of a handful.

It was on Scheu's advice that the Edinburgh socialists deliberately sought to link themselves with the land reform movement by calling themselves the Scottish Land and Labour League, 'more homely, concrete, alluring, less abstract and foreign looking' than anything containing the word socialism would be. But most had moved beyond land reform. Robert Banner noted,

> Nationalisation of the land will take off our shoulders one thief, the landlord, but the rent he drew will have gone into the pocket of his brother the capitalist, in the form of interest, the most grinding and crushing of all.

The Unitarian minister, Alexander Webster, played a part in spreading the message of socialism in north-east Scotland. For him, as for many others, socialism had emerged from the land reform movement, but also appeared as an extension of his religion.

> I was heartily in all these movements, because I felt they were the forms into which spiritual life was running at the time. I did not surrender religion to them, but found them all in Religion.[13]

His little monthly paper, *The Ploughshare*, brings out very clearly the different elements which fed into the nascent socialist movement. It explained Darwin's evolutionary theory; it regularly quoted Henry George; it published extracts from Walt Whitman's *Leaves of Grass* and from Burns; and it criticised an industrial and commercial system in which 'in a world of exhaustless resources ... there is perpetual need for the means of life'. In addition it threw in Irish Home Rule:

> The Irishman can never have a home in Ireland till he has the Government of the country in his own hands, till the class monopoly of land and capital is abolished, and till free scope for his social aspirations is attained. Speed the day![14]

The Land and Labour League did not see their role as being to get involved directly in political campaigns. Rather they were to be there to sow the seeds and propagate the principles of socialism:

> As a result of such activity, it was believed then by many that a sufficiently large body of socialists would be formed who would be so united in good feeling, and who would be so enlightened as to ways and means, that they would be enabled to take advantage of some popular uprising and so guide that movement as to bring in, almost at once, a Socialist State of Society.[15]

Third Reform Act

Popular politics received another fillip with the extension of the franchise in 1884. The campaign to give people in county seats the same franchise as those in burghs never produced the same fervour that the campaigns for the 1832 and 1868 Acts had done, None the less, there had always been an assumption in radical circles that this was business left undone. G. O Trevelyan, who sat for Hawick, had spearheaded a campaign in the the 1870s for equalisation of the county and burgh franchises. The Scottish Farmers' Alliance had rather belatedly come round to supporting the vote being given to agricultural labourers, after the earlier campaign for land reform had brought only the very inadequate Agricultural Holdings (Scotland) Act of 1883 which failed to give either compensation for improvements or security of tenure.[16] The demonstrations which preceded the passing of the 1884 Act were presented as a continuation of earlier struggles. In most of the city demonstrations the veterans of the 1832 campaigns were given pride of place.

With the passage of the Act there was an implicit assumption that the work of reform was more or less complete, despite the fact that because of the intricacies of registration almost half of the male population was still excluded. Once again Gladstone had also blocked attempts to extend the vote to women. Despite big demonstrations in Glasgow in 1882 and in Edinburgh in 1884 there is little evidence of the cause having progressed much. Mary Hill Burton, sister of the historian J. H. Burton, was the leading Scottish speaker at these, but most of the others were from south of the border or the United States. According to James Mavor, the crisis for the women's movement came in 1886 when radicals believed a choice had to be made between pressing the the issue of Irish home rule or of female suffrage: 'The majority of the leaders of the suffrage movement, after a sharp struggle in which there were rumoured hysterical incidents, decided in favour of Ireland'.[17]

What was to prove even more significant than the franchise extension was the 1885 redistribution measure. It created single-member constituencies in most of the big cities. Glasgow, since 1868 a three-member constituency, now became seven single-member constituencies. Edinburgh got an extra member and was divided into East, Central and South, while Aberdeen got a north and south division. Only Dundee remained a two-member constituency. The boundary commissioners went to some length to draw the constituency lines largely on a class basis. It was to transform politics. The new constituencies reflected the increasingly residential segregation of social classes which was taking place and drove politics along the same route. Liberal associations in the past had generally played safe and had spurned working-class candidates on the ground that they would not attract middle-class voters across the city. With many of the constituencies now predominantly working-class this was a policy which was harder to defend and it strengthened the demands of those who wanted more direct representation of labour. It also created new county seats which incorporated many small towns and villages and brought the majority of miners into the political system for the first time.

The changed political situation encouraged trade unions once again to look to the issue of more direct representation of labour. The annual Trades Union Congress at Southport in 1885 had a rather perfunctory discussion of the issue. Some talked of the need to get labour 'well represented by men who would steer clear of all party politicians', while others saw the road to labour representation lying with a balanced selection of both Conservative and Liberal labour representatives. In 1886 the decision was made to form a Labour Electoral Committee which soon altered its name to the Labour Electoral Association, which had a Scottish division. There were also moves to try to get trade unionists elected to municipal councils. The difficulty was as always in raising the necessary resources to campaign and finding candidates who would be in a position to attend day-time council meetings.

Mid-Lanark

The Liberal Party, already deeply divided in Scotland over the issue of Church disestablishment and very badly weakened by the split over Irish Home Rule in 1886, was not in a position to respond either quickly or effectively to these working-class pressures. This became very apparent in the Mid-Lanark by-election of April 1888. Keir Hardie, a miners' agent from Cumnock in Ayrshire, but until recently operating in Lanarkshire, had all the credentials necessary for a working-class candidate. Hardie had been brought up in a home which had been influenced by the republican and secularist movements of the 1870s and where Tom Paine's *The Age of Reason* was reputed to have had a place on the bookshelf. He had, however, become an evangelical Christian and a Good Templar, devoting much energy to the total abstinence campaign. He had begun to come into contact with socialist ideas in 1884 through the activities of the Blantyre draper, William Small, who in his turn had been brought to socialism by Scheu, John Glasse and their circle in Edinburgh. Hardie's initial response to the new ideas was hostile. The temperance and the co-operative movements were 'to be the forces which will eventually elevate the working classes',[18] and he resented the attacks on the Liberal Party. But by the end of 1886 there were signs that socialism together with events in the industrial field were beginning to have their effect on his attitudes. He began to think in terms of a new party that would attract to it the more advanced elements of the Liberals who would shake themselves free of Whig domination, but which would also incorporate elements of socialism. His contacts with London socialists such as Tom Mann and H. H. Champion strengthened the new direction of his thinking. Now the call was to 'Get rid of the idea that the capitalist is an indispensable adjunct to any industrial system'.[19]

The opportunity to test the veracity of Liberal claims to be sympathetic to working-class representation in Parliament came in April 1888 with a by-election at Mid-Lanark. Hardie was an ideal candidate for a predominantly mining constituency around Wishaw and Hamilton, although not all the miners' leaders supported him, an opposition he put down to 'pure spleen'.[20] It was as a Liberal Radical that he offered himself in a letter to Baillie Burt, the chair of the Mid-Lanark Liberal Association:

> Personally I have been a Radical of a somewhat advanced type, and from the first have supported Mr Gladstone's Home Rule proposals.
> The rest I leave to your association in the hope that the desire of the labourers to be represented by a man of themselves will not be overlooked.

Apparently the letter failed to arrive on time and at the selection meeting it was suggested that Hardie had decided against coming forward. A week later he withdrew his application to the Liberal Association, on the ground that the miners' interests were not represented on the Association and that, anyway, the candidate had already been decided upon.[21] Instead, he offered himself as an independent labour candidate.

Hardie could count on some financial support from miners, but he also had the backing of the wealthy Henry H. Champion, a former army officer who had resigned his commission over the attack on Egypt in 1882. Champion for the past year had been advocating the formation of a Labour Party by pushing the line of independence within the Labour Electoral Association. A philanthropic Glasgow lady put up £100 and Champion eventually came up with a further £250 which may well have come from Conservative party circles via the maverick Tory Radical, Michael Maltman Barry. He had the backing also of John Ferguson, but the Irish National League in Lanarkshire remained solidly loyal to the Liberals and the Catholic *Glasgow Observer* showed no sympathy for a 'pack of atheists and socialists'. Never a great administrator, Hardie's campaign was fairly shambolic, but nevertheless it attracted national attention. There were attempts by the Liberals to persuade him to withdraw his candidacy and he met with the Liberal agent Schnadhorst in April and was offered a seat at the next election if he agreed to stand down. This he refused to do, and as a result lost the official backing of the TUC's Labour Electoral Association. A motley group of radicals, disenchanted Liberals and a few Tories rallied to his support. George Carson on the Glasgow Trades Council, which he persuaded to support Hardie's campaign, talked of a new party 'for the attainment of the emancipation of the working classes' and Scottish home rule.[22] The full might of the Liberal press was turned against him and he polled a mere 617 votes.

However, out of the contacts developed during the by-election there grew the Scottish Labour Party. An initial meeting in May under John Murdoch's chairmanship resulted in a conference in Glasgow on 25 August 1888. There had been discussions in the previous year about the possibility of a Scottish miners' Labour Party. The poorly-organised mining unions in Scotland were conscious that many of the English mining areas were returning mining-union officials to Parliament. But this was to be something broader. Immediately after the Mid-Lanark election there was an attempt to come to some agreement with the Scottish Liberal Association over future labour representation but it came to nothing. Hardie now claimed that he had left the Liberal Party, although the tone was still a conciliatory one.

> If the Liberal Party desired to prevent the Labour Party from splitting it in twain, it has an easy way out of the difficulty to adopt the programme the Labour Party had laid out, and it would find the working man heart and soul with it, as good Liberals as they had been hitherto.

The fact that this was a party which had grown out of radicalism and out of the land reform movement was apparent in the choice of vice presidents – John Murdoch, the long-time campaigner for Highland land reform, G. B. Clark, the crofters' MP and campaigner for all radical causes, and Robert Bontine Cunninghame-Graham, MP for North-West Lanarkshire. The last, who was elected president of the party, was the extraordinary 'Don Roberto', writer, poet and aristocratic adventurer. As a politician he has had a rather hostile press. To Mrs Webb, always quick with the acerbic remark, he was 'a poseur – an unmitigated fool in politics'. A recent biographer of Keir Hardie has been even more scathing, 'an erratic aristocratic radical MP [who] ... drew his credentials as a labour leader from his rude remarks about his fellow Liberal MPs ... an upper-class romantic rather than a serious politician'. But he, like so many of the early socialists, had been increasingly horrified by what he had seen of industrial Britain and, like so many other romantics, came under the spell of William Morris. Cunninghame-Graham never lost his admiration for Morris and in the wonderful gem of a description he wrote on Morris's funeral in 1896, 'With the North-West Wind', he wrote of him as 'a pilot poet lent by the Vikings to steer us from the Doldrums in which we now lie all becalmed in smoke to some Valhalla of his own creation beyond the world's end'. He had earned his credentials the previous year when he had his head cracked and was arrested on 'Bloody Sunday' in November 1887 in the Trafalgar Square riots organised in protest against Irish coercion. Even before Mid-Lanark, he had been in touch with Hardie about the need to have 'an organisation in future for election work'.[23]

The new party's demands were advanced radical – adult suffrage, triennial parliaments, payment of MPs, disestablishment, a second ballot and a local veto on public houses. But it also supported land nationalisation and the nationalisation of railways, banks and mineral rights. The programme included home rule all round, which had entered the Liberal radical catechism in the late 1870s when even Gladstone had encouraged it by suggesting that Parliament was 'overwhelmed' with business. He had also rashly promised that 'I will consent to give Ireland no principle, nothing that is not upon equal terms offered to Scotland and to the different portions of the United Kingdom'.[24]

Socialist ideas

There were few who would have unequivocally described themselves as socialist at that August meeting. There were trade unionists, land reformers, a substantial group of Georgites, lots of liberal radicals as well as a smattering of eccentrics. Many wanted to use any new organisation as a pressure group on the Liberal Party.[25] The more committed socialists continued through the SDF and the Socialist League. The first conference of Scottish Socialist Societies was held in Edinburgh in December 1888, to try to united the SDF, the Land and Labour League and groups of Christian socialists. There were four SDF branches from Crieff, Edinburgh, Dundee and Glasgow, four Socialist League branches from Edinburgh, Glasgow, Kilmarnock and West Calder, together with the Glasgow Christian Socialist Society. They agreed to collaborate for propaganda purposes in the Scottish Socialist Federation, with W. D. Tait as secretary. A few months before, French workmen visiting the Glasgow Exhibition had announced themselves as socialists and had been entertained by Edinburgh socialists, with pledges 'to do all in their power to sweep away the frontiers of all countries, and to unite the workers of very nationality for the overthrow of their common enemy, capitalism'.[26]

The revelations of dreadful living conditions for so many of the population revealed in select committee and royal commission reports in the 1880s and by exposés of the lifestyles of many of the poorest pushed others to question the existing system. John Bright's Rectorial address in 1882 followed by the accounts of *Life in One Room* by Glasgow's medical officer of health, J. B. Russell, helped to shock a few more out of Podsnapian complacency. For others specific texts pushed them to socialism. In Inverness it was W. T. Stead's *The Maiden Tribute of Modern Babylon* (1886), with its revelations of the sexual exploitation of children which opened the eyes of a young middle-class woman, Rachel McMillan, to 'the existence of a dark world that ringed her sheltered life'. Soon contacts with the Socialist League in Edinburgh brought her to socialism.[27] In Aberdeen the young compositor, James Leatham, already influenced by the land reform movement and the Georgite writings and speeches, was pointed in the direction of socialism by the Revd Alexander Webster. But it was the American, Lawrence Gronlund's *The Co-operative Commonwealth,* which he read in 1885, which gave him a model of a possible socialist society.[28] Morris continued to charm, and his utopian society of *News from Nowhere* and *Earthly Paradise* with their rural idyll perhaps particularly appealed in Scotland with its hankering for a rural past. Certainly Prince Kropotkin's writings which similarly envisaged a decentralised, democratic society of small farms and small workshops also features on the reading lists of most Scottish socialists.[29]

Most of the young enthusiasts probably got their ideas in abridged form in magazines. As Glasier points out controversial works were 'rarely on the catalogues of libraries accessible to the working class'. Few ploughed through the writings of Ruskin or Carlyle let alone Marxist writing. Glasier recalled 'we had only dim ideas, mainly derived from magazine literature, concerning new currents of thought that were agitating academic art and literary circles'. Edwin Muir, a few years later, got access to Ruskin and Carlyle in a weekly paper, *Great Thoughts*, which, although essentially pushing an anti-socialist message, nevertheless printed extracts of the originals.

While many, like Hardie, saw their socialism as an extension of their Christian belief, a recapturing of the simplicity and the egalitarianism of the early Christian Church, many others came to socialism by way of the secular movement. Tiny eclectic and secular societies had kept alive the ideas of early socialism from the Owenite period through to the 1880s. George Jacob Holyoake was a frequent visitor in the 1860s, with Bradlaugh and the National Secular Society taking up from him in the 1870s. The tailor, Peter Henrietta, was a key figure at the meetings in Glasgow's Eclectic Hall in Dunlop Street and on Saturday evenings he would review and analyse the events of the week from a socialist perspective. Annie Besant, who edited the *National Reformer* and had not yet found either her later socialism or theosophy, visited a number of times to lecture in the 1870s. When Bradlaugh adopted a vigorous anti-socialist position in the 1870s a number of his former disciples began to turn away towards the new movements. A number of them were associated with the Land Restoration League. At Morris's first lecture in Glasgow in 1884 there were, according to Glasier, a few veteran Owenites who had not lost the faith and hopes of their younger days. Those aged Radicals, who were in the most instances Freethinkers, listened enrapt to the unfolding afresh of the ideas of the Communist Commonwealth, and were pathetically eager to communicate their joy in beholding once more in the sunset of their years the glory of the vision which had filled their eyes in the morning glow on the hill-tops long ago.[30]

It was quite common for some to lose their Christian faith and find their socialist faith at roughly the same time. James Leatham was a secularist before he was a socialist. In Glasgow both James Shaw Maxwell and Bruce Glasier came through Freethought activities. In Aberdeen John Paton broke from the Episcopalian Church when preparing for confirmation and then moved to socialism. Tom Bell, influenced by his father's hardening attitudes against the Church, came to so see religion as the great enemy and became a confirmed atheist.[31] He too, like Emanuel Shinwell, got his introduction to socialism by way of the secular society. There were regular lectures from leading secularists such as G. W. Foote, J. M. Robertson, Dennis Hird and Mrs Bradlaugh-Bonner. The Rationalist Press was important in making available cheap scientific works which undermined simple creationist ideas, such as Huxley's *Man's Place in Nature* and Haekel's *Riddle of the Universe*, and many of the young people attracted by socialism liked to think of themselves as scientific and modern. More directly anti-Christian works such as Ingersoll's *Mistakes of Moses* and G. W. Foote's *Brimstone Ballads* gave Tom Bell the ammunition to torment the Salvation Army girls who worked alongside him in a bottling factory.[32]

In the 1890s Robert Blatchford's *Clarion*, which was widely read in socialist circles in Scotland and which pushed a vigorous anti-Christian line tapped into this stream of socialism. His book, *God and My Neighbour*, argued that science had now destroyed the foundations of all religions. How effective it was is difficult to assess. Joseph Burgess believed that Blatchford's arguments had not made a single convert in Scotland and, indeed, were a barrier to very many who still held strong religious beliefs.[33] Others, however, found that Blatchford's writings gave them a rational basis for their existing unbelief or, at least, anti-clericalism. In the early twentieth century, Manny Shinwell claimed that Blatchford's writings, especially *Britain for the British* 'exercised more influence on my political outlook than any other'. The appeal, according to Shinwell, was his 'clear-cut, concise and easily understood language in comparison to Hardie's somewhat prosy, economic jargon'.[34] The Orkney poet, Edwin Muir, deeply wretched in Glasgow, recalled weeping on the top of a tram over the statistics presented in Blatchford's *Britain for the British*. It converted him to socialism:

My conversion to Socialism was a recapitulation of my first conversion [to Christianity] at fourteen. It was not, that is to say, the result of an intellectual process, but rather an emotional transmutation; the poisonous stuff which had gathered in me during the past few years had found another temporary discharge ... Having discovered a future in which everything, including myself was transfigured, I flung myself in it ... My sense of human potentiality was so strong that even the lorry men and the slum boys were transformed by it; I no longer saw them as they were, but as they would be when the society of which I dreamed was realised.[35]

For some the route to Socialism came through that extension of Christianity. A number of clergy were active in the moves toward labour representation and to socialism from an early date. The Revd J. T. Glasse in Edinburgh, the Revd William Mackay in Glasgow, the Revd Alexander Webster in Aberdeen. Dundee had a Labour Church in 1892 meeting in the Thistle Hall, 'to develop the religious life interest in the Labour Movement'. The Labour Church rejected the concept of personal sin as the cause of suffering and boldly asserted that suffering was the result of bad social organisation.

In Glasgow Archie McArthur was president of the Glasgow Christian Socialist League which became linked to the Labour Army. Through the pages of Hardie's *Labour Leader* a young people's club, Crusaders, had been formed. McArthur, Lizzie Glasier, sister of Bruce, and Alex Gossip, secretary of the cabinetmakers' society, and with the help of Carolyn Martyn, a student at the university, developed this, in 1896, into the Socialist Sunday School. By 1900 there were seven branches in Glasgow, one in Partick and one in Edinburgh. The aim was to spread moral teaching rather than a specifically Christian message and to provide lessons in citizenship, focusing on history, ethics and civics. By 1912 there were fifteen branches in Glasgow and eight in Edinburgh and MacArthur published a magazine for them, the *Young Socialists*. It was about propagating ethical socialism. 'The cultivation of emotions appropriate to the co-operative mode of life' is how Fred Reid describes it. According to McArthur's associate, Lizzie Glasier, socialism is 'an idealism ... the highest flight of the ideal into the realm of the practical'. It was a faith – 'a faith based on Divine brotherhood and sisterhood of humanity – irrespective of class, colour or creed'. It was a religion – 'a religion greater than creeds or dogmas'.[36] Socialist Sunday Schools were to continue to be a significant element in the making of socialists in the west of Scotland until the 1960s. The people associated with them, like Hardie and many of his Scottish associates, undoubtedly took the view that socialism was the natural successor to organised religion as the means of achieving the Calvinist ideal of the Godly Commonwealth. Socialism they argued was the new religion which could tap into the religious consciousness of the Scottish people.

There is little doubt that the pre-1914 socialist movement attracted many who were, as Stanley Pierson says, 'socially homeless'.[37] Many were trying to be upwardly mobile, moving away from their father's job to try to be clerks or teachers or shopkeepers. Others were the hairdressers, haberdashers and commercial travellers of what has been called a middle-class proletariat, people who were perhaps particularly vulnerable to the impoverished life of striving for respectability without resources in a strange city. For some the movement gave them a home among fellow spirits who were prepared to discuss politics endlessly. Others sought the fellowship and friendship, the 'hearty intimacy' of the Clarion Clubs and numerous other socialist-linked organisations. Many, on the other hand, undoubtedly revelled in their isolation. An Aberdeen-born barber, John Paton commented,

> Socialists were undoubtedly cranks; they were in a similar category to the strange beings who tore their beards and confessed their sins in public at religious meetings. I became aware of the curious glances of my old companions as they saw me busy selling pamphlets or taking collections at meetings. Plainly they thought my madness had grown upon me; their queer restraint and side glances when we chanced to meet were very eloquent.
>
> But with others, I glowed with righteousness in the face of ostracism. Our zeal and enthusiasm throve upon it. We acquired the air of men set apart; we walked along with a tense air and set expression. We conceived we were the stuff of martyrs.[38]

In the years before 1914, such people were small in number but it would be a mistake to judge their influence merely in terms of numbers. They tended to be the activists, in many cases the brightest, certainly the ones who had the faith to work for a cause against all the odds. By their constant challenging of the common-sense of Liberalism they unsettled increasing numbers, undermined complacency and forced through change.

Notes

1. Donald J. Withrington, '"A Ferment of Change": Aspirations, ideas and ideals in Nineteenth Century Scotland', in Douglas Gifford (ed.), *The History of Scottish Literature*, Vol 3 (Aberdeen, 1988), pp. 54–9.
2. *The Christian Treasury*, Feb. 1875 quoted in Smith, *Passive Obedience*, p. 79.
3. *Good Words*, Feb. 1881 quoted in Smith, *Passive Obedience*, p. 301.
4. J. Bruce Glasier, *William Morris and the Early Days of the Socialist Movement*, (1921), p. 20.
5. Stephen Yeo, 'A New Life: the Religion of Socialism in Britain, 1883–1896', *History Workshop*, no. 4, Autumn 1977.
6. M. J. Crick, '"To Make Twelve O'clock at Eleven": The History of the Social Democratic Federation', Ph. D. Huddersfield 1988, p. 38.
7. E. P. Thompson, *William Morris. Romantic to Revolutionary*, (1977), p. 298.
8. Glasier, *William Morris*, p. 16.
9. Thompson, *William Morris*, p. 743.
10. Glasier, *William Morris*, p. 22.
11. NLS Acc 4965. John Gilray, 'Early Days of the Socialist Movement in Edinburgh', p. 3.
12. Hardie quoted in Lowe, *Souvenirs*, p. 110.

13. Webster, *Memories of Ministry*, p. 31.
14. *The Ploughshare*, 1885–1886, 16 issues.
15. Gilray, 'Early Days', p. 4.
16. *Aberdeen Journal*, 26 January 1884.
17. James Mavor, *My Windows on the Street of the World*, Vol. I, (1923), p. 170.
18. Fred Reid, *Keir Hardie. The Making of a Socialist* (1978), p. 83.
19. *Miner,* May 1887 quoted in Reid, *Keir Hardie*, p. 97.
20. NLS Dep. 176, Vol. 8, Hardie to Champion, 15 March 1888.
21. Francis Johnston Correspondence.
22. Mitchell Library, Glasgow Trades Council Minutes, 4 April 1888.
23. NLS Dep.176, Vol. 8, Hardie to Graham, 15 March 1888.
24. Quoted in M. Fry, *Patronage and Principle. A Political History of Modern Scotland* (Aberdeen, 1991), p. 92.
25. Reid, *Keir Hardie*, p. 118.
26. Gilray, 'Early Days of the Socialist Movement in Edinburgh', p. 11.
27. Yeo, 'A New Life', p. 9.
28. Bob Duncan, *James Leatham 1865–1945. Portrait of a Socialist Pioneer* (Aberdeen 1978).
29. Laurence Thompson, *The Enthusiasts. A biography of John and Katherine Bruce Glasier,* (1971) p. 39; Duncan, *Leatham,* p. 32.
30. Glasier, *William Morris*, pp. 27–8.
31. Tom Bell, *Pioneering Days* (1941), p. 18.
32. *Ibid.* p. 31.
33. S. Pierson, *British Socialists: The Journey from Fantasy to Politics* (1979), p. 74.
34. E. Shinwell, *Lead with the Left: My First Ninety-Six Years* (London, 1981), p. 35.
35. Edwin Muir, *An Autobiography* (1980), p. 47.
36. Lizzie Glasier, *Socialist Sunday Schools: a Reply to the Sabbath School Teachers Magazine* (Glasgow, 1907), p. 7.
37. Pierson, *British Socialists*, p. 1.
38. J. Paton, *Proletarian Pilgrimage* (1935), p. 116.

CHAPTER SEVEN

Making a Labour Party 1888–1900

Socialists were the converted and committed minority. Most trade unionists remained either indifferent or firmly attached to Liberalism. Joan Smith has summed up the 'common sense' of Glasgow Liberalism in the 1880s:

> Most Glasgow working men believed in Free Trade, the iniquities of the House of Lords and all other hereditary positions, loathed landlordism, believed in fairness and the rights of small nations and in democracy and the will of the people.[1]

But there was evidence of a gradual questioning of whether the Liberal Party was any longer the best defender of these beliefs.

Trade unions and politics

Unlike many of the early socialists, Hardie believed firmly in the need for trade-union backing if an independent party was to be successful and he and James Shaw-Maxwell, who had taken over the secretaryship of the Scottish Labour Party and was the key organiser, toured the country trying to attract union support, by presenting it as a 'a party in fact to promote social progress and to try to get shorter hours and more pay'.[2] They found it very difficult to overcome a perception of themselves as extremists, a view not helped by some wild speeches from Cunninghame-Graham. Also, Hardie's vitriolic attack on the general secretary of the TUC, Henry Broadhurst, at the 1888 Congress did little to endear him to the average trade-union official. They were, however, able to tap into growing discontent among many trade unionists at their lack of representation on most public bodies. There were also signs that the issue of church disestablishment, which immersed the Liberal Party in Scotland in 1884–5, was diverting Liberal attention from issues which working people regarded as of greater significance. In the 1885 election Liberal fought Liberal in twenty-three Scottish constituencies, largely over disestablishment.[3]

In 1882 the Glasgow Trades Council had formed a committee to recommend candidates for the School Board who would be prepared to reduce fees, arguing that 'by the proper application of … endowments, the rate charges for the education of the working classes would be lessened'.[4] Throughout 1883 and 1884 there were motions drawing attention 'to the question of being represented by working men in the Town Council and Parliament'. The difficulty, as always, was finding the means to pay for this, since 'the masses have not seen their way in any number of cases to raise what is needed to pay them'.[5] Attempts to rouse some enthusiasm proved difficult, however, and a committee set up to sound out views on labour representation on the Town Council and to raise a £1,000 by 20,000 workers contributing a shilling each, reported that most unions had not bothered to reply.[6] A Labour Representation League was set up, which the union leadership was at pains to distinguish from the Scottish Land Restoration League, that was also trying at this time to raise money for candidates. A few months before, the Trades Council had overwhelmingly rejected a motion in favour of land nationalisation on the grounds that it was 'impracticable at the present time' and that it was better to concentrate on getting reform of the land laws. In the end the Labour Representation League had to admit failure to break 'a nearly general indifference – a sort of stand-aloof feeling'.[7]

The pattern was very similar in Edinburgh. Robert Banner had represented the Consolidated Union of Bookbinders on the Trades Council in 1879 and had sought to extend the scope of the council by having it discuss 'all questions of national importance political and social', but he found himself in a minority of two. Soon he clashed with his own society when he moved an amendment in the council 'to the effect that there was nothing demoralising in Sunday labour' and, in the following year, he was dismissed as their delegate, 'in consequence of the language he used in connection with the late Royal Review'.[8] He soon turned to socialism. When Henry George came to Edinburgh it was the chair of the Trades Council, A. C. Telfer, who presided over his meeting, although the Trades Council remained opposed to land nationalisation.

The reform agitation of 1884 and a visit of Gladstone to the city revealed the extent to which the trade unionists saw themselves as part of the Liberal movement, although there was always frustration at the extent to which whiggish elements dominated the local Liberal Association. The redistribution of seats in 1885 immediately brought demands that one of the three seats should go to a 'bona fide working man … who by being a participator in, knows the circumstances of his own class'.[9] But, in the end, as in Glasgow, Edinburgh working men showed no enthusiasm and a separate association did not emerge. The names of three trade unionists were submitted to the Liberal Association, but none was selected.

A breakthrough was made in Aberdeen. There a number of Aberdeen trade unionists were very active in the local Liberal Association, but, in 1884, the Trades Council was approached with a proposal of a contribution 'towards a fund for the return of a labour candidate'.[10] It was rejected on the grounds that the time was not opportune. But, in September 1884 the TUC met in Aberdeen and the Revd C. C. MacDonald, minister of St Clement's Church and an active campaigner for Highland land reform, preached the pre-congress sermon to the 'representatives of the toiling millions of our country-men who are the heirs of the oppressions and repressions of centuries, the victims of class legislation and of a long-dominant feudalism, uncompromis-ing and unyielding even it is death throes'. He argued that it was not enough to continue to cast votes even for 'the best and largest hearted men of the classes who have hitherto controlled legislation':

> You must represent yourselves. You must do your own work in Parliament and in the other councils and governing boards of the nation. It is thus, and only thus, that you will reap the fruits of the sufferings and struggles of centuries; thus, and only thus, that you will come fully to understand and worthily to discharge the sacred obligations of citizenship; thus, and only thus, that the commonwealth will attain its full strength and grandeur in the union and interaction of the interests and energies of the whole people, and arise in a new aspiration of freedom the champion and the guardian of the rights of man.[11]

It may have been this which brought a change of mind, and in November the Trades Council successfully nominated two of its members for the Town Council, standing as Labour candidates in opposition to an increase in the salary of the chief constable. They complained bitterly about 'the professed Liberals of the city in high stations ... These were the men who patted the working-classes on the back, but gave them nothing ... the working classes were entitled to a fair representation'.[12] A few months later at the school board election, the council's six nominees were elected.

The council, therefore, was in a position of considerable strength when approached by the Radical Association about candidates for the next elec-tion. It was regarded as an invitation to nominate a candidate, only to be told that the Liberal Association would not share the responsibility of nominating a candidate with either the Trades Council or the Radical Association. For many this was the breaking point. Alex Catto, a baker, summed up the feeling:

> It seems to me that we have arrived at that period in our history as working men when we must look to ourselves to get men to represent ourselves. It seems to me that the shop-keeping element in the Liberal Association are wanting to put us out of sight ... and we can show to the Liberal Association that if they can dispense with our help we can manage without them.[13]

They were prepared to run the radical professor of Roman Law at University College London, W. A. Hunter, son of the president of the local co-operative society, against the Liberal Association, if necessary, although no doubt there was much relief when the Radical Association and the Liberal Association both agreed to accept him as the candidate for North Aberdeen for which he was duly elected.

Continuing divisions within Liberalism after 1886 encouraged demands for change. According to Derek Urwin, the party in Scotland 'presented a confused picture of competing factions, and its losses might have been greater if it had not been for the cult of the "Grand Old Man" which in the East of Scotland had been invested with the significance of a political religion'.[14] Gladstone's commitment to home rule for Ireland was highly problematic for many Liberals. As well as sectarian religious suspicion at concessions being made to Catholics, there was a sense of injustice that Ireland was getting more than Scotland and this because the Irish had resorted to violence while Scotland had not. Perhaps, even more, there was a deep suspicion of Irish politicians who were perceived as playing an opportunistic game. John Ferguson, for example, had regularly instructed his supporters to vote Conservative, anticipating Parnell's instructions in 1885. After 1886, however, he was well ensconced in the Liberal Party and, although he had originally been enthusiastic about the Scottish Labour Party, when he came to regard it as a threat to the home-rule cause then he withdrew Irish support.[15]

The range of issues which concerned trade unionists and the effect of the activities of the 1880s can be seen in the instructions given by the Edinburgh Trades Council to their delegate to the inaugural conference of the Scottish Labour Party in 1888. They included among other things first political reform: triennial parliaments and elections all in a single day, adult suffrage and the end of plural voting, simplified registration so that movement between constituencies did not result in disenfranchisement, payment of MPs and election expenses. Then came constitutional reform: home rule all round, abolition of the House of Lords and all hereditary offices to be replaced by a representative chamber and a second ballot. Thirdly, there was land reform, very much in line with the Georgite programme of four shillings in the pound tax on land income, plus the land reform programme of rent courts, fixity of tenure, rent control, the abolition of primogeniture, entail and hypothec and the taxation of ground values and feu duties. In the area of labour legislation there was general opposition to state interference in hours of work, to arbitration courts and to state insurance schemes. While free education was supported there was opposition to school boards getting involved in feeding school children. Finally, the delegate was to support a veto on the drink trade and a proposal that no war be entered into without support of the Commons.[16]

There were moves in 1887 in Glasgow to get collaboration between the Land Restoration League, the Trades Council, the shopkeepers' association and a tenants' defence association to contest up to nine of the city's wards on the platform of taxing the real value of property, taxing unlet houses, moving taxation to taxes on income, a local veto on public houses and smaller salaries for public officials and evening meetings of the town council, but the shopkeepers and the tenants' association regarded this as too radical.[17] The following year, however, with the Scottish Labour Party in existence, the Trades Council agreed to sound out views on whether they should affiliate. In the end, the decision was made not to. But the council sponsored four candidates in the municipal elections of 1889, all except one emphasising their independence. Only Henry Tait, secretary of the Scottish railwaymen, standing as 'a true Radical Liberal and temperance reformer' with the backing of the Liberal Association, succeeded in getting elected.

Rival parties

The Scottish Labour Party continued to try to get a deal with the Liberals. Bargaining with the Liberals for labour representation, rather than striving for ideological independence remained the main political strategy of the SLP. Cunninghame-Graham, Shaw Maxwell and Hardie met privately in January 1890 with Marjoribanks, the Liberal whip. He was prepared to offer Labour the representation of Greenock and two other seats, assuming always that the constituency party agreed, in return for Labour agreeing not to put up a candidate in an impending Partick by-election. When revealed in the *North British Daily Mail*, the compact caused uproar among Liberals, and Marjoribanks proved quite unable to deliver local constituencies. Efforts by George Carson, the secretary of the Scottish Labour Party, and the most active member of the Trades Council, to broker agreements with Liberals in municipal politics met with an equal lack of success.

Now, however, Aberdeen Trades Council tried a new initiative by calling a national conference in Edinburgh to consider the issue of labour representation. In 1886 the president of the Trades Council called for co-operation with working men outside the trade unions to consider 'the organisation of a strictly Political Association to secure more direct representation in Parliament and Public Boards'. He probably had in mind some of the young socialists who were beginning to imbibe the ideas being propagated by Alexander Webster. The Land and Labour League people encouraged trade unionists to focus on the issue of an eight-hour working day to be imposed by act of parliament, something which became a test issue for socialists. In Aberdeen the key influence was Henry Hyde Champion, who had visited the city, where he had family links, in 1887 and 1888 under the auspices of the Scottish Land and Labour League and the Scottish Socialist Federation. Champion wanted to create a party based on Parnell's model of the Irish National Party, concentrating on a single issue. He had been expelled from the SDF when he had suggested that socialism might need to be subordinated to the workers' struggle. He believed that a legal eight-hour day would be the rallying cry for a workers' party. The idea caught on and the Aberdeen Trades Council was the first in the country to declare in favour of a legislative eight-hour day in August 1889. Champion returned to Aberdeen for the first May Day rally of 1890, which was bigger than that held anywhere else in the country except London, and a Labour Committee was set up around a young bank clerk,

George Gerrie, who had made the transition from the secretaryship of the Junior Liberal Association, via the Radical Association to independent labour.[18] The members of the Trades Council unanimously agreed to 'pledge themselves to make the interests of labour the first and determining question in all their political action imperial and local', to sever any connection with the Liberal Association and to 'put their shoulders to the wheel to move the political machine for their benefit as a class'.[19]

It was Gerrie's committee and a committee of the Trades Council which were empowered 'to draw up a programme of labour questions of pressing importance' and to call a national conference. The initial idea was to confine the conference to trade unionists, but after Hardie wrote saying that he had intended calling such a conference, but was willing to accept the Aberdeen one, it was agreed that 'anyone could take part in the conference who was favourable to the labour interest but who was precluded from becoming a trade unionist'.[20]

It was a sign of changing times when the conference of sixty-seven delegates from trades councils and local labour parties, claiming to represent 84,500 members, held in Edinburgh on 8 August 1891, heard attacks on Gladstone as 'the Grand Old Humbug' and as no different from Lord Salisbury and 'all other fossilised types of ancient nobility'. George Carson denounced the Liberals for failing to deliver on their promises of meeting the aspirations of the working class. Much to Hardie's satisfaction, the conference agreed to back financially candidates brought forward by recognised labour bodies, 'and whose candidature is in no wise connected with either of the great political parties'. On Hardie's motion it was also agreed to campaign for payment of MPs and local councillors. An executive of one representative from each trades council, plus a representative from the Scottish Labour Party was appointed to try to establish local labour representation committees around the different trades councils.[21] Out of it there emerged the short-lived Scottish Trades Councils' Independent Labour Party. While the new organisation was committed to backing candidates who were independent of either of the two main parties, there was at the same time concern that they should not put forward labour candidates 'where there was any likelihood of a Tory beating a Liberal or a Radical'.[22] The idea was for trades councils to organise branches among unions and among the unorganised and to propagandise by every possible means.

Unfortunately for the future unity movement, the Stirlingshire miners' leader R. Chisholm Robertson, was chosen as secretary and this ensured the antagonism of Keir Hardie and his allies, with whom Robertson had recently clashed. Robertson was a maverick figure, whom the historian of the Scottish miners describes as a 'stormy petrel' and Cunninghame-Graham referred to as 'Robespierre'. He and Hardie both competed for the dominant position in Scottish mining unionism. The programme for the party consisted of demands for a legal eight-hour day, adult suffrage and reform of the registration laws, payment of MPs and of election expenses, nationalisation of the land, mines and railways, local option, triennial parliaments and a second ballot. Although clearly with a socialist tinge, it is a measure of the extent to which it saw itself as part of a progressive radical movement that in the election of 1892 it supported Peter Esslemont, radical Liberal member of Aberdeenshire East, Sir William Wedderburn in North Ayrshire, Seymour Keay in Nairn, J. Rigby in Forfarshire, J. G. Weir, Crofter candidate for Ross and Cromarty, W. A. Hunter in Aberdeen, T. R. Buchanan in Edinburgh West, W. Birkmyre in Ayr Burghs, J. H. Dalziel in Kirkcaldy, all on the left of the Liberal Party. Among those who could claim a more independent stance, it backed John Wilson, the Midlothian miners' leader in Edinburgh Central, Robert Brodie, president of Glasgow Trades Council in the College Division of the city against the veteran Dr Cameron, Champion in South Aberdeen, Chisholm Robertson in Stirlingshire and Cunninghame-Graham in Camla-chie. The SLP was not so very different. It backed Bennet-Burleigh, who stood as 'Labour and Liberal candidate' in Glasgow-Tradeston, Brodie, who described himself as 'Labour and temperance' and John Woolen in Perth, 'an independent Gladstonian'.[23]

In spite of the divisions and petty tensions among a leadership of prima donnas, the Scottish Labour Party continued to be active. Its 1892 con-ference, with Cunninghame-Graham as president, had as vice-presidents G. B. Clark, John Ferguson, C. A. V. Conybeare, J. Shaw Maxwell, Dr Stirling Robertson from Montrose, who wrote in the radical *People's Journal* under the nom de plume of 'Gracchus'; the journalist Bennet-Burleigh, George Gerrie from Aberdeen and John Ogilvie of Dundee Radical Association. It had delegates from the Single-Tax Association, the Labour Army, Smillie and Small from the Lanarkshire miners and the Revd Alexander Webster from Aberdeen. It sponsored George Carson and Martin Haddow for the 1892 municipal elections in Glasgow and by the spring of 1893 Carson was confidently claiming that 'in Glasgow, Edinburgh, Dundee, Paisley, Falkirk and many other places, the very cream of the Trades Unionists have fallen into line and are devoting their best energies and all the time they can afford to the movement'.[24] Hardie's paper, the *Labour Leader,* was broadening from merely a miners' paper into an effective propaganda weapon.

Disenchantment with Liberalism continued to grow. The decision of the new Liberal government to concentrate on Irish Home Rule aroused little enthusiasm, with the SLP declaring that 'It is of minor consequence to the people of this country, and not to be compared with social legislation or the interests of the unemployed'.[25] It now stood for 'the complete overthrow of injustice, privilege and monopoly, and the co-operative ownership by the workers of the land and the means of production' and its programme was a legal eight-hour day, self-supporting home colonies to provide work for the unemployed, provision for the sick, disabled and aged by means of a graduated tax on unearned incomes, 'land restoration', prohibition of child and married women's labour and of piecework, and free secondary and university education. It also added, in what may have been an allusion to the issue of women's suffrage, that while committed to democratising the system of government political reforms must not 'usurp the place of social and economic questions'.[26]

Meanwhile, the association of the Aberdeen leaders of the Scottish Trades Council's Labour Party with H. H. Champion was causing increasing difficulty. Since the Mid-Lanark by-election of 1888 there had been rumours of Champion acting as a conduit for 'Tory gold'. His association with the maverick 'Tory-radical', Michael Maltman Barry, seemed to confirm this and it was strengthened by Champion's leaning towards the idea of an imperial customs' union, which to many seemed to challenge the sacred cow of free trade. As a result, many of the city's socialists and Liberal trade unionists had refused to back him in the election of 1892. During the campaign there were rumours that the Scottish Trades Councils' Labour Party had been offered £1,000 (some suggested £3,000) by the Conservative Party to contest Liberal seats.[27] Despite this, he polled 991 votes, the highest of any independent labour candidate in Scotland.

Hardie, now the member for West Ham, had switched his attention south of the border and had successfully dominated the Bradford Conference in January 1893 which formed the Independent Labour Party. According to Lowe, the Scottish Labour Party, which was well represented at Bradford, had wanted the name Socialist Labour Party but this was rejected in favour of the blander and more expansive 'Independent'. At a conference in Dundee in October, the Trades Councils' Party sought to find some basis for unity within the Scottish movement, but, before it met, a further scandal exploded, with the revelation of a letter from Champion in which he and Chisholm Robertson were apparently seeking to discredit the Independent Labour Party and present Hardie and his associates as catspaws of Liberalism.[28] Many activists boycotted the conference and, to all intents, it marked the end of the Trades Council Party with a decision to go along with the Bradford programme.[29]

A further effort to unite the fragmented Scottish labour movement was made at the last Scottish Labour Party conference in January 1894. There were delegates from fifty-two trade unions, Edinburgh, Dundee, Falkirk, Glasgow, Govan and Paisley Trades Councils, four branches of the Henry George Institute, five co-operative societies, three Fabian societies, the Glasgow Ruskin Society, several branches of the Social Democratic Federation, one of the Scottish Socialist Federation as well as nineteen branches of the Scottish Labour Party. A resolution was passed calling for 'nationalisation of land and the industrial capital of the nation' and summoning workers 'to support energetically the Scottish Labour Party and every similar organisation which has for its objects the return to parliament and to every representative body representatives who will act irrespective of the convenience of any political party in securing justice to labour and the establishment of a just social order'. An SDF amendment that the words 'the socialisation of the means of production, distribution and exchange to be controlled by the Democratic State in the interests of the entire community, and the complete emancipation of labour from the domination of capitalism and landlordism' be substituted for the last part of the resolution was defeated by 104 votes to 57. The women's ILP, whose president was a Mrs Harper, carried a resolution for the franchise to be given to all women.[30] A national election fund was to be launched to which trade unionists and others were to be asked to contribute.

Significantly, the Scottish Labour Party insisted on retaining its independence and it was not until 1895 that the decision was finally made to merge with the ILP. Its last electoral tussle was fittingly at Mid-Lanark, when Robert Smillie, the miners' leader, offered himself as a labour candidate. It developed into an acrimonious battle. The *North British Daily Mail* attacked 'the handful of windbags who call themselves the Independent Labour Party', who were working hand in hand with the Tories. The Glasgow *Observer* described the SLP as 'a set of the most venomous enemies that Ireland and the Irish people have' and advised that 'every man with Irish blood in his veins should shun it, as he would the bitterest enemies of his race'.[31]

In the general election of 1895 there were five ILP candidates in Glasgow. Robert Smillie had another try, this time in Camlachie, standing against the Liberal temperance reforming councillor, Samuel Chisholm. His vote of 669 was well down on the 1892 support but was enough to prevent Chisholm taking the seat. Shaw Maxwell managed only 448 in Blackfriars and Hutchesontown. Hardie's Labour Army friend, Frank Smith, stood in Tradeston, the radical journalist, J. E. Woolacott, in St Rollox and Professor J. Robertson Watson as an unlikely candidate for Bridgeton. Elsewhere, Alex Haddow stood in Govan, J. L. Mahon in Aberdeen and James MacDonald in Dundee.

As in England, the 1895 election was disastrous for the ILP, with a heavy drain on limited finances and plummeting morale at the results, and nearly threatened its demise. However, it may have strengthened the determination to make gains in local elections. In Glasgow, years of effort at last bore fruit, when in the expanded Town Council of 1896, eight Labour and radical candidates, including the ubiquitous John Ferguson, were returned. They had the backing of a new Workers' Municipal Election Committee, established by the Trades Council but incorporating delegates from the Irish National League, the ILP and the Co-operative societies. In Edinburgh the Trades Council had won its first seat on the Town Council in 1889, but failed to follow it up. In the general election of 1892 it worked with the Scottish Trades Councils' Labour Party and the local Temperance Party to support the Broxburn Miners' leader, John Wilson, against the brewer, William McEwan, in Edinburgh Central. Wilson offered himself as 'representing all shades of advanced Liberal and Radical opinion' and was heavily beaten.[32] His electoral committee blamed the 'spell which McEwan's philanthropy has thrown over the electors', but, none the less, they were hopeful that 'the effects of our propaganda ... had wakened them to the objects we had in view and that time will prove our cause a winning one'.[33] Despite this, however, a motion by a leading Liberal who had bandied around the accusation of 'Tory gold', was carried by the Trades Council and it pulled out of the political activity.

It was probably not coincidental that on the day on which that decision was made, 8 November 1892, the first meeting of the Edinburgh branch of the Scottish Labour Party was held. It included socialists from the earlier Socialist Federation and independent labour trade unionists. James Connolly was in the chair and his mentor, John Leslie, one of the most influential of Edinburgh socialists and one of the leading speakers of the SDF, was one of the secretaries.[34] By 1894 the SDF journal was hopeful that the Trades Council was 'coming into line; and with the influx of new blood must become even more pronouncedly Socialist'.[35] But, in fact, the council remained more or less evenly balanced between Lib-Labs and those who supported independent labour and it was slow to give any lead on political activities.

The Socialist Society steadily permeated the Trades Council in Aberdeen and at the beginning of 1893 as many as thirteen members of the Socialist Society, 'all of them speakers and writers of more than average ability', had been appointed as delegates to the council.[36] Even after his departure from Aberdeen loyalty to Champion and, therefore, hostility to Keir Hardie remained and the Aberdeen ILP, as the branch of the Trades Council Labour Party had become, refused to affiliate to the national ILP. It refused to support John Lincoln Mahon when he stood for North Aberdeen in 1895 and some of the Aberdeen ILP supported efforts to have Maltman Barry nominated as Conservative candidate for the southern division. However, all sections of the labour movement united in the following year to back Tom Mann when he stood in a by-election and polled 2,476 votes against his Liberal opponent's 2,909. The fact that the local ILP intrigued to ensure that Hardie, who was looking for a seat after his defeat in 1895, was not selected as the candidate made Hardie seriously consider resignation from the party.[37]

It seems to have been the new unionist activities among the dockers in 1889 which stimulated moves towards political action among Dundee working men. Cunninghame-Graham, Hardie and Aveling all addressed meetings there and a group of socialists and trade unionists emerged to try to get labour representation. They proposed the London dockers' leader, John Burns, as a candidate, but when the Liberals offered to support him in Battersea he withdrew from Dundee. In 1890, the president and secretary of the the Trades Council were elected to the Town Council as Lib-Labs, with a wage provided by the Trades Council. A branch of the Scottish Labour Party was formed in the city in 1892 and it put up the London socialist tailor, James MacDonald, but against the open hostility of most of the Trades Council. As in Edinburgh, enthusiasm for political action swung back and forth among trade unionists in the 1890s and, in 1895, after MacDonald's second defeat, an anti-socialist motion was passed requiring delegates to have approval from officials of their societies before raising any motion dealing with social or political questions.[38]

New Liberalism

All the signs in the 1890s were of the breakdown of the Labour radical consensus which had survived the vicissitudes of early years. There was a hardening of class attitudes as working-class activists and organisations began to assert their claims to direct representation. Labour, while not as yet offering a programme which was markedly different from that of the left of the Liberal Party was none the less determinedly insisting on its right to be represented even if it meant allowing Conservatives to gain. On the Liberal side, local constituency associations, weakened by the departure of so many of their wealthy supporters to the Liberal Unionists, needed candidates who could pay their own way and were less than willing to take risks. Labour interventions stoked what was often class bitterness. Someone like Samuel Chisholm in Glasgow when frustrated in his parliamentary ambitions by Labour intervention in an election could lash out and denounce the 'socialists' as 'engineered and financed by the publican trade'.[39]

It was not that there were no attempts to modify Liberalism and to make it responsive to working-class demands. The powerful radical wing of the party had a programme of reform which was considerably to the left of the Newcastle programme. It favoured an eight-hours day for miners, abolition of the House of Lords, home rule all round, more land reform and adult suffrage.[40] The 1890s were years when there was a fervour of intellectual activity in Liberal circles about likely future social development. Some, like Lord Rosebery, wanted to avoid getting caught up in competition with Conservatives over social reform issues. They feared that it would lead to a deepening of class antagonism, if the better off were to be taxed heavily to maintain the poor or the less well-off came to expect state help as a right. Others, on the other hand, believed that the whole evolution of society was pointing to greater collectivism and that this should be embraced. Many believed that municipal ownership offered greater efficiency than much of private enterprise and had the additional advantage of maintaining democratic control, and a Liberal-dominated town council in Glasgow embraced a programme of municipal activity in the the late 1890s.

Professor William Smart, at Glasgow University, declared that 'a century of laissez-faire had made laissez-faire impossible' and, therefore, there was now a readiness to accept state intervention.[41] The academic and journalist Henry Dyer argued that 'the middle and upper classes of this country must make up their minds to the fact that if a revolution which may end in chaos is to be avoided, they must prevent the catastrophe by anticipating the demands of the age'.[42] This did not necessarily lead them to socialism or to the Labour Party. Socialism was seen as pushing the collective needs of society before those of the individual. To New Liberals, the creation of a society which would allow the full flowering of the individual was still what mattered, but within an ethical society. Dyer talked of a 'reasonable school of political economy' that 'while rejecting the socialistic programme ... think that the State should intervene for the purpose of mitigating the pressure of the modern industrial system on its weaker members, and extending in great measure to the working classes the benefits of advancing civilization'.[43] The emerging Labour Party raised doubts because its reforms seemed limited, haphazard and not based on ethical considerations. They seemed to focus on narrow class interests and to set the demands of the workers above those of the rest of society. Rather, New Liberals looked to a Scottish tradition of civic regulation and responsibility. It had long been accepted in Scotland that the state (usually the local state) was justified in intervening in society if it was for a moral purpose.

Popular Conservatism

Since 1832 Scotland had proved stony ground for the Conservative Party and the standing joke among Liberals was that all the Scottish Conservative members could squeeze into one first-class carriage of the Edinburgh to London train. The assumption was, according to John Buchan, that 'a working man who was not a Liberal was inaccessible to reason, or morally corrupt, or intimidated by laird or employer'.[44] There were a number of Workingmen's Conservative Associations in the 1860s but they tended to be little more than occasional meetings addressed by country gentry. Things clearly began to change after 1885 and within a decade Conservatives and Unionists had gained 33 of Scotland's 71 seats and, in 1900, for the first time since 1832, had secured a majority of the Scottish seats.

The process of broadening the appeal of conservatism had begun in the 1870s. According to Iain Hutchison, in Glasgow and the west of Scotland the 1880s saw a culmination of a ten-year process of the integration of the Loyal Orange Institution with the Conservative Party, although Elaine McFarland has argued for its being an alliance of convenience rather than actual integration.[45] But, after the Orange Order, the most effective element of popular conservatism was the Primrose League. The first Scottish branch was formed in October 1885, two years after it was launched in England, but the expectation was that Scotland would prove to be fertile territory.[46] The habitations were to be places where different social classes could mix and be entertained, but the purpose was strongly political. Within a year there were reports, particularly from the west of Scotland, that the primrose was much in evidence among working people on 19 April, which the Liberals derisively dubbed 'St Beaconsfield's Day'. Yet the League never achieved the huge

popularity which it did in England, although its membership figures were
many times more than all the socialists and independent labour organisations
put together. Membership figures are uncertain, but there were claims of over
26,000 in the 1890s in more than 150 branches, with significant working-class
membership in Stirling, Aberdeen, Paisley and Bathgate.[47] Some of the
habitations offered opportunities for all kinds of conviviality and meetings
usually ended with musical entertainments. The Partick and Perth habitations
both supported choirs and the 'Salisbury' habitation in Edinburgh West had
an amateur dramatic club. But, despite the success of the party in the 1900
election the number of habitations in Scotland holding regular meetings had
fallen to fifty-two.

Some of the political success came not from conservatism but by way of
Liberal Unionism. The emergence of the new party allowed many to move
out of the Liberal Party while still claiming to be the true carriers of a Liberal
tradition. Catriona MacDonald has shown how Liberal Unionists in Paisley
used the language of 'constitutionalism and class co-operation' to link with
older radical language.[48]

Yet another thread of popular conservatism was that linked with the
extraordinary Maltman Barry, whom Cunninghame-Graham described as
'the most Marxian of Tories and the Toryest of Marxians'. Born in Glasgow
in 1842 he became a journalist on various Tory papers in London. In 1871,
'Citizen Barry' was to be found associating with Karl Marx and his associates
of the First International Working Men's Association. In the 1870s he came
to the view that the Conservative Party was the party which had done more
for the working class, with social legislation such as the factory acts. He also
became an enthusiast for Empire and a supporter of 'Lord Beaconsfield's
foreign policy... and of the imperial idea', as he told the electors of Dundee
when he offered himself as a candidate in 1880. He developed close links
with Champion and through him with Hardie and others in the emerging
Labour Party. Indeed, he liked to claim to be 'the creator of the Independent
Labour Party'. In 1892 he fought Banffshire as a 'Tory Democrat' against the
radical Sir William Wedderburn, largely on an anti-disestablishment ticket.
and in 1895 he sought the South Aberdeen seat, on a programme emphasising the importance of the Empire and proposing social reform, including
old-age pensions and legislation on the eight-hour day. In 1904 he failed to
win the Tory nomination at Montrose against John Morley, but he was
adopted with the support of conservative working men for North Aberdeen
in 1906 where he polled 931 votes.[49]

After 1903 there were undoubtedly working men who were attracted by
Joe Chamberlain's proposals for tariff reform. John Moffat, the Liberal
Unionist candidate for Paisley, could present this in 1905 as the defence of
the worker against capitalists who 'take advantage of the undefended condition of the labourer, to force him to work the longest hours for the least
pay ... to turn him as much as possible into a tool or machine', and as a

barrier to 'the encroaching tide of militarism, capitalism and other "isms" which are threatening them'.[50] The appeal of Barry in 1906 to some of the Aberdeen unionists was his support for tariff reform, and there was an 'Organised Labour' branch of the Tariff Reform League.[51]

Scottish Workers' Parliamentary Election Committee

In spite of the gains in local government and the presence on the Glasgow Town Council of a group of labour 'stalwarts' who were pressing for further 'municipal socialism', there was an air of despondency over the independent labour movement after the defeats of 1895. Bruce Glasier bemoaned the fact that 'all the enthusiasm and glamour seems to have gone out of the movement'.[52] Success in weaning working-class support away from liberalism had been negligible. Even the most committed were failing to win over their unions to any kind of socialism.

The defeat of the engineers in the great lock-out of 1897 may well have been a catalyst for change. The largest and most successful of unions had been humiliated by the united action of employers. Technological changes in the workplace were undermining the position of the skilled worker. He could no longer be so certain that his skill and his union would protect him. There was a greater readiness to look for legislative protection.

It was the indefatigable George Carson at the April 1899 meeting of the recently-formed Scottish Trades Union Congress who moved that, because of the present economic situation and the break-up of the Liberal Party, the time was 'ripe for the consolidation of all working-class movements, and the formation of a working-class political party, whose ultimate object would be the nationalisation of the land, and the means of production, distribution and exchange.' The Congress was largely the creation of the Scottish trades councils, the most vigorous and militant section of Scottish trade unionism. Right from the start socialist activists were well-represented at it. But it was also a product of concern at a lack of attention to Scottish issues in the British TUC. The result was that in January 1900, seven weeks before the famous meeting in the Memorial Hall in London, which is usually taken as the founding meeting of the Labour Party, 226 delegates met in the Free Gardeners' Hall in Edinburgh and formed the Scottish Workers' Parliamentary Election Committee to work 'for direct independent working-class representation in the House of Commons and on local administrative bodies'.

The delegates were from trade unions, the ILP, the Social Democratic Federation and the Co-operative movement. The presence of the co-operative societies was to remain a distinctive feature of the Scottish organisation and the first chairman of the Scottish Workers Parliamentary Committee which resulted from the conference was Henry Murphy of Lanark Co-operative Society. Their presence reflected the extent to which co-ops had become politicised as a result of a decade of battles with private traders' associations trying to keep them out of markets. It also reflects the extent to which ideas challenging old perceptions had been propagated in the pages of the *Scottish Cooperator* by its editor, Henry Dyer.

The new organisation had the usual problem of trying to find a consensus among such a varied group. Robert Smillie, the miners' leader who chaired it, talked of the need for a 'militant independent Working Class Party'; yet others tried, unsuccessfully, to have the word independent dropped. Socialists wanted a commitment to the 'nationalisation of the means of production, distribution and exchange', but that too was negatived. It was agreed to work for 'direct Independent Working-class Representation ... as the logical sequence to the possession of political power by the working classes'. Local committees were formed to work with the new organisation, ruffling the feathers of trades councils and other groups which already had election committees. A programme of what were regarded as pressing issues included a legal eight-hour day, old age pensions, support for the disabled, taxation of land values and 'all other forms of unearned income', state work-schemes to create 'self-supporting industries by which the right to work would be secured to everyone' and a minimum wage.[53] Its manifesto declared that there was a need for a party that recognised that 'the greatness of an empire consists not in the extent of its territories, but in the well-being of its citizens'. The greatest problem of the age, it argued, was the social problem and that 'can only be solved by the workers themselves'.[54]

The new party was formed in the midst of the South African War which was re-uniting radical groups in opposition. Its one candidate in the khaki election of 1900 was the journalist A. E. Fletcher, for Glasgow Camlachie. Because of the special circumstances he was able to garner backing from the whole spectrum of progressive bodies. As well as the ILP and local Liberals, he had the support of the trades council, the United Irish League, the SDF and the Clarion Scouts.[55] He presented himself as a radical as much as a Labour candidate. It was not enough to overcome the jingoist campaign of his opponent.

Despite its protestations of independence, the SWPEC was still caught in the politics of progressive radicalism. In this it was undoubtedly reflecting the prevailing attitudes among the Scottish working classes, still powerfully attached to radical principles. But the formation of the new body was nevertheless immensely important. It was an indication of how far the Liberal Party seemed to be incapable of responding adequately to the growth in working-class organisation and working-class confidence. The evidence of growing class hostility is apparent in the language of both local liberal associations and the labour organisations. Class was becoming a key factor in politics to a greater extent than ever before. But the formation of the new body was also vitally important for the future shape of the Labour Party. The experience of reconciling conflicting views and of balancing socialist and trade unionist concerns, which Hardie got at Edinburgh in January, stood him

in good stead the following month in London. Hardie and the ILP were able
to emerge from the Memorial Hall largely controlling the agenda of the new
Labour Representation Committee and ensuring that the commitment was to
a truly *independent* party in Parliament. The Labour Party had been formed.

Notes

1. Joan Smith, 'Labour Tradition in Glasgow and Liverpool', *History Work-shop*, No. 17, Spring 1984, p. 34.
2. Mitchell Library, Glasgow Trades Council Minutes, 12 June 1889.
3. J. G. Kellas, 'The Liberal Party in Scotland 1876 - 1895', *Scottish Historical Review*, XLIV, April 1965, p. 9.
4. *North British Daily Mail*, 2, 9 February 1882.
5. Glasgow Trades Council, *Annual Report 1883–84*.
6. *North British Daily Mail*, 23, 30 April 1885.
7. Glasgow Trades Council, *Annual Report*, 1884–85.
8. NLS, Edinburgh Trades Council Minutes 6 January 1880, 6 October 1881; Edinburgh Bookbinders' Minutes, 15 June 1880.
9. Circular issued by Edinburgh Trades Council bound with Bookbinders' Minutes, 30 March 1885.
10. Aberdeen University Library, Aberdeen Trades Council Minutes, 21 May 1884.
11. C. C. MacDonald, *Sermon preached on Sabbath 7th September to the delegates attending the Congress at Aberdeen 1884*.
12. K. D. Buckley, *Trade Unionism in Aberdeen 1878–1900*, (Aberdeen, 1955), p. 122.
13. *Daily Free Press*, 4 June 1885.
14. D. W. Urwin, 'Conservative Party Organisation in Scotland', *Scottish Historical Review*, XLIV, 1965, p. 95.
15. James G. Kellas, 'The Mid-Lanark By-Election(1888) and the Scottish Labour Party (1888–1894)', *Parliamentary Affairs*, 18, (1964–65), p. 325.
16. The full programme is printed in *Edinburgh Trades Council Centenary Publication*, (Edinburgh,1959), pp. 48–50.
17. Mitchell Library, Glasgow Trades Council Minutes, 19 October 1887.
18. Gerrie went on to become the first member of an abortive effort by Joseph Burgess to establish a national independent labour party through the pages of a Lancashire-based Labour paper, the *Workman's Times*, 30 April, 6 May 1892.
19. AUL, Aberdeen Trades Council Minutes, 8 May, 2 July, 24 December 1890.
20. *Ibid.* 3 May 1891.
21. *Daily Free Press*, 10 August 1891; *Trade Unionist*, 15 August 1891.
22. *Workmen's Times*, 12 March 1892.
23. Kellas, 'Mid-Lanark By-Election', pp. 326–7.
24. *Labour Leader*, March 1893.
25. D. Lowe, *Souvenirs*, p. 17.
26. Membership Card of Scottish Labour Party 1893.
27. *Workman's Times*, 22 October 1892.
28. The letter was published in Hardie's *Labour Leader*, October 1893.
29. *Daily Free Press*, 9 October 1893.

30. *Glasgow Echo*, 3 January 1894; *People's Journal*, 6 January 1894.
31. David Howell, *British Workers and the Independent Labour Party 1888–1906*, (Manchester, 1983), p. 154.
32. *Scottish Leader*, 16 June, 7 July 1892.
33. NLS, Edinburgh Trades Council Minutes, 11 October 1892.
34. It was Leslie who persuaded Connolly in 1896 to return to Ireland and to organise a socialist party there. N. Davies, *Connolly of Ireland* (Liverpool, 1946), pp. 8–9.
35. *Labour Chronicle*, 15 October 1894.
36. *Workman's Times*, 12 January 1893.
37. H. Pelling, T*he Origins of the Labour Party* (1965), p. 174.
38. Dundee Trades Council, *Annual Report 1894–95*.
39. Maver, 'Local Party Politics and the Temperance Crusade', p. 51.
40. Kellas, 'Mid-Lanark By-Election', p. 329.
41. W. Smart, 'The Municipal Industries of Glasgow', *Proceedings of the Philosophical Society of Glasgow*, XXVI, 1894–95, p. 37.
42. H. Dyer, *The Foundations of Social Policy* (Glasgow, 1889), p. 4.
43. *Ibid.* p. 26.
44. John Buchan, *Memory Hold the Door* (1941), p. 53.
45. Hutchison, *Political History*, p. 122; E. McFarland, *Protestants First*, pp. 160–9.
46. M. Pugh, *The Tories and the People*, p. 128.
47. Janette Moran, ' Scottish Conservatism and the Primrose League 1885–1904', BA. dissertation, Department of History, University of Strathclyde, 1993. This is one of the few detailed studies of the League in Scotland. Pugh, *Tories and the People*, p. 133.
48. Catriona MacDonald(ed.), *Unionist Scotland* (1998), p. 59.
49. J. T. Ward, 'Tory Socialist: A Preliminary Note on Michael Maltman Barry (1842–1909)', *Scottish Labour History Society Journal*, No. 2 (April, 1970), pp. 25–37.
50. MacDonald, *Unionist Scotland*, p. 61.
51. Francis Johnston correspondence. J. F. Duncan to Hardie 12 June 1905.
52. Howell, *British Workers*, p. 162.
53. NLS Mf. Mss 141. Minutes of the Scottish Workers' Parliamentary Committee.
54. *Daily Record*, 21 March 1900.
55. Howell, *British Workers*, p. 163.

CHAPTER EIGHT

Competing for Radicalism 1900–18

The early years of the twentieth century saw a continuing struggle between the Liberal Party and the Labour Party for the radical inheritance. Both sought to claim that they were the true representatives of popular politics and the standard bearers of the moves towards greater democracy. Neither had clearly won by the time war broke out in 1914 and there were many who still pinned their hopes on a broad Liberal–Labour progressive alliance.

Anti-imperialism

At the 1901 conference of the Scottish Workers' Parliamentary Election Committee an earlier decision that sponsored candidates would not appear on the platform of candidates from other parties was reversed, with the result that the SDF withdrew its support for the new organisation. A. E. Fletcher spoke against that earlier decision, arguing that it would debar him from supporting someone such as G. B. Clark, who 'had voted against the South African conspiracy', and the change was clearly an indication of how the war in South Africa had triggered a revival of Liberal radicalism and encouraged talk of a progressive alliance.

Although imperialism had an appeal for many Scots, there had always been a loud and effective anti-imperialist thread within Scottish Liberalism. G. B. Clark in the 1890s continued to denounce the growing pressure which was being applied by Rhodes and his associates on the Boer Republics. In the aftermath of the Jameson Raid he achieved notoriety by publishing papers stolen from the office of Rhodes' solicitor, which hinted at Chamberlain's approval of the Raid. Robert Wallace, the former editor of *The Scotsman*, who had ousted the imperialist Goschen in Edinburgh in 1886, remained one of the fiercest critics of imperialism until his death at the end of the century. His last article in *The Contemporary Review* in 1899 was a scathing attack on 'the seamy Side of Imperialism'. It was aimed against the growing band of Liberal Imperialists and at those, 'to whom the conversion of home heathens and the civilisation of home savages are dreary and insipid occupations compared with doing the same things to even more repulsive aliens, provided they are a thousand miles away and have never been seen by their Quixotic benefactors'.[1]

To many Scottish Liberals, from Campbell-Bannerman down, the war against the Boers was 'a scandalous plot of money seekers using the Government as a catspaw'. A war brought on 'by fraud, force and folly', according to G. B. Clark, and by millionaires 'in the fond hope that they would be able to get cheaper labour and bigger profits'.[2] Aberdeen Trades Council was one of the first trade-union organisations and – one of the few – in October 1899 to protest against the war brought on 'in the interests of Jewish and British speculators',[3] but Dundee, Edinburgh and Glasgow soon followed. Liberals radicals and Labour people both argued that the war would weaken the Empire, and at times the case was less against empire as such than against an immoral empire. James Bryce, the Liberal member for South Aberdeen, argued that the best and surest foundations of imperial strength lay in 'the affection of our fellow subjects', while Keir Hardie, in the same vein, declared, 'You cannot build an Empire of free peoples by force'.[4] A number of Scottish Liberal MPs regularly voted against war policy. G. B. Clark and Sir William Wedderburn, an old India hand, who sat for Banffshire, always did, voting against supplies for the troops alongside people like David Lloyd George. The two Aberdeen MPs, James Bryce and D. V. Pirie, T. E. Buchanan in East Aberdeenshire, Morley in Montrose, J. H. Dalziel in Kirkcaldy, Tom Shaw in Hawick, Dewar in Edinburgh South and MacEwan in Edinburgh Central, Sinclair in Forfarshire and Weir in Ross and Cromarty usually did.[5] S. J. Brown identifies sixteen pro-Boer Scottish MPs, interestingly mostly spread down the east coast constituencies.[6]

Before 1899 there is not much evidence that imperial concerns impinged on Labour, but the war changed that. The South African War brought the issue of imperialism into Labour consciousness and pushed Liberals and some Labour together again. Liberals and Labour combined in 'Stop the war' meetings in the main cities, on more than one occasion ending in bloody riot as students and other 'well-dressed middle-class rowdies' tried to break them up. The Clarion Scouts in Glasgow defied jingoist mobs and organised a meeting which included Hardie, Lloyd George, John Ferguson, McLardy of the Henry George Society, Henry Murphy of the Co-operative Association and A. J. Hunter, the retired secretary of the trades council.[7] Keir Hardie argued for an anti-war alliance between Labour and Liberals like John Morley, rejected for Newcastle but recently triumphantly returned for Montrose.

After the Khaki election which showed a significantly smaller swing to the Conservatives and Unionists in Scotland than in England[8] the voice of criticism became louder. Rosebery's rectorial address at Glasgow, with its suggestion of Britain's divine mission, brought condemnation from many Liberals and from clergy. Campbell-Bannerman's 'methods of barbarism' speech with its echoes of earlier criticism of the army reflected precisely the kind of concerns that many Scottish radicals were expressing. For the first time a clergyman of one of the main churches, James Barr of Rutherford United Free in Glasgow, a future Labour MP, spoke out against the war in a series of five lectures, later published as *Christianity and War*. He argued that the silence of the clergy had been misunderstood and that a considerable number were hostile to the war. Now, he declared, 'the pulpit must resume its ancient office of instructing the nation'. Like most pro-Boers he saw the war as the result of a capitalist conspiracy, but he also tapped nationalist sentiment, with comparisons of Scotland's wars of independence against Edward I of England with the Boer struggle against Edward I of Great Britain.

It was out of pro-Boer activities and the battles over free speech that the Young Scots Society emerged at the end of 1900. The inspirer was Hector MacPherson, who had maintained a strong anti-war line as editor of the *Edinburgh Evening News*. Formerly an admirer of Rosebery, MacPherson parted company with him over his imperialist views. He urged stronger denunciation than most Liberals were prepared to make of the Jameson raid at the end of 1896 and regarded the war as 'both politically and morally wrong'. He hailed the battle for free speech 'on that historic night in the Waverley Market' as comparable to the radical struggles against the 'Dundas Despotism' and denounced the 'Yahooism' which had created a situation where 'the uitlanders on whose behalf we are at war had more freedom of speech than Scotsmen have today in their own country'.[9]

The idea of the new society was that it would 'stimulate interest in progressive politics ... and generally to promote Liberal Principles'. This did not mean the increased state intervention of some of the New Liberals. Macpherson indeed argued that Liberals were leaning too much towards socialism while the Tories were bribing both the landed class and the working class.[10] Tom Shaw, MP for Hawick, as president, gave the inaugural address on 'Patriotism and Empire' in October 1901, calling for greater democracy and warning that patriotism was becoming 'more and more the exclusive property of a growing military caste' encouraged by the fact that Britain was taking on itself the task of 'the policeman of the world'.[11] The Society wanted to recapture the position of Cobden, Bright and Gladstone with its rejection of unilateral action in international affairs. It immediately courted controversy by inviting John X. Merriman, former Prime Minister of the the Cape and opponent of the war, to address them. *The Scotsman* led the resulting outcry. On the other hand, the veteran radical Morrison Davidson dedicated his *Africa for the Africanders* to the Young Scots Society 'in the hope that they may be able in some measure to expiate Scotland's heavy share of the guilt of the most sordid and generally infamous war ever waged even by the Pirate Empire'.

Home Rule

The second progressive issue on which middle-class and working-class radicals could combine was home rule for Scotland. The moves to grant home rule to Ireland in 1886, while splitting the Liberal Party, stimulated Scottish demands for home rule, although John Murdoch had a decade before prophesied that the Gaelic revival would 'fan the flame of nationality'. A Scottish Home Rule Association was founded in May 1886. The moving force behind it was an Edinburgh solicitor Charles Waddie, who had published a list of complaints about Scottish legislation which was held up in Westminster. Significantly, Professor J. S. Blackie chaired the first meeting and G. B. Clark was a key member. Blackie in the 1880s had revived the issue declaring that,

> Scotland had the right to demand that her public business shall be conducted seriously on Scottish ground, in a Scottish atmosphere, and under Scottish influences, not hustled and skimmed over hastily in an Imperial parliament.[12]

An all-party movement in 1884 had succeeded in getting the government to accede to the appointment of a Secretary for Scotland.

The demand from the SHRA was now for 'home rule all round', a federal system, a 'United States of Great Britain'.[13] It reflected both resentment at Ireland being treated as a special case and the continuing frustration at the failure of the imperial parliament to deal with what were seen as pressing Scottish issues. In Aberdeen, the Trades Council, the Junior Liberal Association and the Radical Association collaborated in a home rule demonstration at the end of 1886 and the Association, against Waddie's advice, gave support to Hardie's Mid-Lanark campaign. The new Scottish Labour Party made home rule one of its objectives and Hardie and the Lanarkshire miners' leader, Robert Smillie, both became vice-presidents of the Association.

W. A. Hunter, MP for North Aberdeen and G. B. Clark, the MP for Caithness, had raised the issue in Parliament in 1886. Clark continued to bring in motions over the next few years, with some success, in that the majorities against fell from 121 votes in 1889 to a mere 18 in 1893. All the Liberal associations in Scotland incorporated home rule all round in their objectives. By 1891 Charles Waddie was explaining *How Scotland lost her Parliament and what became of it*, with a strongly nationalist message. In 1894 Sir Henry Dalziel's motion was actually carried by 180 votes to 170. Many linked the campaign to frustration at the House of Lords blocking of Liberal measures and could tap into the power anti-landowner sentiments. Sir William Wedderburn told Aberdeen Liberals that,

> It was impossible that they could ever get for Scotland land reform or temperance reform or equality of religion or anything else as long as they had to ask in a House [of Lords] which was dominated by English Tory squires, English bishops and English brewers. they would never get what the Scottish people wanted without Home Rule for Scotland and they could not get Home Rule for Scotland as long as the House of Lords had a veto on the proposal.[14]

In the next few years campaigning was left to a handful of the committed, such as Morrison Davidson, who, although he had lived in London for a quarter of a century, still liked to believe that Scotland had a different set of values from those in 'Godless England': 'William Wallace, the stainless knight of Elderslie, was the Scottish Kruger and Steyn, Botha, de la Rey and De Wet rolled into one', while an Englishman 'of the regular John Bull pattern' was 'an unreasoning anti-Boer'.[15]

For some Liberals, constitutional reform was central to the continued identification of the Liberal Party as the main progressive force. John M. Robertson, the Liberal MP for Greenock, wrote in the new Labour newspaper, *Forward*, home rule would bring 'a new era of democratic reform'. At the Glasgow conference of the Young Scots in 1907 the issue of Scottish home rule came to the forefront, and they issued a Home Rule manifesto. The complaints were largely about the failure of the existing political system to deliver long-called-for Scottish legislation on land-reform, temperance, housing, education and poor law reform. To these were added some new, recent grievances. Bruce's Scottish Antarctic Expedition of 1904 had received only meagre support and that only after a tremendous outcry. The national art collections were inadequately funded and the meteorological museum on Ben Nevis had been forced to close because of the withdrawal of a small government grant. The campaign gained encouragement from the success, in 1908, of Vernon Pirie's private member's bill for Scottish home rule which was carried by 257 votes to 102.

Once the Lords' veto was removed by the Parliament Act of 1911 the demand was for an immediate home rule bill and there was talk of putting up home-rule candidates in by-elections and a declaration that 'Only by the formation of a strong Scottish Nationalist party can Scotland hope to secure an adequate recognition of her needs.'[16] A deputation from the Young Scots' Society in 1912 to lobby Scottish MPs on devolution led to the formation of a Scottish Home Rule Council, which included among its members, the editor of the ILP newspaper, *Forward*, Tom Johnston, and Roland E. Muirhead, the wealthy backer of the moves to independent labour. In 1913 the International Scots Home Rule League was formed aimed at mobilising cross-party support to maintain pressure on the Liberal government to deliver home rule for Scotland.

Temperance

A third area where links between Liberalism and Labour were maintained was in the temperance movement. The temperance crusade had motivated a generation of Liberal radicals since at least the 1850s and 1860s. Temperance was seen as the means to both moral regeneration and to economic regeneration for individuals. Drink was the road to the moral degeneracy of individuals, but it was also seen as creating many of the social problems which had to be tackled at the end of the century. As Irene Maver has shown, someone like Glasgow's United Presbyterian Lord Provost, Samuel Chisholm, had no doubt that 'slumdom' was the product of the drink trade and 'if social and temperance reformers could settle the drink question on a total abstinence basis, then the necessity for housing operations would be wholly removed'.[17] Six thousand Good Templars marched to Bannockburn field in 1897 to protest against an enemy 'More to be feared by the Scottish people than the enemy faced by our forefathers in 1314'.[18] The majority of Labour activists declared a commitment to temperance, but rather than the prohibition which many of the most committed middle-class reformers favoured, Labour came to focus on control of the number of licences through municipalisation of the trade and local option. The winning of a Scottish Local Veto Act in 1913 weakened a pillar of Liberal support, although enthusiasm for municipalisation of public houses remained part of the Labour programme.

Land reform

The fourth area was the continuing demand for land reform. While the 1886 Crofters' Act had gone a considerable way to meeting the grievances of the Highlands, the tenant farmers of non-Highland counties lacked similar rights. With unemployment high in 1903 and 1905 the issue revived. It is a measure of how far Labour still continued to accept traditional economic analysis that they too argued for the creation of smallholdings as a solution to urban problems. The Liberal government was trying to get a measure through which would extend the provision of the Crofters' Act to the whole of Scotland and to create smallholdings, but it was blocked by the Lords. The young Tom Johnston, editor of *Forward*, began publishing a series of articles on 'Our Scots Noble Families', which blamed the plight of urban workers on the depredations of generations of the landed class:

> We who think that the land should be owned by the State, we who think that no man has a right to enclosure for sport while other men starve by the wayside for lack of food, we who *know* that the lands of Britain belong to the Crown (and through the Crown to the people), we who know that the land has been pillaged and stolen by ducal brigands, we who still pay rents to the descendants of these brigands, we who are chased from the mountain sides by their keepers and from the burn-sides by their water bailiffs – we, are *we* the Robbers?

Johnston's biographer has rightly described it as 'one of the most searing assaults on the landed class ever written', a tone which mixed old-fashioned radical liberalism with biblical-inspired fervour.[19] He excelled even Lloyd George in his denunciation of 'the Dukes':

> Those low, mean, despicable, contemptible, wretches, clutching like Shylocks their blood money from the land their ancestors stole; those whining, ungentlemanly, non-moral cowards surfeiting themselves in the plenty they have wrung from the poor; ravishing from aged labourers their pitifully small pensions; playing on the ignorance of the people to escape taxation.[20]

Published in book form in 1909 amid the bitter debates over Lloyd George's 'People's budget' with its taxes on landed wealth, it attracted much attention and led to the establishment of a new Highland Land League with the ubiquitous G. B. Clark as president and Johnston as vice-president. One hundred thousand gathered on Glasgow Green in September 1909 in what Joan Smith as called 'the last great demonstration in the Liberal reform tradition' to call for the passage of the budget, and 'end to the House of Lords' and 'Home rule all round'.[21] The League was committed to land nationalisation by gradually removing the rights of inheritance. But with the Liberal government trying to push through measures for land reform the tendency was to reaffirm the links with radical Liberalism.

A 1911 Small Landholders (Scotland) Act extended some of the protection of the 1886 Act to small tenants throughout Scotland and gave to the board of agriculture substantial new powers of compulsion on landowners to force the creation of new smallholdings.[22] Predictably, the process of change was at snail's pace and after seven years the board of agriculture had only created some 500 new holdings. Discontent remained in the congested Highland areas and there were continuing challenges to landowner authority particularly in the outer isles with land-raids. The *Highland News* in 1913 noted 'ample evidence of a coming revolt'.[23]

Although land reform linked with nationalisation of the mines was a central issue in the Midlothian by-election of 1913, the new Highland Land League markedly failed to stir significant popular support outside the Highlands and few of Johnston's colleagues in the ILP shared his enthusiasm for the issue. It was a sign that urban labour was turning inwards in its concerns and concentrating on the social problems of the cities.

Labour organisations

It was agreed initially that the two committees, the London-based LRC and the Scottish Workers' Parliamentary Election Committee, should operate separately, with Ramsay MacDonald, secretary of the LRC confirming that the area north of the Tweed was the responsibility of the Scottish body. But problems quickly arose because trade-union membership spanned the border and some national unions had their headquarters in Scotland. MacDonald, ever anxious about the resources of the LRC, began to press for unions to include Scottish membership in the calculation of the levy due to the LRC. Within a few months MacDonald was suggesting that the two committees be 'centralised in one'.[24] The Scottish committee, dependent on voluntary contributions for its finances, also had the problem of asserting its authority over the various other bodies which were already in existence to get working-class candidates returned. Powerful groups such as the Glasgow Trades Council or the miners' unions paid little attention to the new body. Calls to create a single Scottish Workers' Party, which would consolidate the various groups fell on deaf ears, although the Committee in 1902 became the Scottish Workers' Representation Committee.

There was no formal Liberal–Labour pact in Scotland such as MacDonald and Herbert Gladstone had agreed for English constituencies. Previous attempts had made clear that on the Liberal side it could not be delivered. None the less, the Liberal leadership still showed a willingness to try. The Scottish Liberal Association set up a conciliation committee in 1904 to 'direct its attention, not merely to obviating electoral disputes between Liberal and Labour candidates, but [it] should also endeavour to unite all the progressive forces'.[25] In the end, it was never asked to act and any approaches to Labour met with firm assertions that there would be no co-operation with any other political party. Labour paid the price in the election of January 1906 when only two Labour candidates were returned, compared with the twenty-seven in England. George Barnes, the secretary of the ASE, won a three cornered-fight in Glasgow-Blackfriars and Hutchestown, with support from some of the United Irish League and disgruntled Liberals, while Alexander Wilkie, a member of the executive of the LRC, won alongside a Liberal in two-member, Dundee. Wilkie and his supporters presented themselves as the progressive wing of the Liberal Party, 'pushing them on to work' and he studiously avoided the use of the word 'Labour' in his manifesto.[26] Nine other Labour and miners' candidates went down to defeat.

The failure of the Liberals and Labour to agree a pact in Scotland was an indication of the growing class hostility which was coming to the fore in Scotland. The Liberal leadership could do little to persuade local constituency associations to select Labour candidates. Lanarkshire Association regularly refused to accept miners' candidates even in predominantly mining constituencies. Wilkie had expected to get Liberal Association backing when he offered himself in Dundee, but a section of the local Liberal leadership balked at the prospect and went for the usual London barrister.[27] Liberal hostility hardened as Labour interventions in by-elections caused Liberals to lose seats to the Unionists. Dundee Liberals threatened to discontinue their payments to party funds unless socialism was confronted and there were calls for 'a crusade against socialism'. The Scottish Liberal whip warned that 'unless the Liberal party stood upon its own legs its very vitals would be consumed and it would fall between two stools, and disappear as an active force in British politics'.[28] Some of the bitterness stemmed from local politics, where there were signs of increasing polarisation into anti-socialist and socialist camps over the issue of municipalisation and rate-backed expenditure, with elements of local Liberalism combining with Unionists to keep Labour candidates out.[29]

Both the Scottish Workers' Representation Committee and its British counterpart, the LRC, remained federations of labour organisations. There was no individual membership of them and not all labour organisations affiliated to them. The trade unions played a key role alongside the ILP. In addition there were bodies such as the Women's Labour League, the Fabian

Society,[30] the British Socialist Party and the Socialist Labour Party. Indeed, the superficial impression is of an extraordinarily active labour movement in these years. There were social activities in groups such as the Clarion Scouts, rambling clubs, choirs such as the Clarion Glee Club, the South-Side ILP choir, the Partick Socialist choir, speakers' clubs and drama societies. On Sunday evenings in Glasgow hundreds would pack into the Albion Halls or the Pavilion theatre to hear speakers from the whole spectrum of left-wing ideology. Hardie's paper, the *Labour Leader*, was published in Glasgow until 1904, when it moved to Manchester, but Tom Johnston started the *Forward* newspaper in 1906 to publicise the whole range of socialist views. The Civic Press and the Reformers' Bookstall kept up a continual flow of left-wing pamphlets. Blatchford's *Clarion* was widely circulated and Clarion vans and *Forward* vans toured the country. But there was not a great deal to show for all the activity. In the early twentieth century few Labour people made it on to town councils. The 'stalwarts' had all been swept off Glasgow Town Council by 1901. After the death of John Ferguson in 1907 relationships with the United Irish League broke down and all seven Labour candidates in the 1908 election went down to defeat.

Elsewhere the story was of bickering and back-biting often as much over personalities as over policies. In Aberdeen Joseph Duncan of the ILP could barely bring himself to deal with Thomas Kennedy of the SDF. It was not uncommon for the SDF to try to recruit in the same week and in the same area as the ILP.

Relations between the Scottish Committee, which in 1906 became the Labour Party (Scottish Section), and the Labour Party (as the LRC now was) National Executive Committee in London continued to prove difficult and, increasingly, a number of Scottish unions sought affiliation to the Labour Party. Scottish decisions to contest John Morley's old seat in Montrose and to try to get the second seat in Dundee against the advice of the London NEC intensified the antagonism. When the miners' unions decided to affiliate to the Labour Party in 1908 there was really little future for the Scottish body and, amid much recrimination against the SDF and against those who were 'treating Scotland as a province', the Scottish Section agreed to ask to become a committee 'directly financed and controlled by the Labour Party'.

The Labour vote doubled in the January 1910 election, but such an advance was small compared with the advances being made in Wales and elsewhere and it brought no extra seats. The second election of that year brought a further gain of West Fife, thanks to very effective organising by the miners' political agent. A series of conferences in 1911 and 1912 tried to pinpoint the causes of Labour failure in Scotland. Among the reasons identified were a lack of effective and continuous organisation between elections; an over-concentration on Lanarkshire at the expense of other areas; and divisions produced by religious sectarianism, which some suggested was not helped by taking up 'political issues' (by which was implied Irish Home Rule) rather than economic ones. There was also a fear of letting in Unionists in three cornered fights. What could happen was revealed in a by-election in 1912 in Gladstone's old seat, Mid-Lothian, which was, of course, of immense symbolic importance to the Liberals. A Liberal majority of 3,000 was over-turned when 2,413 votes went to the Labour candidate and a Unionist crept in with a majority of 32. Any possibility of a Liberal-Labour agreement was shattered.

The ILP

The Independent Labour Party was the liveliest of the organisations affiliated to the Labour Party, although membership was difficult to maintain. It had made major advances among trade unionists in the 1890s and eight of the eleven members of the parliamentary committee of the STUC, formed in 1897, were ILP supporters. By 1908 there were 130 branches in Scotland and it was claimed that membership had doubled in the couple of years since the Liberals came to power. Dundee had 130 members in 1910, although many of them were in arrears; Arbroath had 56 thanks largely to the activities of John Addison, 'the great apostle and high priest of socialism in this district', as the local paper described him.[31] Forfar had twenty and Montrose a mere fifteen, which had soon fallen to only six stalwarts, who complained of the 'very uphill work' in maintaining the branch.

The ILP was very much a party of the skilled working-class, certainly in Glasgow and the west of Scotland, where its main strength was. In many ways there was always limited sympathy for the poorest sections of the population. There was, for example, little urgency for an extension of the suffrage either to women or to the excluded forty per cent of the male population. Hardie thought that after 1884 the franchise was no longer an issue and 'only the details remain to be adjusted'. There was a concern that neither women's votes nor the 'slum vote', if granted, would help socialism.[32]

It was in the years from 1908 onwards that the ILP emerged as unques-tionably the leading radical and socialist organisation. It then became, as Joan Smith has argued, 'the heir to radicalism'.[33] It focused on local government and in that sense also it was within a radical tradition which had argued against centralism and that the nearer government was to the people then the more it would be responsive to democracy. Enthusiasm for municipalisation had waned after 1902 as complaints about the rate burden became louder. But in 1908 a proposal to use the profits of municipal activities to reduce the rates rather than prices, something which was not previously allowed in Scotland, roused resistance. The ILP in Glasgow became the strongest defenders of the power of local government as it came under attack from the political right. Municipal enterprise now became municipal socialism. For Tom Drife of the ILP, writing in *Forward*, municipal socialism was to be the means of eradicating poverty. It would even out the fluctuations in the economy. Municipal workers would not be dismissed during slumps, wages would be reduced and 'this would ensure a steady demand for goods of all kind. And this, again, would almost abolish depression'. It would end the constant struggle for existence and give men the opportunity 'to strive to excel in other ways'.[34] Hardie enthused about the vista of municipal authorities taking over 'coal mines and wheat fields' and 'serving its citizens 'with bread, water, houses, clothing, and fuel' and anything else that was required. Thus, he argued, would the city be 'in a fair way to solving many of the most ghastly problems of our modern civilization'.[35]

It was John Wheatley, the ex-miner turned small businessman, elected to the extended Glasgow Town Council in November 1912, who came up with the scheme that most caught the imagination,with the proposal to use the common good fund, boosted by the profits of the municipal trams, to finance a programme of housebuilding. He proposed 10,000 four-roomed cottages to be rented at £8 per year.[36] Support for municipal housing became the benchmark of future labour candidates and municipalisation became the 'essential strategy in the gentle, uphill climb to the peaks of socialism'.[37] The Glasgow Labour Party put housing at the top of its political agenda, calling for the provision of 'healthy housing ... at rents which they could afford to pay' if necessary through subsidy, before there was any more slum clearance. Working-class cottages should be financed from the common good fund and a fair rent court should be established.[38]

The ILP had to face constant sniping from the left, from the purist elements of the Socialist Labour Party and from John Maclean and his associates in the Social Democratic Party, as the SDF had now become. The latter wanted all the emphasis to be on socialism and on the creation of a united Socialist party which would not modify its political goals in order to attract mass support. Maclean argued that the Labour party was 'a miserable caricature of Marxism'. There is no doubt that in the industrial unrest of the pre-war years there were those who were attracted by the militant tones In 1911 Glasgow was the strongest centre of the SDP in Britain outside London, with Maclean attracting large numbers to his classes on Marxist economics.[39] In Dundee it was reported that a 'strong and enthusiastic branch' existed, which was attracting ILP people.[40] But entrenched hostility to all but a few trade-union leaders and Maclean's inability to co-operate with others, other than on his own terms, ensured that the challenges from the far left were seen off.

Although local trades councils would try to pull together the various organisations at elections times, this was rarely easy. None was prepared to sacrifice their autonomy to some wider body. In Glasgow the attempt to create a city-wide Labour Party went on for years before a constitution was eventually agreed in March 1912. But even then, the local trades council refused to withdraw its existing affiliation with the National Labour Party and there was persistent rivalry. In spite of this, the better organisation did bring success in the elections for a new corporation in Glasgow, much enlarged by the annexation of neighbouring burghs. Twelve Labour members were elected at the November 1912 elections, rising to eighteen by 1914. It was these who built on the foundations laid to create a coherent political strategy based on municipal socialism.

Advances were being made in local government in all the major Scottish cities. Edinburgh elected its first Labour councillors in 1909 and on the eve of war had six. Over Scotland the Labour Party could claim 69 town councillors and 13 county councillors in 1915. Perhaps more significant in the long term were the improvements in organisation after an abhorrence of canvassing had been overcome. Thanks to the arguments of Tom Johnston and others, it came to be recognised that the soap box was not enough. Local Labour Parties took on the task of organising and co-ordinating There was also an increased determination to ensure that as many potential supporters as possible were actually registered. In Lanarkshire, the miners' organiser Duncan Graham flooded the registration courts with claims for lodgers to be admitted to the register until a deal was forced upon the other parties. Finally there was a Scottish Advisory Council, with Ben Shaw as secretary. At its inauguration in 1915 it oversaw fifteen divisional Labour parties, fifteen local labour representation committees, several miners' political associations, the Scottish ILP council, twelve Women's Labour League branches, three Fabian Societies as well as trades councils and trade unions.

Women's suffrage

Labour, particularly through the ILP, also took up the cause of women's suffrage. A few stalwarts, like Priscilla McLaren who remained active through her seventies, had continue to push the campaign for women's rights in the years after 1886, with nothing very obvious to show for it. But there is evidence of quiet advances being made. The Scottish Women's Co-operative Guild petitioned for the vote in 1893 and the Scottish Women's Liberal Federation pressed for women to be allowed to sit on town councils. When the latter failed to win this in 1900, the focus switched back to the suffrage. A new Glasgow and West of Scotland Association for Women's Suffrage was formed in 1902. Branches of the new more militant Women's Social and Political Union, launched by the Pankhursts in 1906, also quickly took off in Scotland.

Many of the activists in both wings of the women's movement were associated with labour organisations. Tom Johnston's *Forward* provided a forum for pro-suffrage articles and consistently argued that the success of socialism required 'complete democracy'.[41] Not all were so enthusiastic. There were real fears that women, particularly if there was a property-qualification in their suffrage, would prove to be a conservative force and that they were not likely to do much to push forward the cause of socialism. Others argued that any franchise reform had to go beyond women and ensure that the more than forty per cent of adult men who were still excluded should also be brought in. Despite splits in the WSPU the cause spread, particularly in 1909. Leah Leneman concludes that by the end of that year there can have been few in any corner of Scotland who was not aware of the issue of 'Votes for Women'.[42] While most of the activists were middle-class and while the 'unladylike' behaviour of the more militant appalled many a working man, there were growing signs of working-class women taking up the issue. Also, while there may have been limited sympathy with physical-force campaigns, the crass brutality of the police on many occasions was guaranteed to arouse some sympathy among those who had little reason to respect the police. The riot when police tried to arrest Mrs Pankhurst at a meeting in Glasgow's St Andrew's Halls in March 1914 was pretty widely blamed on police incompetence and did much to undermine the legitimacy of the government's obduracy. The issue became linked to home rule when Scottish Liberals agreed to insert a women's suffrage clause into the private member's Home Rule Bill which was being debated. The effect was to have women's suffrage overshadow the central issue of home rule.[43]

War

When the war broke out the leadership of the ILP quickly adopted an anti-war stance and parted company with the Labour Party. They continued the arguments of pre-war Liberal radicals that it was secret diplomacy and the machinations of foreign office officials which was largely responsible and that the only gainers were likely to be the industrialists and the financiers.[44] Not all ILP supporters went along and branches folded and membership slumped to around 3,000.[45] On the other hand it had support from much of the local trade-union leadership. It also attracted Liberal radical dissenters associated with the Peace Society, such as the Revd James Barr. Despite the restrictions of war-time legislation, *Forward* effectively maintained its anti-war position, finding it inconceivable that Britain should be on the same side as Tsarist Russia.

The war also brought out an awareness of profiteering and sharpened views that the real enemy was capitalism, which had 'no notion of … commonweal … can have no patriotism, since its very nature is such, leech-like for profit irrespective of any national or social consideration'.[46] Wheatley and the ILP organised a rent strike of nearly 20,000 tenants in November 1915. It was justified because the tenants 'respected all law which was just and fair', but did not respect the law which, allowed increases in rents at the present juncture'.[47]

These were the months when Clydeside began to earn the epithet 'red' and there were many signs of an intensity of feeling that the sacrifice being asked in the war was not an equal one. There was much sympathy for MacLean's anti-war stance and protests at the 'malicious and vindictive' sentences passed on him and others. The gradual extension of conscription made the ILP a focus for widespread protest alongside the No-Conscription Fellowship. It was condemned in the Trades Council 'as dangerous to the stability of the nation and totally opposed to the principles of British freedom', as a 'violation of civil liberty and a menace to working-class interests'.[48] It was rejected by the STUC, the Scottish Labour conference and the Labour conference.[49] From 1916 onwards there was growing support for moves towards a negotiated peace. Helen Crawfurd of the WSPU helped launch the Women's Peace Crusade in June 1916 and by 1917 membership of the ILP was beginning to recover and, for the first time, was beginning to make inroads well away from the industrial heartlands. By 1918 the ILP in Scotland had about a third of the total British membership.

Revolutionary socialism had been effectively marginalised before 1914. Most parts of the BSP, including the paper, *Justice* , became enthusiasts for war. Although individuals were to play key parts in offering leadership during the sometimes bitter industrial struggles over dilution of labour, at no point did they seriously challenge the dominance which the evolutionary socialism of the ILP had over the labour movement. It was on social issues, such as housing and rent, rather than workshop issues, that the ILP was at its most effective and ILP activists were the ones who most effectively took the lead in these. Although much attention was devoted to Maclean, many ILP people, like James Maxton, ended up in prison for conscientious objection. The revolution in Russia undoubtedly produced a frisson of excitement throughout the labour movement, but it stirred hope of Russia entering the modern democratic world rather than hopes of its being emulated in Britain.

The war years also showed that support for Scottish home rule had not really abated. The policy of the STUC was to call on the Parliamentary Labour Party to support 'the enactment of a Scottish Home Rule Bill'.[50] The same spirit of nationalism forced Arthur Henderson and the Labour leadership in London, much against their better judgment, to concede a separate Scottish Council of Labour with a considerable amount of autonomy. At the same time, the war undermined even further the organisation of Scottish Liberalism, but also much of its moral authority. The more radical elements were disenchanted by Lloyd George's political tactics and by his gung-ho determination to accept nothing less than unconditional surrender. Liberalism was thrown into disarray while the ILP was able to emerge as the natural successor to advanced liberal radicalism.

Notes

1. *Contemporary Review,* LXXV (June 1899), pp. 782–99.
2. *Daily Record,* 23 August 1900.
3. Richard Price, *An Imperial War and the British Working Class. Working-Class Attitudes and Reactions to the Boer War 1899–1902* (1972), p. 83.

4. Peter Warwick, *The South African War: the Anglo-Boer War 1899–1902*, (1980), p. 252.
5. *Times*, 31 July 1900.
6. Stewart J. Brown, ' "Echoes of Midlothian": Scottish Liberalism and the South African War', *Scottish Historical Review*, 71, (1992), p. 171.
7. *Daily Record*, 7 March 1900.
8. 1.9% in Scotland compared with 2.9% in England on an old register. See H. Pelling, 'Wales and the Boer War', *Welsh History Review*, 4, 1968–9, p. 363.
9. Hector MacPherson, *The Gospel of Force* , (Young Scot Publication No. 6, Edinburgh 1903), p. 2; *Hector Macpherson. The Man and His Work. A Memoir by his Son* (Edinburgh, 1915), p. 16.
10. *Edinburgh Evening News*, 1 January 1901.
11. Thomas Shaw, *Patriotism and Empire*, (Young Scot Publication No. 1, Edinburgh 1901), pp. 8, 13.
12. Quoted in *60 Points for Scottish Home Rule* (Young Scots Society, n.d.).
13. James Mitchell, *Strategies for Self-Government*, p. 70.
14. *Daily Free Press*, 30 November 1897.
15. Davidson, *Africa for the Africanders*, p. 7.
16. *Young Scots Handbook 1911–12*, pp. 6–13.
17. Quoted in I. Maver, 'Local Party Politics and the Temperance Crusade; Glasgow 1890–1902', *Scottish Labour History Society Journal*, No. 27, 1992, p. 47.
18. T. C. Smout, *A Century of the Scottish People*, (1986), p. 146.
19. Quoted in Graham Walker, *Thomas Johnston* (Manchester, 1988), p. 8.
20. *Forward*, 18 September 1909.
21. *Scotsman*, 20 September 1909.
22. John Brown, 'Scottish and English Land Legislation 1905–11', *Scottish Historical Review*, 47, 1968, pp. 72–85.
23. James Hunter, *The Making of the Crofting Community* (Edinburgh, 1976), pp. 190–5.
24. NLS, Scottish Workers' Parliamentary Election Committee Minutes, 6 January 1900.
25. Edinburgh University Library, Scottish Liberal Association, Minutes, 30 March 1904.
26. *Dundee Courier*, 12, 17 January 1906; *People's Journal*, 20 January 1906.
27. W. H. Fraser, 'The Labour Party in Scotland' in K. D. Brown (ed.), *The First Labour Party, 1906–1914* (1985), p. 46.
28. NLS, Elibank papers, Mss 8801. Master of Elibank to Lord Knollys, 7 November 1906.
29. *Ibid*. J. P. Croal to Elibank, 9 July 1907.
30. The Fabian Society was surprisingly slow to grow in Scotland. A Glasgow branch was founded in September 1901 with the future Scottish organiser of the Labour Party, Ben Shaw, as its secretary, and his wife, Joanna, on the committee. Its membership remained firmly middle class, with people like the academic Thomas Jones, the journalist Tom Johnston, the ex-journalist and schoolteacher MacNeill Weir, the ILP shipowner James Allan, the businessman R. F. Muirhead, the future Lord Provost, Daniel MacAulay Stevenson. It was eight years later before an Edinburgh branch was formed with the Revd John Glasse as the honorary president and John Young, soon to be a councillor, as chair.

31. *Arbroath Herald*, 1 May 1908.
32. J. Smyth, 'The ILP in Glasgow 1888–1906. The struggle for Identity' in A. McKinlay and R. J. Morris (eds), *The ILP on Clydeside 1893–1932 : from foundation to disintegration* (Manchester, 1991), pp. 44–7.
33. Joan Smith, 'Taking the Leadership of the Labour Movement' in McKinlay and Morris, *The ILP on Clydeside*, p. 70.
34. *Forward*, 28 August, 18, 25 September 1909.
35. J. Keir Hardie, *The Common Good. An Essay in Municipal Government*, (Manchester, n.d.), pp. 6–8.
36. John Wheatley, *Eight-Pound Cottages for Glasgow Citizens* (Glasgow 1913).
37. Smith, 'Labour Tradition in Glasgow and Liverpool', p. 36.
38. *Glasgow Labour Party Constitution*, 7 April 1915.
39. Smith, 'Leadership of the Labour Movement', p. 74.
40. Arbroath Public Library, Scottish ILP Federation. District Committee No 3. Minutes 5 July 1908 to 9 February 1918.
41. Leneman, *A Guid Cause*, pp. 42–3.
42. *Ibid.* p. 90.
43. *Ibid.* pp. 191–2.
44. *Forward*, 19 September 1914.
45. C. Harvie, 'Before the breakthrough, 1888–1922', in I. Donnachie, C. Harvie and I. S. Wood (eds), *FORWARD! Labour Politics in Scotland 1888–1988* (Edinburgh, 1989), p. 24.
46. Tom Johnston, *The Huns at Home during Three Years of the Great War*, quoted in G. Walker, *Thomas Johnston* (Manchester, 1988), p. 41.
47. Gordon Brown, *Maxton*, p. 60.
48. Mitchell Library, Glasgow Trades Council Minutes, 5 January 1916, 7 March 1917.
49. William Kenefick, 'War Resisters and Anti-Conscription in Scotland: an ILP Perspective' in C. Macdonald and E. McFarland, *Scotland and the Great War*, (East Linton, 1999), pp. 59–80.
50. *Forward*, 5 July 1916, 7 March 1917.

CHAPTER NINE

The Radical Inheritance since 1918?

There is considerable debate over who were the more than forty per cent of men who were excluded from the franchise before 1918 because of the intricacies of the registration procedure. Some historians argue that it was the poorest and most mobile and that these were potential Labour supporters. Yet others have argued that the barriers to registration affected all social classes and that no one political party was particularly disadvantaged. What is certain is that it was mainly the young who were excluded, the under thirty-fives living at home with their parents or moving regularly.[1] The 1918 Representation of the People Act removed most of the barriers to registration in order to deal with the problem of soldiers. It was clearly unacceptable that those at the war front or just back from it should be kept off the register, while 'shirkers' at home might be on it. It also admitted women over 30 who, themselves or their husbands, were owners or occupiers; some 40 per cent of the electorate. The result was that the Scottish electorate increased from 779,012 in December 1910 to 2,205,383 in November 1918, a 183 per cent increase. The new electorate then were mainly first-time voters, most of them with no great political awareness and no family tradition to look to for political guidance. The test for all political parties was who was going to be able most effectively to organise and rally this new constituency.

The Conservatives and Unionists were at some advantage. They had for some time before 1914 recognised an emerging world of mass politics in which there was less and less room for lengthy, reasoned speeches. It was a politics which required slogans and symbols which could immediately and briefly capture attention. Among the advice given to organisers of the Primrose League, the most successful example of mass political mobilisation, had been not to waste time in political argument, but to allow the masses the experience of being near the great. By the end of the century, the Conservatives had commandeered the union flag as one of their own symbols and had effectively used the slogans of patriotism and imperialism. They had also for long realised the importance of party organisation, of keeping details of potential supporters and ensuring that they turned out at election time.

Liberals were wedded to older forms of politics and they were slow to adjust. An inherent belief that politics were about rational debate within an educated electorate made them cling to older patterns of electioneering. Gladstone had introduced some of the elements of modern politics at Midlothian with his whistle-stops to address the crowds. But the core of it was still the lengthy speech to be reported in full in the press. They frowned on oversimplifying political debate, on crude sloganising and on extensive canvassing. Even more critically, Liberal organisation was crumbling. In local politics they had been losing ground to anti-socialist conservatism for some time before 1914 and with no parliamentary election for eight years, many local associations barely existed. In addition the Asquith/Lloyd George split at the top was reflected at all levels of the party. It was in no position to fight an effective election campaign and Lloyd George's ruthless use of the 'coupon' to ensure that his supporters were returned merely confirmed what was already on the cards.

Labour had inherited some of the distaste of the Liberals for canvassing and electoral organising. Many still believed that the right message, delivered often enough and with sufficient fervour from the soap-box, could win the masses to socialism. But some of the reticence about organisation had gradually been eroded by 1914 and in many places the mechanisms to cope with the new political scene were in place. The party was also helped by the spread of trade unionism, which had more than doubled its membership over the previous decade. The party's new constitution, which, for the first time in clause four committed it to 'the nationalisation of the means of production, distribution and exchange', gave power very firmly to the trade-union wing. It was able to present itself as the trade-union party and it was no doubt to their union branch and to the shop stewards that many of the new voters turned for electoral guidance. But the struggle over who would most effectively speak for the new democracy was far from over.

Labour breakthrough

Labour could congratulate itself in December 1918 that its vote in Scotland had increased tenfold, but there was disappointment that this had only resulted in seven MPs. There was some comfort in the fact that many of its other thirty-nine candidates had come a close second to coalitionists and that the Liberal Party was clearly in a vulnerable position. There were also gains being made in municipal politics. In the west of Scotland campaigns over the now notorious problems of housing were paying dividends and Labour won forty-four of Glasgow's city council seats in November 1920, when again due to boundary changes the whole council had to be elected. The extent of Labour's growth was apparent in the 1922 general election when with just over half a million votes and twenty-nine MPs, it became the largest party in Scotland. Most spectacularly of all it took ten of the fifteen Glasgow seats, while the Liberals held none.

There is a debate on how the success in the west of Scotland can be accounted for. Iain MacLean in his *Legend of Red Clydeside* sees it as less to do with the persuasiveness of socialist arguments, as with the increasing effectiveness of Labour organisation. In particular, he argues that the end of the Irish crisis with the recognition of the Irish Free State and of Northern Ireland had removed the factor which for Catholic population of Irish descent in the West of Scotland had constantly diverted attention from local social issues. Now they could turn to Scottish politics and Labour were the gainers. A recurring thread in the ILP was the idea that there was something particularly democratic and egalitarian about the Scots, a view usually linked to presbyterianism and its democratic church structures. It was another of the features which it had drawn from the nineteenth-century radical tradition. But thanks to the work first of John Wheatley and then of Patrick Dollan, it also sought to be inclusive and to win over Catholic workers. Wheatley had founded the Catholic Socialist Society in 1906 and, despite resistance from the clergy, the ILP had begun to make inroads into the Catholic community. In the 1920s Labour was able to inherit the very effective Irish political machine in the city. While no doubt it helped, Alan McKinlay is right to challenge McLean's view and to emphasise the much longer-term perspective which is necessary to understand what was an ILP success.[2] In 1922 it was able to present itself as the party which was concerned with social issues, which could span the sectarian divide, whose anti-war stance was now of much less significance and which had the necessary organisation to deliver the vote.

Home rule hopes

The Clydeside ILPers who were seen off by cheering crowds from Glasgow's St Enoch Station on Sunday 19 November 1922 had the sound of 'The Red Flag' ringing in their ears but they carried with them as much radicalism as socialism. Patrick Dollan declared that 'Not since the Reform Act of 1832 had so much enthusiasm been evoked at a political demonstration'.[3] In theory at least, most were abstainers who had included temperance reform in their manifestoes. They were committed to land nationalisation and they were firm believers in the need for Scottish home rule. The 1918 Labour manifesto had continued the commitment to a parliament in Edinburgh. Labour activists and trade unionists had joined businessmen and a mixed band of both Radicals and Conservatives in September 1918 to revive the Scottish Home Rule Association, to campaign against the centralised system of British government which was 'inefficient and inconsistent with national sentiment'.[4] The Labour link was firmly there, however, with the veteran R. B. Cunninghame-Graham as president, and Roland E. Muirhead, ILPer and financier of *Forward* as secretary. Appeals to President Woodrow Wilson to 'support Scottish self-determination' and allow Scottish representation at the peace conferences fell on deaf ears, but by 1920 the Association had the backing of 47 co-operative societies, 38 trade-union branches and 24 branches of the ILP.

Like nineteenth-century radicals, they were quickly frustrated by the difficulties in getting any change in a parliament dominated by English Conservatives. A few remaining Liberal Radicals such as J. M. Hogge, a founder of the Young Scots, tried to rally support for a Scottish constitutional convention, but the post-war depression kept popular attention fixed on social and economic issues not constitutional ones. Labour gains were consolidated in the 1923 election with all but Motherwell of the Lanarkshire seats being won and gains in Midlothian and Peeblesshire and Renfrewshire, as well as in some traditional radical Liberal burghs like Dunfermline and Kirkcaldy. When MacDonald's minority Labour government failed to take up the issue of Scottish home rule, the Gorbals ILP MP, George Buchanan, introduced a private member's home rule bill in May 1924, as the first step to a federal structure all round. A rally in support in Glasgow's St Andrew's Hall heard Maxton declare that a Scottish Parliament was required 'to make English-ridden, capitalist-ridden, landowner-ridden Scotland into the Scottish Socialist Commonwealth'.[5] When the speaker allowed the bill to be talked out, the consequent parliamentary uproar brought the suspension of Maxton, Kirkwood and Stephens.

The failure of Labour to deliver revived the idea of a constitutional convention and meetings of what was termed a Scottish National Convention were held to plan future strategies. Two years later, the Revd James Barr, another who had made the journey from radical pacifism to Labour, and who sat as Labour Member for Motherwell, the last Lanarkshire bastion to fall to Labour, moved another home rule bill which proposed dominion status for Scotland and the end of Scottish representation at Westminster. Again a Scottish Convention of MPs, trade unionists, local councillors had given its backing and Tom Johnston acted as seconder, but again it was talked out with even less consideration than Buchanan's bill.

There were signs of Labour enthusiasm for home rule waning, as people like John Wheatley came to believe that the immense social problems of inter-war Scotland could not be solved from its own resources and that British solutions were necessary.[6] Similarly, faith in municipal socialism had also begun to wither. Local variation in services and rates seemed less acceptable and the demand increasingly was for national uniformity, and this involved centralisation of decision making. The ideals of municipal socialism lingered on in smaller communities like Kilsyth and Tom Johnston's Kirkintilloch, but the big cities looked to the state to provide most of the resources for their regeneration. No doubt also, having sniffed the realities of power at Westminster, the Labour party had justified hopes of regaining it. Whatever the cause, for the next decade and more Labour showed little interest in the issue of home rule.

Nationalism

The failure of the Barr measure stimulated a revival of popular nationalism, when the young Glasgow student, John MacCormick, launched the Glasgow University Scottish National Association, largely a breakaway from the Labour Club. In the following year at the Bannockburn rally, he joined with the veteran radical of many causes, Roland Muirhead, to form the National Party of Scotland. The need for a new party had been discussed at the various conventions, as hopes of Labour delivering on its commitments faded. Both Roland Muirhead and his brother Dr R. F. Muirhead, despite their ILP credentials, had come round to the idea that this was the only way to carry the issue forward. Feeding into it were remnants of Gaelic revivalism and Highland Land Law Reform through the Scottish National League, formed in 1919 around the Hon. Ruariaidh Erskine of Mar, and William Gillies, a republican businessman, Gaelic playwright and former secretary of the Glasgow Fabians. The League stood for 'complete national independence'. A third element could trace its roots to the pre-war Young Scots, with T. H. Gibson, who had recently resigned from the Scottish Home Rule Association to join the Scottish National League because he felt that the Association was too closely associated with the ILP. Cunninghame-Graham added to the continuity with earlier movements by becoming president of the new party and his close running of Stanley Baldwin in the Glasgow Rectorial election of 1928 gave welcome publicity to the new movement. The Scottish Home Rule Association, after some debate, agreed to dissolve.

The National Party of Scotland appealed to many who had grave doubts about a Labour Party which was increasingly aligned with the trade unions and with the industrial working-class of the west of Scotland. Intellectuals, journalists, students, penniless aristos, small-town solicitors, whose vision of the ideal Scotland was often shaped in 'kailyard' mythology were among those attracted to it.

The Conservatives and Unionists tended to see nationalism as a product of the left, while others, such as Herbert Grierson, professor of Rhetoric at Edinburgh, saw sinister Roman Catholic influence at play.[7] But Scottish Unionists were keen to make a bid for the working-class vote drifting away from Liberalism. The Unionists' conference of 1925 and 1926 was prepared to contemplate constitutional reform by altering the composition of the House of Lords and, as Iain Hutchison and Chris Harvie have argued, a distinctive strand of Scottish Conservatism committed to state interventionism was developing.[8] A few Liberals and Conservatives united in the Scottish Party at the end of the 1920s, presided over by the Duke of Montrose, and committed to permeating the Liberal and Unionist parties in favour of some measure of devolution. They included Sir Andrew MacEwen, a Liberal, former provost of Inverness, Daniel Macaulay Stevenson, Fabian and former Lord Provost of Glasgow, Andrew Gibb, Unionist professor of Scots law at Glasgow University. But the decision of most of the predominantly working-class Cathcart Unionist Association in July 1932 to affiliate to the Scottish Party was condemned by the Unionist establishment as 'narrow foolish nationalism'.[9]

In 1934, and at the cost of about a fifth of its membership, MacCormick led the National Party of Scotland into a merger with the Scottish Party to form the Scottish National Party, calling for 'a Parliament which shall be the final authority on all Scottish Affairs'. Jack Brand regards the decision as mistaken, seeing the alliance with the Scottish Party as 'a return to an older style of politics', appealing to notables, rather than the mass appeal which, however ineffectually, the National Party of Scotland had tried to achieve.[10] It took decades to again win back support in the industrial heartlands of Scotland.

Coping with crises

Many writers comment on a lack of confidence among the middle class in Scotland in the 1930s, as the economy was battered by a combination of mismanagement and global financial and economic crises. There was little real enthusiasm for political change. Jennie Lee found 'all the finest people in the grip of a kind of spiritual paralysis' when she visited her native Fife.[11] The Labour Party was back to a mere seven seats in 1931 from its thirty-six of 1929, and there was little readiness for battles with the huge national government majority. There was also no patience within the Labour Party for local deviations and years of battles with the ILP finally led to its disaffiliation in 1932. The Labour Party thus lost that element of the party which most incorporated the strand of nineteenth-century radicalism and ethical social-ism which had been so important a factor in Scottish popular politics since the 1880s. Some searched for it in the Communist Party, but only a few could relish the combination of Stalinist discipline and political opportunism which was a feature of its history in the early 1930s. The Labour Party itself became almost exclusively identified with the industrial working class

The gradual revival of the economy in the second half of the 1930s brought a revival in Labour fortunes and confidence. The invasion of Abyssinia by Mussolini, the Spanish Civil War and the growing concern at the rise of fascism in Europe allowed different elements of the Left to strive for a popular front to resist. Once again much effort was expended on peace movements and in rallying to the League of Nations. But there were always tinges of nationalism around them. There was a revival of interest in devolution, with Tom Johnston resuscitating the old argument that efficiency of government demanded some devolving of power from Westminster. For many Labour still seemed to offer the better prospect of real constitutional change. The opening of St Andrew's House in Edinburgh for the new Scottish Office with a flock of new civil servants and the ever-enhancing power of the Secretary of State led to echoes of earlier criticisms of the abuse of power, with Tom Johnston and others arguing that there was a lack of democratic checks on state power.[12] An all-party campaign for devolution in the summer of 1939 was overtaken by the war.

War and its aftermath

The second world war brought many changes. The SNP splintered over what stance to take on it, while at the same time there was growing unrest at MacCormick's rather dictatorial style of party management. Pacifist elements succeeded in rallying a mix of support to oust him from the leadership in 1942. MacCormick's supporters formed a new Scottish Convention, which succeeded in attracting some new support from outside the usual nationalist circles. The aim was to win over the support for home rule which existed within all the existing political parties and, as thoughts turned to reconstruction after the war, there was an attempt to create some kind of consensus to tackle Scotland's problems. A 'Declaration of Scottish Affairs' initiated by William Leonard, a former tutor in John MacLean's Marxist economic classes and now MP for Glasgow St Rollox, called for a Scottish parliament to deal with Scottish domestic issues.[13]

The SNP, despite the lack of MacCormick's organisational and oratorical skills, made quite a strong showing in various war-time by-elections, eventually winning a parliamentary seat at Motherwell just before the end of the war. But this did nothing to endear the movement to the Labour leadership and the war confirmed the party as firmly centralist. Creating the National Health Service, taking control of the commanding heights of the economy, pulling out of India left little room for constitutional refinements. Apart from Shinwell, the old ILP elements had all but disappeared from the centre of the party. It was the Fabian vision of efficient, expert-run socialism which came into its own, not the ethical, democratic (not to say romantic) socialism of the Scottish tradition. Nationalisation of industries with centralised control made Labour's centralising tendencies even more pronounced.[14]

In this atmosphere it was again nationalism which tried to stir populist support with MacCormick's plans for a 'Scottish National Assembly'. Some 600 delegates from unions, churches and town councils, together with people like the nutritionist Sir John Boyd Orr and the writer Naomi Mitchison, from outside the usual political circles, met in Glasgow in March 1947. Indeed, according to Jack Brand, it was largely a middle-class affair which overwhelmingly called for a single-chamber Scottish parliament within the UK.[15] A second Assembly agreed to launch the Covenant, declaring the need for 'reform in the constitution of our country ... to secure good government in accordance with our Scottish traditions'. Starting with a symbolic signing in the Church of Scotland's Assembly Hall in October 1949, 50,000 names were appended in the first week and eventually some two million in all were claimed. To MacCormick it was 'a demonstration of national unity as the Scots might never have hoped to see':

> Unknown district councillors rubbed shoulders and joined in pledges with the men whose titles had sounded throughout all the history of Scotland. Working men from the docks of Glasgow or the pits of Fife spoke with the same voice as portly business-men in pin-striped trousers.[16]

But MacCormick's association with Liberals and Unionists was seen by an increasingly beleaguered Labour government as part of an anti-Labour, anti-nationalisation campaign, and the government made clear that the party's long commitment to home rule was no more. In 1950, for the first time in its history, there was no mention of home rule in Labour's manifesto. It was a position reconfirmed throughout the 1950s. Efforts to maintain the momentum of the Covenant foundered and the few branches of the Covenant Association had little sense of direction. The SNP and related strictly nationalist organisations meanwhile were torn apart by internal disputes.

Michael Keating concludes that there was probably less that was distinctive about Scottish Labour in the 1950s than at any other time in its history. The policies and the party organisation were both more or less completely integrated into the British party.[17] Trade union domination ensured that the bulk of its Scottish MPs were older, solid (even stolid) trade-union loyalists, often with a myopic parochialism spiced with the rhetoric of a largely mythical 'red' past. In local government in most areas which they controlled the policies pursued were far from radical and even further from socialism.

Labour may have paid some price for its determined Britishness, because in 1955, for the first time, the Unionists, as Scottish Conservatives always called themselves gained the majority of Scottish seats (thanks mainly to boundary changes): 36 to Labour's 34 with now only one Liberal in Orkney and Shetland. But the party, too firmly identified with the grouse moors and the ever-unpopular landed classes, despite the efforts of many within it to get across a different image, failed to build on its success and instead began an accelerating decline. With the Scottish economy creaking in the late 1950s there was a swing back to Labour and the clinging to Union was stronger than ever. The Scottish Labour conference of 1959 firmly rejected devolution over the protests of some of the ablest of the younger delegates. The more populist tradition of moral crusading was taken up by the Campaign for Nuclear Disarmament. It linked many shades of politics in marches to the American bases at Holy Loch and Castle Douglas. It gained from the injection of ex-communists of the 'New Left', who had pulled out of the Communist Party in the aftermath of the crushing of the Hungarian uprising in 1956. It was helped by the left-inspired folk-song revival, which introduced many for the first time to the songs of Scotland's radical and industrial past and stirred nationalism. The Labour Party reacted badly to these pressures and the rejection of unilateralism by the party conference in 1962 revealed how Labour was no longer able to harness popular idealism.

Nationalism rises

The nationalist movement was reviving and fissures within it were being closed after the death of MacCormick in 1961. More importantly, groups of young nationalists were determinedly setting out to create a mass party by establishing branches across the country.[18] The first signs of its bearing fruit were in West Lothian, when in a by-election in 1962 the SNP candidate, William Wolfe, came second ahead of both the Conservatives and Liberals. By the 1964 general election they were able to put up fifteen candidates, in 1966 twenty-three.

Labour was now dominant in Scotland and in the 1966 election their vote together with a small contribution from the Communists added up to more than fifty per cent of the popular vote, something which not even 1945 had delivered. With the Conservatives no longer serious contenders for an effective opposition, nationalism became the main challenger to Labour dominance. By 1968 the SNP could claim 484 branches and 120,000 members, compared with fewer than 2,000 before Labour came to power. According to Andrew Marr the new supporters were mainly 'the kind of skilled working-class and lower-middle-class voter who disliked the somewhat authoritarian nature of the Labour Movement but had no feeling for the Tory cause either – the sort of mildly stroppy individualists who, in other parts of Britain during the 1960s, gravitated to Liberalism'.[19] The SNP also began to pull into it the young who were protesting against the Vietnam war and workers who were rebelling against trade-union autocracy and dominance of the Labour Party. The accusations of 'Tartan Toryism', which Labour flung at it, no longer stood up to examination.

The culmination was the victory of Winnie Ewing at Hamilton in November 1967. Her victory, although short-lived, was particularly significant because Hamilton was the one Lanarkshire constituency which had an unbroken record of Labour control since 1918, even in the black year of 1931. It was quickly followed by 103 Nationalist gains in municipal elections in central Scotland, thirteen of them in Glasgow.[20]

The shock of Hamilton jolted the leadership of both the other parties. Encouraged by some of the younger MPs organised in the Thistle Group and desperate to revive declining Tory fortunes, Edward Heath in the evocatively named 'Declaration of Perth' quickly pledged a Scottish Assembly. A committee was set up under Sir William McEwen Younger which proposed a part-elected, part-nominated Scottish assembly. A constitutional commission was then established under Heath's predecessor, Sir Alec Douglas

Home, to work out the details. Its proposals in 1970 for a 'Scottish Convention' of 125 members to do some of the work formerly carried out largely by the Scottish Grand Committee were shelved when the Conservatives were returned to power in 1970 and when the nationalist threat seemed to have subsided.

Since many of the SNP converts were ex-Labour people antipathy to devolution within Labour was strong. As Scottish Secretary, Willie Ross, would have no truck with home rule. But there were moves within the STUC, with the miners' leading the way in pressing for a campaign for a Scottish Parliament. Harold Wilson rather unwillingly responded with a Royal Commission, an obvious delaying tactic. With the Conservatives back in power in 1970, Scotland could unite in anti-Toryism largely behind Labour. But campaigns for Upper Clyde Shipbuilders and protest at the continuing decline in the traditional Scottish economy all acquired a nationalist tinge in their rhetoric. A strong home rule campaign began to gather momentum among Labour MPs.

The Kilbrandon Royal Commission in 1973 offered a variety of solutions and launched yet another round of debates on possible structures. It was followed almost at once by the SNP victory of Margo MacDonald in the Govan by-election. Its significance was soon overshadowed by the miners' strike which brought down the Heath Government, but in the subsequent elections the SNP picked up six seats and then eleven behind the slogan, 'It's Scotland's Oil'. It convinced Wilson that some form of devolution had to be offered. What emerged, after endless internal wranglings, was what has been called a 'Toytown Assembly' with little power, which was excoriated by an increasingly pro-home rule Scottish press. A group, including the MPs Jim Sillars and John Robertson, broke away from Labour in 1975 to form a new Scottish Labour Party, which proposed to offer a combination of socialism and nationalism. For a brief but lively three years it attracted radical young people only to be torn apart by Trotskyist infiltration and to disappear with Sillars' defeat in the 1979 election.

Devolution

The second half of the 1970s found all the political parties split over devolution. Labour and Conservatives had powerful protagonists on both sides, while the SNP was split between those who were willing to accept devolution and the fundamentalists who argued that nothing short of independence was acceptable. The failure to get the Scotland Bill passed in February 1977, because of a revolt by twenty-one Labour rebels, led to huge gains by Nationalists in the May local elections. But not, as it proved, to a great upsurge of popular protest. The continued haemorrhaging of support at constituency level strengthened the Labour government's backbone and a new bill was brought in. Opponents plugged away with what became known as the 'West Lothian' question, of whether, after devolution, Scottish MPs should be allowed to vote on English issues. An amendment from the Scots-born Islington South MP, George Cunningham, was carried which required at least 40 per cent of the electorate to support the assembly in a referendum.

The referendum came in March 1979 after a bitter winter of industrial strife and clear signs that the Labour government was on its last legs. The Labour Party was divided on the issue both among MPs and in the constituencies. The Conservatives, still committed to devolution, urged a 'No' vote and the promise of something better from themselves. A powerful 'Labour Vote No' group also emerged around Brian Wilson, Robin Cook and Tam Dalyell. On the other hand, a loose Alliance for an Assembly group included the Conservative MP Alick Buchanan-Smith, who had resigned from the shadow cabinet in protest at Thatcher's rejection of any devolution, the Liberal MP Russell Johnston and the Communist general secretary of the STUC, Jimmy Milne. In the end, the majority in favour was 80,000 but less than 33 per cent of the electorate had supported it. A motion of censure from the SNP, the act of 'suicide pilots' as one of their number described it, brought down Callaghan's government and ushered in eighteen years of Conservative rule.[21]

It also gradually ushered in new approaches to politics as individuals and groups sought ways around the 'elected dictatorship' of Conservative rule. Fifty Labour MPs out of Scotland's seventy-one members were powerless in the face of Thatcherism's advance and powerless to halt the destruction of many of Scotland's industries. There again began to be talk of the need for a Scottish Convention to challenge Westminster's authority. Others talked of another home rule referendum and of disruption of Parliament. The suggestion that the Conservative 'mandate' did not run in Scotland was increasingly made. On the other hand, the SNP lost ground. As generally happens, with the Conservatives in power, it was Labour which seemed the obvious focus of opposition. A mixture of individuals began to return to the idea of a convention and, in May 1980, the Campaign for a Scottish Assembly was launched at the suggestion of Jack Brand of Strathclyde University's department of politics. It involved academics, trade unionists and Labour MPs. A few were nationalist, others from the Labour home rule wing, and a few communists and ex-communists. It was committed to achieving cross-party co-operation and it gradually began to break down SNP and Labour, suspicions. The magazine *Radical Scotland* gave it a very effective forum. But, while all could unite in anti-Conservatism, it proved very difficult to maintain a balance between SNP and Labour. There were also suspicions that any assembly would threaten the position of the entrenched power of Labour-dominated local authorities. But as the Conservative government's curbing of their power continued they too, through COSLA, came round to supporting the idea of an assembly.[22]

In 1987 the Campaign for a Scottish Assembly proposed a Constitutional Convention to draw up 'a practicable blueprint' for an assembly and six months later it issued the grandly-named and powerfully-written *Claim of Right*.[23] Its title deliberately paralleled the 1689 justification for ousting James VII for 'having turned a legal limited monarchy into an arbitrary despotic power' and the 1842 protest by the General Assembly at the infringement of the Church's 'liberties and privileges'. It began with the assertion that 'Parliamentary government under the present British Constitution had failed Scotland and more than Parliamentary action was needed to redeem the failure'. The Union, it argued, had always threatened the survival of a distinctive Scottish culture, but particularly so from the middle of the nineteenth century and although there had been some strengthening of Scottish institutions of government since 1885 it had 'been accompanied by an increasing centralisation and standardisation of British government practice which has more than offset any decentralisation of administrative units'. The English constitution, where the concept of parliamentary sovereignty as a protection against arbitrary royal power had now become largely unchallenged prime ministerial power, was 'an illusion of democracy' and was 'now experiencing a progressive diminution of accountability'. 'Constitutional Conventions', it argued, in a careful choice of words, 'may be, but are not necessarily, challenges to Government'.

By the end of the 1980s the imposition of a poll tax on Scotland a year ahead of England poured petrol on already smouldering discontents. Produced in response to the fears of a rate-payer revolt in Scotland following yet another revaluation of property, it produced the greatest popular defiance of authority since Chartism. By the end of its first year 700,000 warrants had been issued for non-payment of the tax and hundreds of thousands of others had delayed payment until the last moment. Groups within the Labour Party began calling for civil disobedience, disruption of Parliament and asserted 'Scotland's right to self determination on such a basis as the people of Scotland themselves decide'.[24]

The Scottish Convention

The STUC took the lead in pushing Labour towards support for the Convention, and by the end of 1988 the leadership of the Labour Party had come round to the idea of cross-party talks about a Convention. The tentative moves were accelerated when the Nationalists chalked up a remarkable victory over Labour in a Govan by-election. The effect also, however, was to strengthen the resistance of those within the SNP who would brook no compromise short of independence and the SNP decided not to participate. In March 1989 in the Kirk Assembly Hall in Edinburgh the Convention met to assert 'the sovereign right of the Scottish people to determine the form of

Government best suited to their needs'. Labour and Liberal MPs, regional and district councillors, the STUC, joined with Communists, Greens, Church representatives, Gaelic language associations and others under the joint chairmanship of the former Liberal leader, David Steel and an early Labour supporter of home rule, Harry Ewing. With the SNP and the Conservatives boycotting, it was Labour which dominated the Convention, but as James Mitchell has argued, there was also a determination by all those who were involved to make it work and to reject what was seen as the sectionalism of the SNP.[25] Within eighteen months it had come up with the broad outline of a scheme for a Scottish Parliament based on a mixture of first past the post and proportional representation. The Labour Party committed itself to it and there was a steady spread of support in all parties for some kind of devolution.

At the beginning of 1992 an opinion poll suggested that half the Scottish population was prepared to consider the option of independence. Both Nationalists and Labour were confident that time was on their side. The Scottish media was at the forefront of a new, broadly based nationalism. The SNP jauntily talked of 'Scotland Free by 93'. It proved a false dawn. The expectation that the coming election in 1992 would see the ousting of the Conservatives was rudely shattered and, to much consternation, the Conservative share of the vote actually rose in Scotland. Gloom, despondency, anger, mutual recrimination between the opposition parties followed. There was talk of civil disobedience and of boycotting the Westminster Parliament. New organisations, such as Scotland United, were formed to call for a referendum. But no real groundswell of protest was generated. Or, at any rate, no apparent groundswell. What there was was what James Mitchell calls 'the slow undercurrents of change'.[26] It was apparent in the 'Democracy Demonstration' of December 1992 when something like 40,000 people marched in Edinburgh during the meeting there of European heads of government. Organised by a STUC-led umbrella organisation, the Campaign for Scottish Democracy, it brought together activists, but also pulled in many who had not been greatly involved in politics since the 1960s. The message was 'Scotland demands democracy'.

Over the next few years the theme of democracy was regularly repeated, with talk of finding new ways of reflecting grass-roots democracy. By the time of the next election in 1997 there had clearly emerged a determination that the 'mistake' of 1992 would not be repeated. Tactical voting ensured that not a single Conservative MP was returned for a Scottish seat. A referendum showed a clear majority in all regions of Scotland in favour of a Scottish Parliament and, accepting what was called 'the settled will of the Scottish people', as its first major act, the new Labour government delivered the Scotland Act 1998, with the ringing opening, 'There shall be a Scottish Parliament'. A recent poll suggested that 96 per cent of all Scots wanted a Parliament whose members worked together without concern about party lines and which was responsive to the people. Whether the Scottish Parliament elected on 6 May 1999 will deliver 'a new contract or covenant between people and Parliament and develop the new institutions we need for a new kind of democracy' only time will tell.[27]

Notes

1. M. Childs, 'Labour Grows Up: The Electoral System, Political Generations and British Politics, 1890–1929', *Twentieth Century British History*, Vol. 6 (2), 1995, pp. 123–44.
2. Iain McLean, *The Legend of Red Clydeside* (Edinburgh, 1983); Alan McKinlay, '"Doubtful wisdom and uncertain promise": strategy, ideology and organisation, 1918–1922' in McKinlay and Morris, *ILP on Clydeside*, pp. 133–5.
3. Gordon Brown, *Maxton* (1988), p. 11.
4. Quoted in Jack Brand, T*he National Movement in Scotland* (1978), p. 175.
5. Brown, *Maxton*, p. 161.
6. Richard J. Finlay, 'Unionism and the Dependency Culture: Politics and State Intervention in Scotland, 1918–1997' in Catriona M. M. MacDonald (ed.), *Unionist Scotland 1800–1997* (Edinburgh, 1998), p. 102.
7. Compton Mackenzie, *My Life and Times. Octave Seven 1931–1938* (1968), p. 20. Both Mackenzie and Erskine of Mar were Roman Catholic.
8. Iain G. C. Hutchison, 'Scottish Unionism between the Two World Wars', in MacDonald, *Unionist Scotland*, pp. 83–92; C. Harvie, *No Gods and Precious Few Heroes* (1981).
9. Brand, *National Movement*, pp. 217–8.
10. *Ibid.* p. 227.
11. Harvie, *No Gods and Precious Few Heroes*, p. 98.
12. Finlay, 'Unionism and the Dependency Culture', p. 105.
13. J. Mitchell, *Strategies for Self-Government. The Campaigns for a Scottish Parliament* (Edinburgh, 1996), p. 87.
14. C. Harvie, 'The recovery of Scottish Labour, 1939–1951' in Donnachie, Harvie and Wood, *FORWARD*, p. 78.
15. Brand, *National Movement*, p. 244.
16. John MacCormick, *The Flag in the Wind* (1955).
17. M. Keating, 'The Labour Party in Scotland, 1951–1964' in Donnachie, Harvie and Wood, *FORWARD*, p. 87.
18. Brand, *National Movement*, pp. 258–9.
19. Andrew Marr, *The Battle for Scotland* (1992), p. 117.
20. Brand, *National Movement*, p. 262.
21. Marr, *Battle for Scotland*, p. 163.
22. Mitchell, *Strategies*, p. 116.
23. Written largely by the retired Scottish Office civil servant, Jim Ross.
24. Marr, *Battle for Scotland*, p. 200.
25. Mitchell, *Strategies*, p. 130.
26. *Ibid.* p. 282.
27. The words are those of Canon Kenyon Wright, one of the key figures in the Scottish Constitutional Convention. *Sunday Herald*, 4 April 1999.

Index